Andaman and Nicobar Islands

India's Untapped Strategic Assets

Andaman and Nicobar Islands

India's Untapped Strategic Assets

Sanat Kaul

INSTITUTE FOR DEFENCE STUDIES & ANALYSES
NEW DELHI

PENTAGON PRESS

Andaman and Nicobar Islands: India's Untapped Strategic Assets
By Sanat Kaul

First Published in 2015

ISBN 978-81-8274-774-6

Published by
PENTAGON PRESS
206, Peacock Lane, Shahpur Jat,
New Delhi-110049
Phones: 011-64706243, 26491568
Telefax: 011-26490600
email: rajan@pentagonpress.in
website: www.pentagonpress.in

Branch:
Prime Arcade
Office #11
1154 Saifee Street
Opp. M.G. Road, Camp
Pune-411001
Email: pentagonpresspune@gmail.com

In association with
Institute for Defence Studies and Analyses
No. 1, Development Enclave,
New Delhi-110010
Phone: +91-11-26717983
Website: www.idsa.in

Printed at Aegean Offset Printers, Greater Noida, U.P.

Contents

Preface

My writing this book was more by accident than design. It all began with a seminar which I attended at the Institute of Defence Studies and Analysis (IDSA) on Andaman & Nicobar Islands. At the seminar during the Q&A session I asked quite a few questions, which is not my normal habit. Thereafter, I was invited by the Director to his office and during this informal discussion an offer was made to write a book on the strategic challenges of Andaman and Nicobar Islands. I accepted the offer readily. Although, I was given 18 months to write this book I took a considerable time more for which my apologies to IDSA.

I have spent four years of my life in these islands. From 1975 to 1977 I was posted in Car Nicobar as Deputy Commissioner. This out of the way remote island had hardly any communications in those days. There was no TV, no telephone except for a 25 line PBX for the island, no air connection and a very poor inter-island ship service connecting the Nicobar Group with Port Blair. With all the isolation I had a wonderful time in the company of the Nicobarese and the Officers of the Indian Air Force (IAF). I spent another two years from 1991 to 1993 in Port Blair when things had changed completely and the lifestyle was very different. We had good telephone connectivity to the entire country as well as abroad. Air services connecting Port Blair to mainland India had improved. However, it still felt like a remote outpost of India with no strategic planning.

The reason I took up the challenge to write this book was not out of nostalgia but more out of dissatisfaction. I am dissatisfied with the system in which we function and we should not blame it on the democratic process only. There appears to be no strategic planning in our system even at the official level. It had no vision and it produced nothing of any consequence. We miscalculated our one way friendship with China, and even after the 1962 defeat, we learnt nothing. The Island Development Authority (IDA) set up by Prime Minister Rajiv Gandhi and service by the Planning Commission has been a total disappointment in spite of having all the major cabinet ministers on it. It had no vision and it produced nothing of any consequence. The Look East Policy of Prime Minister Narsimha Rao in 1991 was a step in the right direction but it overlooked the importance of these islands. This book is one such attempt at looking into our strategic depth to see where we can leverage some advantage.

The Andaman & Nicobar Islands offer a strategic advantage to checkmate our reverses on our northern and western borders. I have mentioned in this book that if a proper policy is drawn and implemented we could, perhaps, turn the tables on the Chinese. This will happen only if we carefully leverage the potential that these islands offer. With Great Nicobar Island near the western entrance of the Malacca Strait and India's relationship with its eastern neighbours in good health, we have potential to increase our strategic depth in Indo-Pacific. The book describes the Chinese Malacca Dilemma which could be our advantage.

Finally, I have tried to show what India achieved in the North East in the 1950s by a policy driven initiative by creating the North East Frontier Agency (NEFA) with the mandate to have effective jurisdiction up to the McMahon line. This finally led to successful creation of Arunachal Pradesh. By pursuing another policy driven initiative for these islands we could leverage the latent potential. This can be achieved by creating a new administrative setup.

I am grateful to Lt. General Bhopinder Singh, Lt. Governor of these islands during my visit in 2012 for his frank discussion. I am also grateful to Lt. General Marwah Commander-in-Chief of the Unified Command (CINCAN), Vice Admiral Murlidharan DG Coast Guards, Mr. Anand, the current Chief Secretary, Mr. Vivek Rae and Mr. Shakti Sinha, the former Chief Secretaries of Andaman and Nicobar Islands. Admiral Arun Prakash, the Former Chief of Naval Staff, Admiral Premvir Das, former Fortress Commander and the current Deputy Chief of Naval Staff. I am also thankful to Mr. Sanjay Singh, former Secretary Ministry of External Affairs (MEA), Ms. Navreka Sharma, India's former Ambassador to Indonesia, and Ms. Veena Sikri and Mr. Rajiv Mittal India's former Ambassadors to Bangladesh. I am also grateful to Mr. Naresh Chandra former Cabinet, Home and Defence Secretary as well as India's Ambassador to US for discussing with me some finer points of my hypothesis and giving suggestions.

I am grateful to Sheela Bajaj Sahi who went through the draft and offered useful suggestions. I am also grateful to Air Marshal Naresh Verma, who has been a dear friend since our days together in Car Nicobar for fixing many appointments. I am, however, most grateful to Prof. D.B. Gupta, currently at National Council of Applied Economic Research (NCAER), who went through each page of my draft meticulously and offered suggestions. The staff of IDSA has been very helpful especially Ms Sumita Kumar and Mr. Vivek Dhankar. I would also like to make a special mention of Mandeep Singh Gauri who helped me with the typing, corrections and computer work for which I am very grateful to him. Thanks are also due to my wife Ranjana and daughter Mahima who put up with my excuses for not doing work relating to her marriage and to my son Ishan, who during his visit from London, where he lives, went through some parts of the draft. Finally, my thanks goes to Shri N.S. Sisodia, the former Director-General of IDSA who offered this book project to me and Dr. Arvind Gupta the current Director-General who has been extremely helpful in all matters and took keen interest in the progress of my work.

Sanat Kaul

Abbreviations

ASEAN	Association of South East Nations
CICIR	China Institute of Contemporary International Relations
DGCA	Director General Civil Aviation
EEZ	Exclusive Economic Zone
EHL	Ellong Hinengo Limited
GNI	Great Nicobar Island
IMB	International Maritime Bureau
IMO	International Maritime Organisation
IOR	Indian Ocean Region
LAC	Line of Actual Control
LEP	Look East Policy
LOC	Line of Control
LTC	Leave Travel Concession
LTTE	Liberation Tigers of Tamil Elam
MEA	Ministry of External Affairs
MHA	Ministry of Home Affairs
MOU	Memorandum of Understanding
NDU	National Defence University
NEFA	North East Frontier Agency
NM	Nautical Miles
NSA	National Security Advisor
ONGC	Oil and Natural Gas Commission
PLA	Peoples Liberation Army
PLAN	Peoples Liberation Army Navy
PRC	Peoples Republic of China (Mainland China)
RC	Republic of China (Taiwan)

SLOC	Sea Lanes of Communications
UN	United Nations
UNDP	United Nations Development Programme
UNGA	United Nations General Assembly

List of Maps, Photographs and Table

CHAPTER 1

Introduction

> *"I have carefully gone through the correspondence between External Affairs Ministry and our Ambassador in Peking and through him the Chinese Government. I have tried to pursue this correspondence as favourably to our Ambassador and the Chinese Government as possible, but I regret to say that neither of them has come out well as a result of this study. The Chinese Government has tried to dilute us by professions of peaceful intentions. My own feeling is that at a crucial period they managed to instil in our Ambassador a false sense of confidence in their so called desire to settle the Tibetan problem by peaceful means. There can be no doubt that during the period covered by this correspondence the Chinese must have been concentrating for an onslaught on Tibet. The final action of the Chinese, to my judgment, is little short of perfidy. The tragedy of it is that the Tibetans have put faith in us; they chose to be guided by us; and we have been unable to get them out the meshes of Chinese diplomacy or Chinese malevolence. From the latest position, it appears that we shall not be able to rescue Dalai Lama. Our Ambassador has been at great pain to find an explanation or justification for the Chinese policy and actions."*
>
> (Extract from Text of Sardar Vallabhbhai Patel, Deputy Prime Minister and Home Minister of India's letter to Jawaharlal Nehru on November 7, 1950).

India as a country has a long land border with Pakistan, China and Nepal and also with Myanmar and Bangladesh. In the north, the Himalayan Range provided the barrier between India and Tibet but after the Chinese aggressive takeover of Tibet, the Chinese border has come in contact with the Indian border which is always under tension. The 1914 McMahon Line drawn between India and Tibet is not acceptable to China as a border. With Pakistan there is a dispute over Kashmir which has led to tension on the border. With Nepal, Bhutan, and Myanmar the borders are peaceful. With Bangladesh the border is peaceful though full settlement is yet to be carried out. However, India also has island territories both in the Arabian Sea and in the Bay of Bengal which are both peaceful. The Andaman & Nicobar Islands are two archipelagos which form a chain between Myanmar and the Straits of Malacca and consist of 572 islands, islets and rocks. The importance of these islands which lie between Myanmar and the western entrance of Straits of Malacca has not been fully appreciated from the strategic

Map 1: Chinese Territorial Claims over India and South China Sea

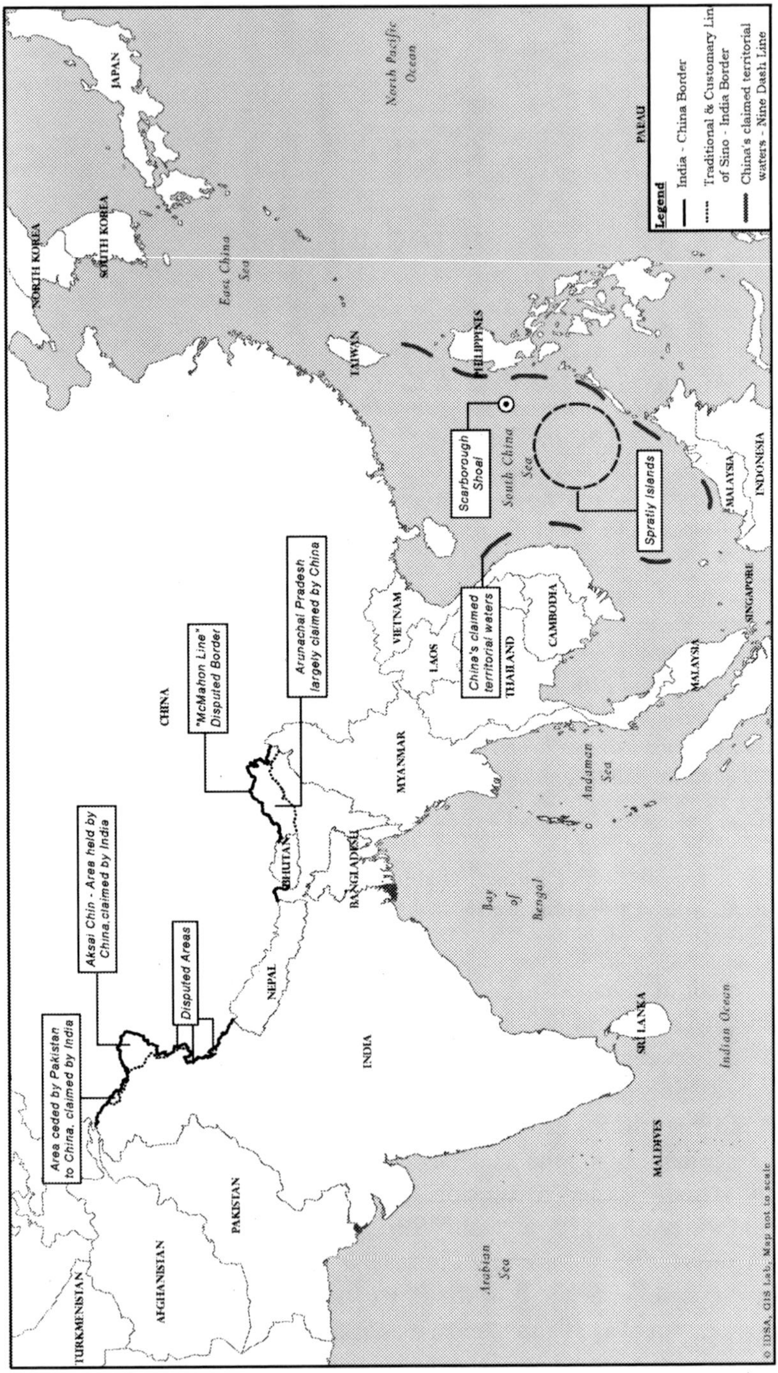

angle. This book is therefore, an examination of the advantages of leveraging the potential of these islands in the present day security scenario in view of China and Pakistan breathing down India's neck.

The strategic importance of Andaman & Nicobar Islands can therefore, be discussed in following ways:

- Chinese encirclement of India and our difficulties in North and West. The critical location of the Great Nicobar Island which gives us tremendous advantage over Straits of Malacca, a Sea Lane of Communication (SLOC) critical to trade and movement of oil from Gulf to South China Sea, East China Sea and the Pacific.
- The two archipelagos consisting of 572 islands, islets and rocks that form a chain gives India its strategic and economic importance in the Bay of Bengal as well as in the Indo-Pacific region.
- These islands also provide India with tremendous economic potential for tourism, fisheries, forests and enable India to add about 30 per cent of its additional Exclusive Economic Zone (EEZ)[1] post UNCLOS III of 1982 which will bring future benefits from undersea mining and potential oil and gas.
- The advantage of India's settled maritime boundaries with its neighbours in the east.
- India and growth of regional groups in the Indo-Pacific.
- Naval diplomacy and defense initiatives in the Indo-Pacific.
- Boosting our Look East Policy (LEP) of 1991.
- Display of India's soft power vis-à-vis the Indo-Pacific Region.

In order to appreciate the full strategic and economic value of these islands, it is necessary to do a review of existing policies and strategic threats. There is a need to assess whether the policy of '*Masterly Inactivity and Benign Neglect*' being followed so far needs to be replaced by a policy of '*Proactive Development*' by leveraging its potential with a forward strategic policy in mind. The comparative analysis with Mauritius, Caribbean Islands and even coastal resorts of Thailand like that of Phuket is necessary to evaluate the hidden wealth of these islands through controlled tourism. It may also be pointed out that out of a coastline of 7,517 kms, a coastline of over 1,962 kms comes from the Andaman and Nicobar archipelagic chain of islands.

Late K.M. Panikkar, an intellectual and India's Ambassador to China in the pre-communist regime in the late 1940s as well as to the communist regime stated in 1959 that the "possession of Andaman & Nicobars gives protection to the East Coast and gives adequate control of the Bay of Bengal". He had also mentioned that "India should not neglect these islands and develop suitable naval and air force facilities."[2]

Historical Background to India-China Dispute

The strategic importance of Andaman & Nicobar Islands has to be seen in the light of its proximity to the Straits of Malacca. The fact that Great Nicobar Island is only 80 miles from the western entrance of Straits of Malacca has its own implications. The Chinese leadership is quite aware that whoever will control the Straits of Malacca will be able to choke the supply line of Peoples Republic of China (PRC). While the Indian land borders are embroiled in disputes and stalemates, it is its maritime borders that bring a ray of hope to resolving the issues and, perhaps, turning the tables. This is, therefore, an important issue for strategic analysis.

Mistakes of the past have to be either forgotten or corrected. First, India made its strategic mistake in referring the Kashmir incident of October 1947 to the United Nations (UN), a matter which UN could not resolve; Second, India helped China in building a road in Aksai Chin by providing food for their troops sent on mules from India over the Himalayas; Third, by recognition of Tibet as "a region of China" in the famous Panchsheel Agreement of 1954 without seeking a quid pro quo on the border issue, India unilaterally surrendered all its assets in Tibet. These consisted of posts of Agents in Lhasa, Gyantse and Gartok, along with troops, about a dozen government rest houses and a telegraph line running from Lhasa to India since the days of the Young Husband Expedition of 1904. This policy of giving into Chinese aggressive postures exists even now on the land frontier i.e. 4,057 km Line of Actual Control (LAC), one of the longest and highest in the world to exert pressure on India. Over 600 "transgressions" implying intrusions have been recorded over the years and a policy of appeasement continues. In this connection analysis by Claude Arpi, an India-China expert on Chinese brazenness and India's preference for continued engagement with China, is interesting where he has established that Chinese have realised that India has become submissive by show of force.[3]

Having shocked India in 1962 by an armed aggression through a perceived impenetrable wall of the Himalayas in which they have still retained 35,000 sq km of uninhabited territory in Ladakh (Aksai Chin), the Chinese withdrew in Arunachal Pradesh (erstwhile NEFA) which they occupied in war, a territory of 93,000 kms which they still claim as theirs. This is so because they do not accept the McMahon Line, signed at the Simla conference of 1914 between the British, Tibet and China. Over time the Chinese have built very good relations with India's neighbours on the land frontiers. The boundary agreement signed between Myanmar (then Burma) and China in 1961 is on the basis of the McMahon Line of 1914, in spite of the Chinese claim of 'unequal treaties' with the British.[4] They signed a boundary agreement with Pakistan in 1963 in which Pakistan gave away 5000 sq km of land in Gilgit/Baltistan region, disputed territory between India and Pakistan to China. This takes the wind out of India's diplomatic strategy followed under Nehru. The McMahon line is the accepted international

Map 2: Chinese Held Territories in Kashmir

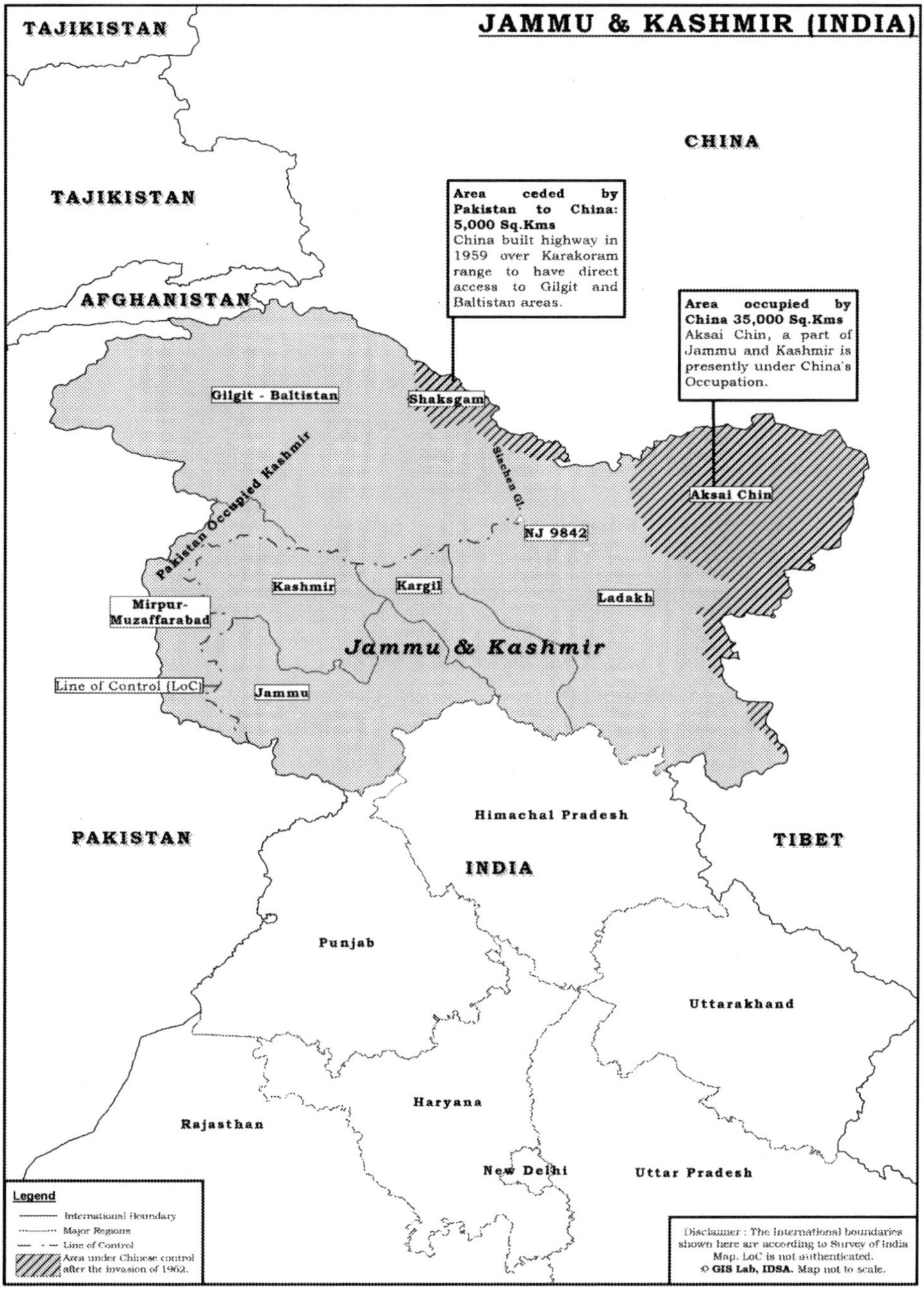

boundary since 1914 when Simla Agreement was signed between India, China and Tibet as equals. It is true that the Chinese representative who had plenipotentiary power and letters of Credentials initialed the agreement but the government of China did not ratify it. However, the Tibetan Representative, who sat as an equal with full plenipotentiary powers, signed the agreement based on the McMahon Line.

The famous economist John Kenneth Galbraith, who was then the Ambassador of United States to India (selected by President John Kennedy), supported this line by his announcement on October 27, 1962 that that US supports the McMahon Line. Again after 50 years, the US Ambassador to India, Nancy Powell, reconfirmed this in 2012 in Guwahati in India.[5] The forcible military occupation of independent Tibet by the Chinese forces from 1950-59, culminated in the Dalai Lama seeking refuge in India, something that Sardar Patel, India's Deputy Prime Minister predicted in his letter to Nehru.[6]

India under Nehru was, however, not prepared to take up the matter at the UN in spite of a request by the Tibetans in order not to offend the Chinese.[7] It was El Salvador which took up the Tibetan case at the UN with a draft resolution entitled "Invasion of Tibet by Foreign Forces" and lost as India was not forthcoming in its support. In 1961, Malay and Ireland joined El Salvador and Thailand to request the UN to adopt a resolution on similar lines. US and UK, the then two major powers, looked to India to provide a lead in this issue but Nehru was very lukewarm towards it and did not support the resolution.[8] The Western powers, following Nehru's lead, did the same in spite of the fact that they did not recognise the communist regime in China and the resolution never got passed. However, India gave refuge to Dalai Lama in 1959 which put India-China relations into a freeze which continues even now in spite of the rhetoric by the governments of either side that relations are improving and trade is booming (trade between India and China is yet another story). The net result was to bring Chinese borders common with India's. The prediction made by Sardar Vallabhbhai Patel, Deputy Prime Minister and Home Minister of India in a letter dated November 7, 1950, ignored by Nehru came through within a decade. The 1962 War by China over their claim of Indian territory was a result of this issue. The Chinese War against India over the Himalayas was in two theatres—the Eastern Theatre consisting of erstwhile NEFA (now called Arunachal Pradesh) and the Western Theatre which is called Ladakh (a part of Jammu & Kashmir (J&K) state). After occupation of NEFA, the Chinese retreated fully in the eastern theatre but they retained 5000 sq km in the western theatre. One reason for withdrawing from the eastern theatre was perhaps due to the effective administration of India over the tribal population, which was not the case in the western theatre. This will be further discussed in Chapters 9 and 10.

India-China Conundrum and Andaman & Nicobar Islands

After a series of diplomatic blunders in the last 65 years India needs to reassess its strategy, consider its strong and weak points and correct the course of its foreign policy. This assessment of strategic implications of Andaman & Nicobar Islands will fall into one such correction which, if implemented properly, could change the course of history of the country. It will also give India the strategic leverage to discuss the border issues in the land areas from a position of strength. India has seen from past experience that China appreciates a country which speaks from a position of strength and not necessarily friendship. Andaman & Nicobar Islands came to India on the departure of the British in 1947 and the Indian Government followed a policy of 'Masterly Inactivity' and 'Benign Neglect' (discussed later in Chapter 8). These Islands however, may be able to give India the "position of strategic strength" if it decides to follow appropriate policies.

The over fifty year old war of 1962 has left a permanent scar on India's psyche, difficult to undo in spite of government claims that all is well.[9] (In spite of Minister Jairam Ramesh's most unwarranted comments in China in 2010 with regard to security issues with China[10]). How can India move on with China and Pakistan joining hands in "bleeding India to death by a thousand cuts"?[11]

Map 3: India-Malacca and South-China Sea

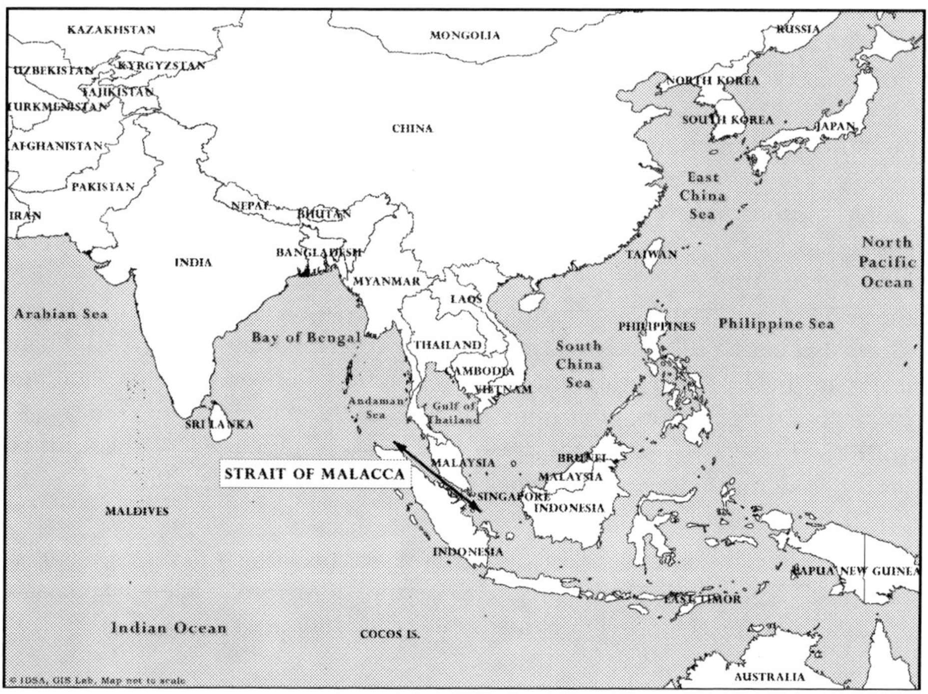

The geopolitical scenario for India is indeed depressing, a mess created by its own politicians and Nehruvian diplomacy. Chinese Communist Party (CCP) meanwhile, has no compunctions in supplying nuclear technology to Pakistan in spite of having signed the Non Proliferation Treaty (NPT) (the Chinese claim that they did all this before signing the Treaty is dubious) and helping regimes like the Army Junta which ruled Myanmar for 50 years while India's foreign policy allowed its goodwill with Myanmar to get dissipated. India's official protest, if any, has not been heard loudly even in India regarding the Chinese building of the Karakoram Highway and the pipelines for gas and oil all the way from Gwadar to Kashgar in Xingjiang through the territory of Pakistan Occupied Kashmir, Gilgit and Baltistan which has been accepted as disputed territory between India and Pakistan by China and mentioned in its border agreement with Pakistan in 1963. (See Appendix 1, Article 6).

There is also a view held by some persons directly involved in strategic issues that high volume of trade between India and China will lead to greater cooperation between the two countries and will ease out border differences over time. This view, however, is not supported by facts on ground. As Prashant Kumar Singh and Rumel Dahiya state in their article on Managing India-China Relations "Rising Trade Volumes have not stopped China from trading additional friction points like stapled visas for residents of (J&K) and damming of Brahmaputra. There is a view that prosperity has made China more assertive."[12] Further, it also appears that China wants to leave the boundary dispute unresolved as a deliberate move to keep India off balance as already 37 rounds of talks have been held at various levels over 30 years.[13] As security analyst Bharat Karnad[14] points out in his article "A frog in the hot water" that the Chinese way of cooking a frog is to put it in water and heat it, but slowly. If the water is heated quickly the frog will jump out of the vessel. If the heat is turned on gradually the frog will luxuriate in the comfort of warm water, unmindful of its final fate. He feels that India is perhaps like the frog mentioned above. In the same article, he goes on to say "the National Security Advisor (NSA) Shivshankar Menon, apparently oblivious to the developments adversely affecting India's vital national interests in the Indian Ocean Region (IOR), declared the other day that 'maritime rivalry with China is not inevitable.' Such pronouncements do nothing, of course, to prevent New Delhi appearing foolish, confirming the Chinese estimation of this country as a 'push over state'. We are once again shocked and reminded of the Chinese profligacy during October, 2012 when they crossed the unmarked Line of Control (LoC) by 19 kilometres in Ladakh.

Therefore, to checkmate China's aggressive designs along with their all-weather friend Pakistan, utilising the strategic importance of Andaman & Nicobar Islands appears to be an obvious alternative strategy for India to adopt.

Chinese Perception of the Straits of Malacca

According to Sithara Fernando,[15] "China's most important maritime concerns in its relations with South Asia are oceanic trade transit points for western China, the sea lanes connecting the Straits of Hormuz and the Straits of Malacca which carry its energy imports."[16] Further according to Che Lin,[17] "China's National Security and peaceful development demand that the Indian Ocean be incorporated into the national security strategy because China's trade, investment, energy, religion, territory and territorial seas are intimately linked to Indian Ocean."[18] Further the Chinese position in the Pacific Ocean is not so good with Japan and US being somewhat hostile to it. It, therefore, looks to the Indian Ocean to avoid further entanglement in the western pacific and avoid the hostile maritime theatre dominated by the US. In any case 80 per cent of China's oil supply comes from the Gulf. And hence the 'Malacca dilemma' for China is real. This has been explained further by the scholars of China Institute of Contemporary International Relations (CICIR) and Renmin University when they state that since the problems arising out of the Western Pacific Region due to the presence of Japan and China are difficult and not likely to be resolved in the short term, the Indian Ocean will be an important passage to bypass the US Military's Pacific chain. As Wang Lirong[19] states "access to Indian Ocean is a perfect option for China to reduce its dependence on waterways on the western Pacific and to breach the West island chain lock".

While China is fast catching up as a maritime power even at cutting edge level, its main interest is to protect it's maritime interests. These include South and East China seas issues and securing its strategic waterways like the Straits of Malacca. The Peoples Liberation Army Navy (PLAN) has over time made two revisions to its strategic guidance since 1987 with the first being securing East and South China Seas and the other being securing its waterways in which Straits of Malacca is the most important.[20]

With US becoming more active in South and East China Seas' disputes, the Chinese Navy is likely to show its potential capacity to create problems in the Indian Ocean. The Straits of Malacca is certainly a major choke point for China and it is here that the Indian state should leverage its advantage. Herein lies the importance of Andaman & Nicobar Islands which forms a chain from Malacca western entrance to Myanmar.

Next in importance comes the danger from non-state actors like pirates in Somalia and even in Straits of Malacca.

Security Consequences of Policy of Benign Neglect and Masterly Inactivity

Security of these islands is not ensured by a policy of benign neglect. There have been many reported cases of anti-nationals and terrorists using these islands as a safe haven. According to Ramtanu Maitra[21] in early February 2005 India apprehended 34 Arakan separatists from Myanmar hiding in Landfall Island in north Andaman. They were a part of the Arakan Army illegally residing in these islands and were regrouping there.

Bertil Lintner[22] confirms that more than 70 Arakanese had been apprehended in the "Long Island" in the Andaman Islands and 145 guns ceased. There was also the *Operation Leach* mounted by Indian Intelligence wherein they were aided by Arakanese rebels who used the Andaman Islands. In this connection, Nandita Haksar[23] had written a detailed book called *Rogue Agent*.

There are also reports amongst the intelligence community that the banned Liberation Tigers of Tamil Eelam (LTTE) has been using these islands as an arms depot as they could operate in these islands quite freely. While security in these islands has been loose, with deterioration in the security scenario in Bangladesh, Nepal, and Bhutan and also northeast states of India like Manipur, Nagaland and Tripura, misuse of these islands as safe havens has been a casualty. To say that these islands are cut off with high seas and therefore safe is not acceptable in the present day reality. This is similar to the false notion of the impenetrable Himalayas prevalent in the 1950s. LTTE had a Wing called 'Sea Tigers' which was their navy. The sea tigers of LTTE had strong links with African pirates. Therefore, like the Himalayas, Andaman & Nicobar Islands should not be considered safe and impenetrable any more due to their isolation.

It has also been reported that foreigners from Myanmar, Bangladesh and Sri Lanka have permanently settled in the Andamans using fake Indian "Ration Cards", which have become identity cards for Indians for many purposes. According to these unofficial reports even as early as 2003 about 50,000 foreigners had settled in various islands of Andaman. Nicobars have very little problem of this nature but there have been reports that Thai fishermen come and live with friendly Nicobarese of Southern Nicobars. With little to do in these islands as employment is not easily available, and they do not have technical skills, they generally turn to unlawful activities.

The Security Apparatus

The Indian Coast Guards set up in 1978 as an armed force of the union by the Coast Guard Act remained grossly under equipped. One cannot, therefore, eliminate the possibility of occupation of one of the deserted islands by unlawful or unwanted elements. However, of late, especially post Mumbai attack from the sea by terrorists from Pakistan on November 26, 2008 there has been a marked improvement. This issue is discussed further in Chapter 8.

About a third of India's EEZ is around the Andaman & Nicobar Islands but the coast guards are not equipped properly to manage its surveillance. In the last ten years, the Coastguards, the Fishing Federation and the Indian Ocean Tuna

Commission (IOTC) have received several complaints about foreign vessels illegally fishing in India's waters. According to a study by the University of British Columbia (UBC) in 2010, it is estimated that India incurs a loss of US$ 150 million to 200 million per year due to illegal and unreported fishing in India's EEZ. The Fisheries Sector contributes about two per cent of India's GDP. It can be assumed that a very large portion of this theft is from EEZ of Andaman & Nicobar Islands as a very large number of poachers are from Myanmar, Thailand etc. including the far off Taiwan.[24] The meager coastguard deployment in Andaman & Nicobar Islands is certainly not based on the proportionate size of its EEZ and the estimated loss due to poaching.

The role of Indian intelligence needs a special mention. This is so because they have not been very resourceful in their work of intelligence gathering in these islands as they followed extremely negative policies which are in fact detrimental to both security and growth. This was by not allowing tourism to come up in uninhabited islands. They have by this logic, cut their own limbs of information gathering. The policy of benign neglect was reconfirmed by the Intelligence Bureau (IB) when in 1992-93 Madhavrao Scindia, then Tourism Minister, persistently requested them for opening of more islands for tourism, especially for foreign tourism but the Intelligence Bureau disallowed opening of any uninhabited islands. The fact that all these uninhabited islands which are without surveillance can be a great attraction to terrorists and such unlawful groups along with accompanying illegal and underground activities was of no significance to them. Maldives, a country which has 26 islands with only a few inhabited, has on the other hand adopted a policy which is contrary to the Indian one. It allows tourism only in uninhabited islands so that there is no cultural clash with the local residents. It is unfortunate that the Indian Intelligence and the Ministry of Home Affairs (MHA) discouraged promoting tourism in these islands when from their angle it can be a source of intelligence gathering. If high end tourism is promoted as is being done in Bhutan or the Caribbean it could become a great source of intelligence. Low end tourism, however, with large numbers can be detrimental to both security and environment. Ultimately, it is the model of tourism that one adopts and implements properly that determines the outcome. This issue is discussed in greater detail in Chapter 9.

Need for Proactive Policies

Showing India's physical presence in these islands is very important. The recent Chinese military occupation of Paracel Islands in South China Sea where the Chinese have suddenly put a civilian governor in the garrison city of Sansha, with their flag and supported by their navy, is a case in point of having actual jurisdiction over one's own under governed territory. Having experienced the Chinese land grab over un-administered territory like Ladakh in the Western Himalayas of India, which they occupied in 1962 and continue to occupy still,

India has not learn its lessons. In comparison, territories of the present Arunachal Pradesh which were under active governance of India in 1962 as the result of a forward policy adopted in the 1950s were returned. Only 38 of the 572 islands and islets are inhabited and uninhabited islands being prohibited for tourism promotion is an outdated and absurd notion of Indian intelligence. This will be discussed further in Chapter 9.

The Nicobar Islands

The Nicobar Group of Islands are crucial to India's security scenario and pose yet another challenge. The MHA has prohibited these islands both to Indians and foreigners for the last 60 years. While the Indians can go with the permission of the local Deputy Commissioner at Port Blair and Car Nicobar, foreigners require an approval of the MHA, which is a near impossible task for the ordinary visitor. In addition, due to no air service and extremely poor inter-island shipping, these islands remain isolated within India and more so with foreign countries which are nearer than the Indian mainland.[25] While the Government of India has provided good governance over these islands, lack of development and integration can lead to isolation which could result in a North-East India like situation.

These 12 inhabited and three uninhabited islands of the Nicobar group have had very little jurisdiction by the Indian Administration. As an anecdotal reference it may be recounted that when Chief Commissioner Mr. A.K. Ghosh[26] visited the small isolated islands of southern Nicobars like Kondul or Little Nicobar in the fifties, the village Captain or headman came out holding a Union Jack to welcome him as he had no idea that the British had left. The Union Jack was then taken back and the Indian flag was handed over. In a similar way another anecdotal incident in which the author was involved happened in 1976, when in a planned discussion meeting the leader of the Planning Commission commented on a scheme in which exercise books, pencil and erasers were provided free to tribal school children of Nicobars. He also made a remark that a scheme like this spoils the tribals and he expressed a desire to scrap the ongoing schemes. Since the author was the Deputy Commissioner of Nicobars he replied stating that they may cancel the scheme and assured them that Nicobarese would not miss it as they do not seek free gifts from anyone. They are proud people and they will buy these items for their children. However, he further questioned them whether they could tell where Nicobar Islands were without looking on the atlas. He further asked whether they were aware that these islands may have remained crown property or had gone to Pakistan due to their proximity to East Pakistan (Bangladesh now). He also mentioned that the moment there is some unsettling secessionist activity like in the north east India, the Government of India goes to them with bagsful of money. Having heard him there was a silence followed by some whispering amongst themselves and then the leader announced 'passed'.

The purpose of mentioning this anecdotal reference was to show how shallow the understanding and appreciation of our own officers was with regard to these islands.

The author can add two more personal anecdotes regarding the isolation of these islands and the lack of surveillance that existed. In 1975, when he was first going to Car Nicobar to take over as Deputy Commissioner of the Nicobar Group of islands he took the overnight inter-island ship called *Yerwa* from Port Blair. In the morning he was called by the Captain of the ship to the deck and informed that a foreign ship was in the territorial waters. As there were no Coast Guards or marine police it decided to overtake the ship. The ship had moved away from India's territorial waters and after a chase *Yerwa* caught up with it. It was a beautiful ship with a New Orleans registration. The occupants were called out by loud speakers to find out why they were in Indian territorial waters. They returned the request by throwing a paper wrapped in a stone across to *Yerwa* which said that they were not in India's territorial waters and left full stream. Being a civil ship it was decided that nothing could be done to apprehend them and they were allowed to go and the matter was reported to higher authorities.

Similarly, in 1975-76 the author got a report of an abandoned ship grounded on the south coast of the Great Nicobar Island towards Straits of Malacca. The matter was reported to all concerned on wireless but no reply came in spite of reminders. In the meantime, two tugs came from Straits of Malacca, pulled the ship out and towed it away while the local authorities could only watch from air with the help of Air Force aircraft. This incident shows how sovereignty of a country can be violated even by a foreign commercial company when effective control is missing.

Strategic Significance of Andaman & Nicobar Islands in the Present Day Scenario

While the importance of Straits of Malacca as one of the 10 SLOCs in the world will be discussed in later chapters, the significance of these islands can only be stressed as they form a virtual chain in the Bay of Bengal and extend India's land as well as maritime borders right up to Straits of Malacca. The two outstanding full length airstrips at Car Nicobar, which is an air force base and at Port Blair, which is a naval base along with two shorter airstrips at Diglipur in North Andamans and Campbell Bay in the Great Nicobar Island, offer a very wide coverage for aerial surveillance. The ports of Port Blair, Mayabandar in the Andamans and Nancowry in the Nicobars offer the navy outstanding natural harbours and can be very useful for naval fleets. The Nancowry Harbour is very deep located far south with Islands of Karmota and Nancowry on either side with two openings on either side.

The Indian Navy's 2009 Indian Maritime Doctrine clearly states that China is seeking to strategically encircle India. It is here that India's strategic advantage lies in the Andaman & Nicobar Islands. Chinese commentators readily acknowledge India's superior geographical position in the Andaman & Nicobar Islands just like the Chinese have in Tibet which they occupied by military force in 1959. Further, a Chinese commentator sees the establishment of Andaman & Nicobar Integrated Command in 2001 as a potential challenge to them. As Liu Jianzhong writes, 'By virtue of its geographical advantage, India has taken a lead in enhancing its control over the western exit of Straits of Malacca between Malaya peninsula and the Sumatra Island.[27]

Ma Ying[28] from the Shanghai Institute of International Studies (SIIS) states that the geopolitical-political position of Andaman & Nicobar Islands is such that being only 80 miles from Straits of Malacca it is like an unsinkable super carrier. As a matter of fact, with four air strips in these Islands there may be no need to keep an aircraft carrier in the Bay of Bengal. It is also like a protective screen and guards India's SLOC. The Military Command at the Andaman & Nicobar Islands is seen to be part of an exclusionary policy of India designed to keep extra-regional powers out. It could provide a check on China's westward expansion into the Indian Ocean.[29] Further as Shi Chunlin of Dalian Maritime University (DMU) states that while India's increased military deployment plays a role of guardian over Straits of Malacca and can monitor in peacetime the transit of Chinese warships and merchant vessels, in wartime the Indian Navy could quickly seal off the Straits of Malacca and other passages entering the Indian Ocean from the east. Liu Quing[30] of the National Defence University (NDU) goes further and states that "based on the 2009 Indian Maritime Doctrine Andaman & Nicobar Command could not only direct a distant blockade against China on the western side of the Straits of Malacca, it could also launch a naval offensive ashore against the Chinese mainland."

The Indian interest in the Straits of Malacca is further enforced by India's Look East Policy (LEP) of 1991. India's oil interests with Vietnam in South China Sea and the offshore blocks that Indian companies have acquired in areas like the Sakhalin Islands off Vladivostok in Eastern Russia and even the oil blocks off the Venezuela coast require that the Straits of Malacca remain open, peaceful and within India's capacity to ensure that no unwanted power tries to block it. Protecting the western entrance of the Straits of Malacca is not only in India's interest but falls into its blue water capabilities as the Great Nicobar Island (GNI) tip is only 80 miles from it. While it is true that in 2006 the Indian Fleet Review showcased its blue water capability with over 50 naval vessels including an aircraft carrier, submarine and advanced stealth frigates, India is yet to consolidate its naval presence in Andaman & Nicobar Islands. Setting up of a new Naval Air Base Baaz in Campbell Bay in the Great Nicobar Island in 2012 is a step in this direction. According to Sahkuja[31] India's preparations are for a blue water navy. It may be pointed out that South China Sea, claimed by China, has had presence of Indian Naval Ships. In 2000, a naval flotilla of five ships including a submarine was sent to South China Sea with port calls at Singapore, Vietnam, South Korea, Japan and Indonesia. This was seen as a challenge to China by the Chinese authorities. In three separate steps Indian Naval Ships were sent to South China Seas-to familiarise them with a potential theatre of operation. *The Economist* magazine has stated that the US Navy finds the Indian Navy up to North Atlantic Treaty Organisation (NATO) standards.[32]

In addition to the strategic location of these islands India should also consider the possible hydro-carbon potential of these islands. The Andaman Sea basin is located between the well explored and mature hydro-carbon producing provinces of Myanmar in the north and Sumatra (Indonesia) in the south. Both these areas contain major gas production fields viz Yadana and Yetagun in Myanmar and Arun in Indonesia.

The exploration activities in the Andaman Basin commenced in 1959 by the Oil and Natural Gas Commission (ONGC) Ltd. of India with about 4,533 sq kilometres of the islands covered by reconnaissance survey. The Andaman Basin should be considered as the frontier area for hydro-carbon exploration. So far 21 wells have been drilled and some gas has been discovered which was considered sub-commercial. Geological formations of Thermogenic and Biogenic nature were found, similar to Yadana and Yetagun gas fields in Myanmar and Arun gas field in Sumatra. It is generally felt that continued exploration activities will definitely prove availability of commercial hydro carbon in the Andaman Basin.

This book has been divided into 10 chapters. The purpose is to explain to the readers the role that these islands can play in India's Strategic Conundrum with China and Pakistan bent upon keeping India down as part of their foreign policy. Only if India leverages the advantages and potential of these islands as part of the LEP, can it perhaps, be in a position of some strength and in a position to counter some aggressive designs. Chapter 2 provides a brief description of these islands, with a detailed history of Nicobar Islands, which the author feels need more attention due to their proximity to the western entrance of the Straits of Malacca. Chapter 3 describes the importance of Straits of Malacca and the issue of the Malacca dilemma of China and how it is trying to reduce its dependence upon it. Chapter 4 goes into the importance of the maritime boundary agreement which India has with its maritime neighbours in the East. Chapter 5 is all about South China Sea, the Chinese claims, issues with ASEAN and Japan. Chapters 6 and 7 describe India's civil and military regional groups and naval diplomacy. Chapter 8 is about the shift in India's defence policy with reference to the LEP of 1991. Chapter 9 discusses the inadequacies of civil policy towards these islands while Chapter 10 offers a policy prescription.

NOTES

1. Exclusive Economic Zone provided by UN Convention on Law of the Seas III.
2. See C. Raja Mohan *Samudra Manthan: Sino-Indian Rivalry in the Indo-Pacific,* CEIP, Washington DC, 2012.
3. See Claude Arpi, "Intrude, Violate and then offer to discuss", *Pioneer*, April 26, 2013.
4. McMahon Line at the border between Tibet and India on the eastern side based on Tripartite Shimla Conference called by the British Indian government in 1913-14, held over six months where China, Tibet and India sat as equals with each representative carrying their credentials. McMahon Line was the border proposed by Mr. McMahon, Secretary of State, who was leading the Indian delegation over the India-Tibet border. This Line was also to divide Tibet into inner and outer Tibet on the lines of what Russians did to Mongolia in 1930, dividing Mongolia.
5. http://www.indianexpress.com/news/us-on-arunachal/1048314/0
6. The occupation of Tibet in 1950-59 was without any doubt an armed aggression on an independent country. The British myth of giving suzerainty to China over Tibet was created by their fear of the Russians taking away Tibet as part of the then Great Game. The Government of India under Nehru with Pannikar as India's Ambassador to pre and post-communist China, conveniently converted the concept of suzerainty into sovereignty.
7. The Tibetan request to take up the matter at the UN had to be carried out by a member of the UN. India was the Dalai Lama's obvious choice . However, Nehru was not interested in taking up their case at all as he did not want to upset the new communist regime in China.
8. R.S. Kalha, "Tibet as a factor in Sino-Indian relations", *Journal of Defence Studies,* 6 (4), October 12, 2012, pp. 7-26.
9. Claude Arpi, *Born in Sin: The Panchsheel Agreement: The Sacrifice of Tibet,* Mittal Publications, New Delhi, 2004 gives a detailed analysis of how we sacrificed our own interest in 1954, signing of the Panchsheel Agreement.
10. Jairam Ramesh, while visiting China said that policies of Government of India were "alarming" and the Government was paranoid of Chinese businessman entering the Industrial Sector in India. www.rediff.com/news/report/rameshs-chin
11. The concept of thousand cuts to bleed India to death was propounded by Zulfikar Ali Bhutto, former Prime Minister of Pakistan.
12. Prashant Kumar Singh and Rumel Dahiya, "Managing India-China Relations", in Rumel Dahiya and Ashok Behuria (Eds.) *India's Neighbourhood:Challenges in the Next Two Decades* Pentagon Security International, 2012, pp. 55-94.
13. Brahma Chellaney, "Can you hear the Chinese whisper grow louder", *Times of India,* December 4, 2011.
14. Bharat Karnad, "A frog in the hot water", *Asian Age,* March 29, 2007, p. 7.
15. Sithara Fernando, "China's Post-1978 Maritime Relations with South Asia: Towards Greater Cooperation", *Strategic Analysis,* 36 (3), May-June, 2012, pp. 461-476.
16. Sithara Fernando, Ibid.
17. Please see Toshi Yoshihara, "Chinese views of India in the Indian Ocean: a geo-political perspective",*Strategic Analysis,* 36(3) May-June, 2012, p. 491.
18. *Journal of Chongqing Socialism College.*
19. Wang Lirong (9), p.50, as cited in Toshi Yoshihara, "Chinese view of India in the Indian Ocean: a Geopolitical Perspective",*Strategic Analysis* 36 (3), May-June 2012, p. 492.
20. You Ji, "The Chinese Navy: Regional Power and Global Reach", *Strategic Analysis,* 36(3) May-June, 2012, p. 479.
21. Ramtanu Maitra, Asia Times Online Ltd, 2005.

22. Bertil Lintner, *Great Game East: India, China and the Struggle for Asia's Most Volatile Frontier* HarperCollins, 2012.
23. Nandita Haksar, *Rogue Agent: How India's Military Intelligence Betrayed the Burmese Resistance,* Penguin Books, New Delhi, 2009.
24. Rohini Mohan, "The Great Indian Tuna Robbery", *Tehelka,* March 03, 2012, pp. 12-13.
25. The policy of Isolation of the Nicobar Group of Islands started by the British and followed by the Government of India has in a way paid dividends as there has been no exploitation by the Indian bureaucracy and traders and the Nicobarese have been allowed and encouraged to join the mainstream.
26. Mr. A.K. Ghosh, ICS, was the Chief Commissioner of Andaman and Nicobar Islands from 1949-53.
27. Quoted from Toshi Yoshihara, no. 17, p.495.
28. Ma Ying, "An analysis of India's Maritime Strategy", *Pacific Journal* 18 (6), 2010.
29. Ren Huaifeng, "The intervention of extra regional powers in the changing security dynamics of south sea region", *Forum of World Economics & Politics,* 5, 2009, p.55.
30. Liu Quing, "The 'String of Pearls' Strategy: India's Assessment and Response", *South-Asian Studies Quarterly,* 2, 2010, p. 26-27.
31. Vijay Sakhuja, "Emerging Contours of Asian Naval Powers", *Opinion Asia,* February 05, 2007, p.16.
32. *The Economist,* March 30–April 05, 2013, p.11.

CHAPTER 2

Background of Andaman & Nicobar Archipelagos

Andaman & Nicobar Islands are two archipelagos of 572 islands/islets starting from the southern tip of Myanmar (South of Coco Islands of Myanmar) to the north-western tip of Sumatra divided by the 10 degree channel and include EEZ of about 5,95,217 sq km which is about 30 per cent of India's EEZ. These islands came to India on the departure of the British in 1947 but their strategic importance both from the security angle and potential economic advantage has never been fully appreciated by India. The Japanese had occupied the islands without any resistance, the only part of British-India occupied by Japanese, for about three and a half years till they lost the World War II. For example, while India became independent in 1947, the Royal Air Force (RAF) continued to maintain a Staging Post with an airfield at Car Nicobar up to about 1956 when they decided to leave for their own reasons. The Government of India, for various reasons decided to leave these islands to their own fate maintaining a minimum level of administration but not encouraging any major economic and security activity. Besides the remoteness of this island chain, in the post-independence period, India's financial capability was also very limited to fund the islands. Hence, India adopted a policy of masterly inactivity and benign neglect which has continued even up till now.

As a general background to Andaman & Nicobar Islands the following details bring out the salient features. There is a full administrative set up in all the 38 inhabited islands and some minimal presence in a few uninhabited islands of the Police and Forest Department.

MAPS AND DISTANCES

Administrative set up of Andaman & Nicobar Islands

General Information

Andaman Islands: Capital: Port Blair

Location: Bay of Bengal 920° to 940° East Longitude, 6° to 14° North Latitude

Map 4: Andaman Islands

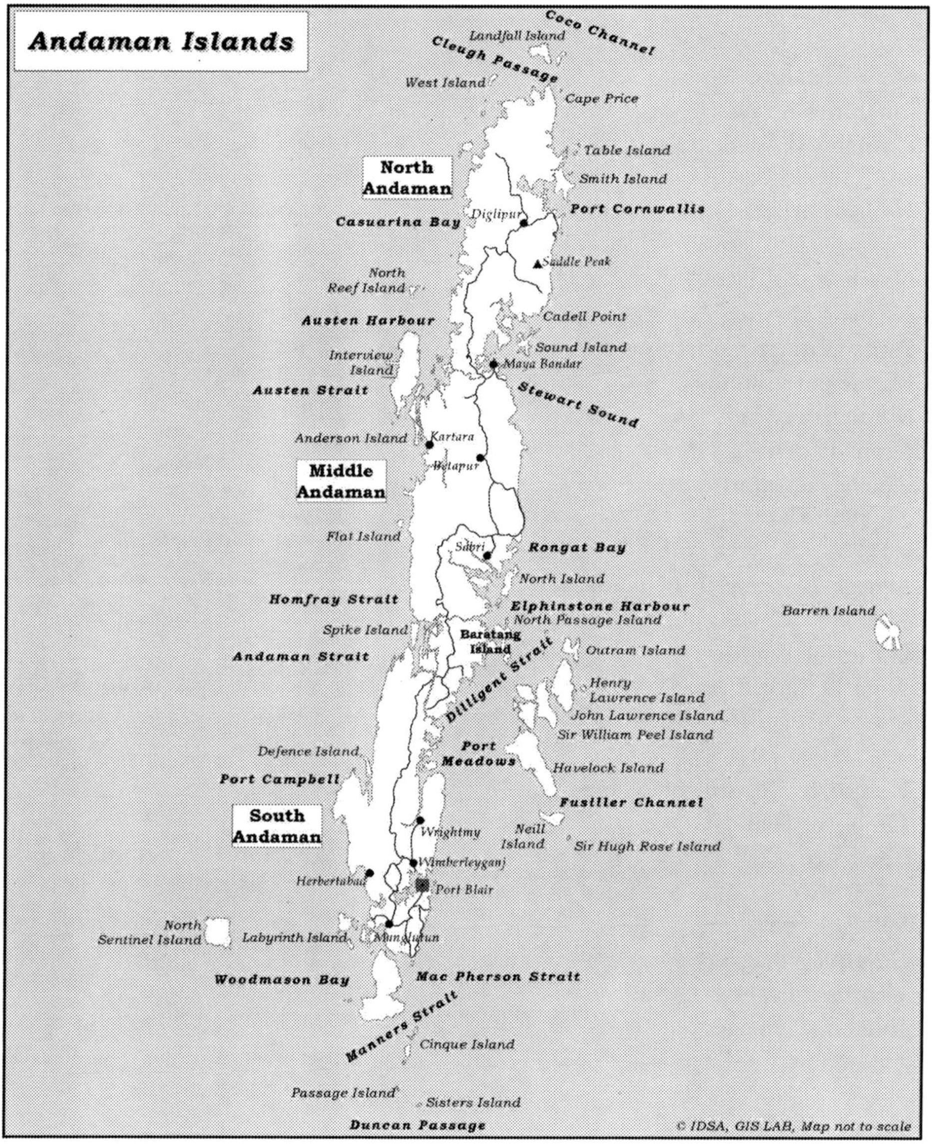

Area South Andaman District:	3,106 sq km
N & M Andaman District:	3,302 sq km
Nicobar District:	1,841 sq km
Total Area:	8,249 sq km
No. of Islands:	572
Inhabited Islands:	38
Un-habited Islands:	534
No. of Districts:	3 South Andaman Districts
North & Middle Andaman District	
Nicobar District	
Parliamentary Constituency:	One
Municipal Councils:	One
Municipal Wards:	18
Gram Panchayats:	67
Panchayat Samities:	Seven
Zilla Parishad:	Two

Length & Breadth of Andaman

Group of Islands:	
Total Length:	467 km (Maximum Width: 52 km, Average Width: 24 Km)
Length & Breadth of Nicobar Group of Islands:	
Total Length:	259 km (Maximum Width: 58 km)

Villages:

Revenue villages:	204
Census villages:	547
Inhabited villages:	501
Uninhabited villages:	46

Population
(Total as well as Sub-division-wise):

Total population:	3,56,152
• South Andaman Sub-Division:	2,08,471
• Mayabunder Sub-Division:	62,736

- Diglipur Sub-Division: 42,877
- Car Nicobar Sub-Division: 20,292
- Nancowry Sub-Division: 13,562
- Campbell Bay Sub-Division 8,214

Literacy rate of males and females (Total as well as sub-division wise):

- South Andaman District: 1,55,403
- North & Middle Andaman District: 71,197
- Nicobar District: 26,535
- Total Male Literates: 1,46,831
- Total Female Literates: 1,06,304

Police Stations

Police stations are spread all over the inhabited islands. The crime rate is negligible.

BACKGROUND OF ANDAMAN ISLANDS

Mythologically, the name Andaman is presumed to be derived from Hanuman, the monkey God, who was known to the Malays as Handuman. Since pre-historic times, these islands were the home of aboriginal tribes. The tribes of the Andaman group of islands are the Great Andamanese, Onges, Jarawas and Sentinelese, all of Negrito origin, while the tribes of Nicobars are the Nicobarese and Shompens, both of Mongoloid stock.

The first settlement on the islands by the British took place in 1789, which was abandoned in 1796. The second settlement which was basically a penal settlement was taken up in 1858, after the first War of Independence in 1857, followed by the settlement of convicts including Moplas, some tribes from Central and United Provinces, refugees from erstwhile East Pakistan, Myanmar and Sri Lanka as well as ex-servicemen. The islands become known in India as "Kala Pani" or black waters due to the penal settlement and its terrible living conditions.[1]

These islands, blessed with natural beauty, 86 per cent forest cover, beaches, undulating creeks, crystal clear water with corals and unpolluted environment command the first place to visit for tourists. This archipelago of more than 572 islets and islands with 37 inhabited islands stretches over a length of more than 700 km from North to South. The topography of the islands is hilly with exotic flora and fauna. The sandy beaches, fringed with coconut palms, and the sea around the island offer excellent scope for adventure water sports including scuba diving and game-fishing. These green islands could attract many nature-lovers, and bird-watchers from all over the world. Adventure tourism like trekking, island camping, snorkeling, scuba diving etc. can become the major attractions here.

Location Bay of Bengal

92° to 94° East Longitude

6° to 14° North Latitude

Capital Port Blair

Highest Peak-Saddle Peak – 732 mtrs

Climate

Tropical and humid, humidity ranges from 70 per cent to 90 per cent with a gentle breeze blowing at all times. The weather is generally pleasant with a mean minimum temperature of 23°C and mean maximum of 30°C.

Access

By Air: Port Blair, the capital city of Andaman & Nicobar Islands is poorly connected with direct flights from only Chennai, Kolkata and Delhi (via Bhubaneshwar) in India. Foreign tourist charter flights are also permitted to land at Port Blair subject to the fulfilment of guidelines of the Director General of Civil Aviation (DGCA). A few islands are also interconnected by helicopters operated by Pawan Hans. However, not many seats are available in these small helicopters. There is a differential tariff structure, one for islanders which is subsidised and the other for the rest. Recently a sea plane has been introduced to a limited number of destinations.

Port Blair is 1,200 km from mainland India (Chennai or Kolkata). Air connectivity is limited and expensive and is two hours by jet aircraft from either place. There is very little connectivity within the islands in spite of four airstrips available from Diglipur in the north Andamans to Campbell Bay in the Great Nicobar Islands in the south. Only recently a passenger helicopter service has started with very limited capacity. While Andaman is within the Directorate General of Civil Aviation (DGCA) Group Disbursal Guidelines which forces airlines to connect to North-East, J&K and Andamans, the services are not adequate and only Port Blair is being touched in spite of Car Nicobar providing an excellent airport. Earlier Indian Airlines used to have a weekly service from Kolkata, Port Blair, Car Nicobar, Chennai. This is no more there. Further due to free pricing, air tickets can be prohibitive during seasons.

By Sea: Regular passenger ship services are available to Port Blair from Chennai, Kolkata and Vishakhapatnam. There are three to four sailings for Kolkata and Chennai and one sailing for Vishakhapatnam every month.

Chennai – Port Blair:	Journey time about 60 hrs.
Kolkata – Port Blair:	Journey time about 66 hrs.
Vishakhapatnam - Port Blair:	Journey time about 56 hrs.

Map 5: Connectivity to Andaman & Nicobar Islands

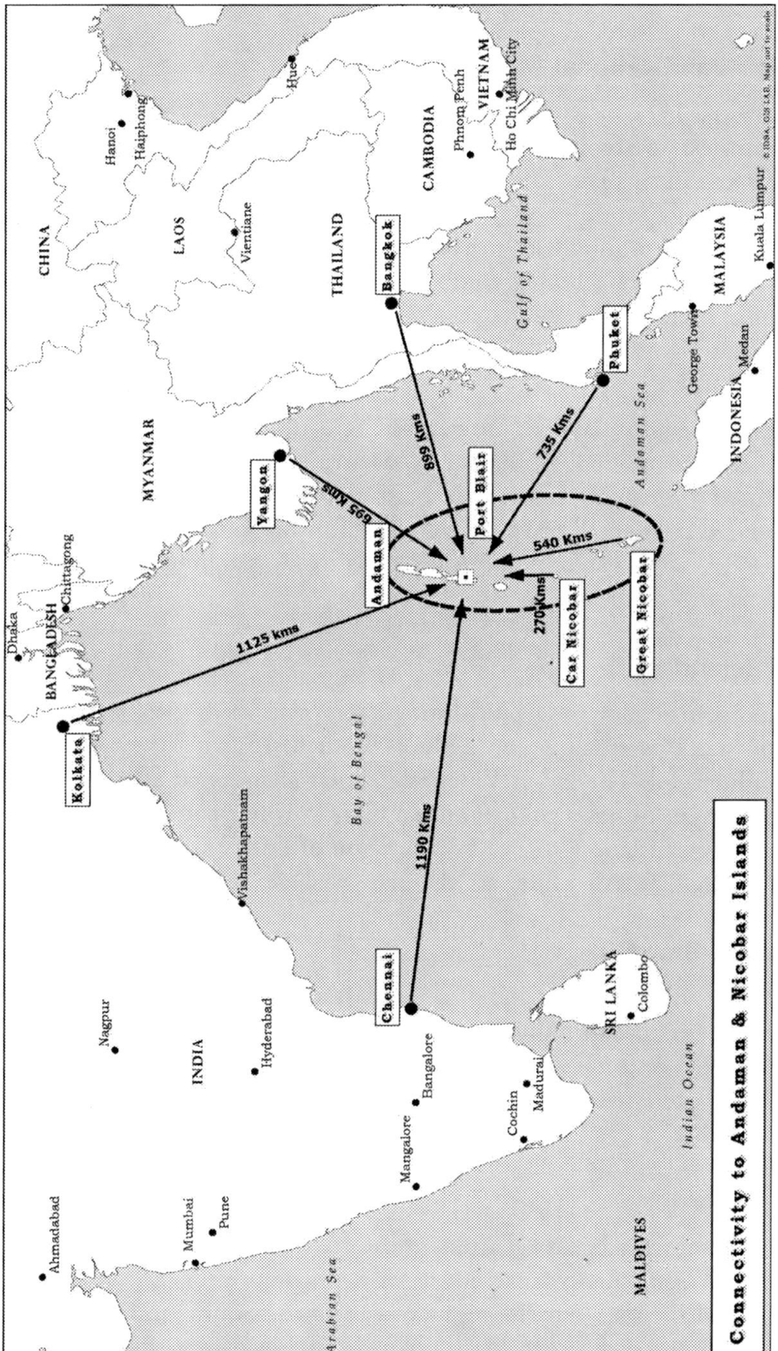

Some Features of Port Blair

Cellular Jail: National Memorial

The Cellular Jail constructed by the British in 1906, located at Port Blair, stands mute witness to the atrocities meted out to the freedom fighters, who were incarcerated in this jail. The name 'Cellular' was given as this jail is made up of individual cells for solitary confinement of the prisoners. Originally, it was a seven pronged building with the central tower acting as its fulcrum and a massive structure comprising honey comb like corridors. This jail has been declared a 'National Memorial'.

Ross Island

Once the seat of British power and capital of these islands where the Commissioner resided, it stands now as a ruin of the bygone days with the old structures almost in debris but held tighter by roots of trees which have surrounded it. A small museum named 'Smritika' holds photographs and other antiques of the British relevant to these islands. It is an important place of tourist interest.

Viper Island

Notorious for chain gang punishment, this island was used as an open jail for the convicts as well as freedom fighters by the Britishers prior to construction of the Cellular Jail. The jail at Viper Island was abandoned after the construction of Cellular Jail. It has a gallows atop a hillock, where condemned prisoners were hanged. Viper Island also saw assassination of Lord Mayo, the Viceroy of India in 1872, by Sher Ali, who was also hanged here.

Chatham Saw Mill

The Chatham Saw Mill, one of the oldest and the largest Saw Mills in Asia, is built on a tiny island named Chatham and is connected to the main island by a bridge. It is a storehouse of timber like Padauk, Gurjan, Marble, Satin Wood, etc. This island has the second largest wharf of these islands and is near the Haddo Wharf.

Mount Harriet

Once the summer Head Quarters of the erstwhile Chief Commissioners during the British Raj, this place is ideal for a fascinating distant view of the other islands and the sea. It is the highest peak in the South Andamans (365 metres high). One can trek up to Madhuban through a nature trail and can find rare endemic birds, animals and butterflies. Conducted tours to Mt. Harriet are available from Andaman Teal House.

Distances from Port Blair

- 1,255 km from Kolkata to Port Blair
- 1,190 km from Chennai to Port Blair
- 1,200 km from Vishakhapatnam to Port Blair
- 735 km from Phuket to Port Blair
- 899 km from Bangkok to Port Blair
- 1,687 km from Singapore to Port Blair
- 695 km from Yangon to Port Blair
- 1,843 km from Malacca to Port Blair

Other islands of the Andaman group are poorly connected but the Nicobar is much worse. The main islands of the Andaman Group from Port Blair to Diglipur in the north are connected by a road which is the only highway in the Andamans but is under orders of the Supreme Court to be closed due to the fact that it passes through the territory of Jarawas, a primitive tribe under protection of Tribal Regulation Act.

The potential wealth of these islands and EEZ has not been determined. However, if oil can be found offshore between Nicobar and Sumatra, there is no reason why the Nicobars should not have it. It has also been recorded that the sea around Andaman & Nicobar Islands is part of one of the four areas of the world that contain extensive deposits of magnesium nodules.[2]

THE ANDAMAN STORY

The Settlements

Prior to the 18th Century the Andaman Islands were not colonised unlike the Nicobars where the Danes started settlement but failed. In Andamans prior to the British, certain primitive tribes like the Andamans, Jarawas dominated these South Andaman Islands while Onges, another primitive tribe lived in Little Andaman Island. Yet another primitive tribe lived and continues to live in Sentinel Islands and is known as Sentinelese. They are still hostile to other human beings.

It was in the 19th Century that the British Government of India decided to use Port Blair as a Penal Settlement for its convicts. This started the inhabitation of these islands. Over time the now famous Cellular Jail was built between 1896 and 1906 and the convicts who completed their sentence were allowed to stay back and were allotted agricultural land. The government allotted agricultural land to the convicts under Section 5 of A & N Regulation, 1926. The convicts came from all parts of India and as they settled they started to intermarry across religious and linguistic groups due to shortage of marriageable couples, especially females. This led to growth of a composite culture and Hindi became the lingua franca. Later Indian freedom fighters were also incarcerated here. Thereafter, there were many waves of settlements in these islands. The Bengalis of erstwhile East

Pakistan came after independence and were settled in islands around Port Blair. The Bhantaus of Uttar Pradesh, a community engaged in robbery and dacoity, were sent by the British, Myanmarese who revolted against the British were sent to these islands, and Karens of Myanmar were also brought in by the British. The Moplahs of Kerala were deported after the Moplah rebellion in 1921. Then post-independence there was natural migration in search of better living by Tamils, Malayalis the Telugu people and people of Ranchi.

The penal settlement was abolished in 1945 when the British re-took the islands from the Japanese and gave free pardon to all the convicts. They were offered repatriation to mainland India but most settled in the Andamans.[3]

During the Japanese occupation from 1942-45, the islands were renamed Shaheed & Swaraj Deep Islands. A provisional government under the Indian National Army (INA) with Subhash Chandra Bose as its head was made in charge nominally while the Japanese military commanders ruled over the islands. General Loganathan of the INA was appointed Governor. Since the Japanese were opposed to the British in World War II, they allowed Subhash Chandra Bose to raise the Indian flag at Port Blair on December 30, 1943. Hence, while India attained independence on August 15, 1947, the Andaman Islands had already raised the Indian flag in 1943.

Post-independence as there was a feeling in some sectors of government that these islands are very isolated from mainland India and very insecure, a strategy to settle ex-servicemen was made by the Central Government. About 300 families of ex-servicemen were settled with land in the Great Nicobar Island with a view that they will provide the necessary intelligence against any untoward happenings. The ex-servicemen were settled along the coast from Campbell Bay to Indira Point (earlier known as Pygmalion Point).The resettlement of ex-servicemen in the Great Nicobar Island was carried out in a systematic manner by the Ministry of Rehabilitation, Government of India in coordination with Director General Resettlement (DGR) of the army. Each soldier was provided with free land and cattle and a resettlement organisation was set up with a Resettlement Commissioner in Port Blair working under the Chief Commissioner (Now elevated to Lt. Governor) with his officers in Campbell Bay.

The main aspect of this resettlement was strategic. By putting ex-servicemen in Great Nicobar it was felt India would create a small group of well trained Indians who would be able to provide the initial intelligence to any undesirable activity in that area. The only other residents of Great Nicobar Island are a small group of Nicobarese tribals who were so isolated and backward that they were not considered a strategic asset. Another group of tribals, very primitive are the Shompens, whose number is in a couple of thousands if not hundreds. While they are friendly, they are shy and unable to communicate. Therefore, was putting 300 families of ex-servicemen a good decision in 1970? Yes, when there were few alternatives and government budgetary resources were very poor this alternative was perhaps, the best. This settlement so far away had its own problems. In 1975 the ex-servicemen even went on strike for their demands. The issues were then sorted out.

It may also be stated that at the time of independence in 1947 the issue of Andaman & Nicobar Islands had come up. There was a proposal by the British to keep these islands as Crown Colonies like the Caribbean or Pacific Islands and not make them a part of India. In fact, there was a thinking that these islands may be kept with Pakistan due to its proximity to East Pakistan (now Bangladesh). There was also an internal discussion in Britain to keep them with Myanmar. At one stage the British also thought of keeping these islands with themselves due to their strategic importance.[4] There is also a rumour that Bishop Richardson, a leader and Bishop of Nicobar Islands had sent a telegram to the British requesting that Nicobars be kept a part of Crown. Promptly, Bishop Richardson was made a member of Rajya Sabha (Upper House) of the first Indian Parliament.

Photo 1: Rt. Rev. Bishop Richardson (June 06, 1888 to June 03, 1978)

(Padma Bhushan), Founder – Father of the Nicobar Islands
Bishop of Andaman & Nicobar Islands & Leader of Nicobar Group of Islands
(Photograph taken by the Author)

The Andaman & Nicobar Islands became a part of India at the time of its independence. They were made into a Union Territory and were administered directly by the Central Government under the MHA. The MHA has always had a lot of fire- fighting to do within the country with political issues coming up in various states. Since these islands were peaceful and showed no signs of threat and secession the MHA followed a policy of 'Benign Neglect'. and Masterly Inactivity'.

The Nicobar Group consists of 12 Islands inhabited by the Nicobarese tribe and another five which are uninhabited. These tribes are more akin to Myanmarese in features, have their own language and could be termed as a progressive group. The island of Car Nicobar, south of the 10 Degree Channel and northern most of the group, is the administrative headquarter for these islands and the last

Map 6: Background of Nicobar Islands

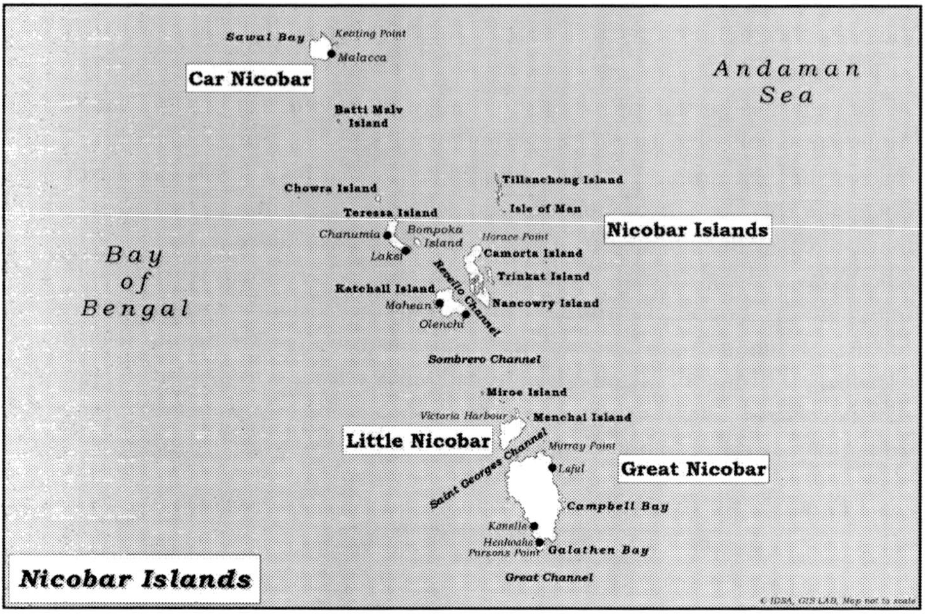

island of Great Nicobars is above six degrees. The Nicobarese tribals' genesis is not known but they speak their own dialect and have their own tradition and customs. A large part of the population is Christian with few Muslims but some in remote islands follow their old beliefs. Even the Nicobarese of Christian faith continue to follow their old traditions.

History of Nicobar Islands

The Danes

The Nicobar Islands were known to sailors for their abundant coconuts. By mid 17th Century the tropical islands were looked upon as a prize and a rich source of resources and funds. After having made well in Mauritius and St. Halena it was felt that more such prizes would be welcome. The strategic location of Nicobar Islands in the Bay of Bengal and at the mouth of Straits of Malacca made it even more attractive. Consequently, the first colonial power to take interest in these islands was the Danish Government through its Asiatic Company. It is recorded that in November 1754, an assembly of high-ranking Danish officials including Director of the Danish Asiatic Company and Governor Krog, who represented the Royal Danish colony of Tranquebar in India, considered the outcome of a recent report submitted to the Danish Government at Tranquebar by Priest Husfeld, a Moravian missionary who had recently returned from the

Nicobar Islands. The report described the Nicobars as an excellent place for planting pepper, cinnamon, sugarcane, coffee and cotton. Further, besides their local resources of coconuts and areca nuts, the islands were said to be located suitably to become a centre for Indian trade and the ship-building industry due to their abundant timber resources.

The Danish Moravian Missionaries tried settlements in the Nicobar Islands four times in different islands over the period 1755 to 1851 but failed every time. The reason for their failure is not clear, but it appears from all evidence that they could not get over the climatic conditions and malaria fever which some of them contracted and the support from their government was also poor. However, the remnants of their stay are hardly there except for wild cows found in Car Nicobar, Nancowry and some other islands. Since the Nicobarese do not domesticate these cows, nor do they drink cow's milk or eat their meat, they have been allowed to go wild and have multiplied over the years. The second evidence of their stay is the fencing used by the local people. Nicobarese keep a lot of pigs. Some are domesticated and some wild. In both cases the pigs are found all over the islands. Since Nicobarese are also settled agriculturalists and plant maize and other crops besides coconuts, they need to protect their fields from their pigs which are allowed to roam around free. For this they have a special type of fencing for the agricultural plots which they consider to be pig proof. This fencing is a crisscross made of small wooden sticks in the design and is strong enough to withstand a pig's attempts to enter it. According to Bishop Richardson, this fencing was introduced by the Danish Moravian Missionaries. Besides these two indications there is no particular evidence that the Danish were in Nicobars.

The term "Danish period" broadly refers to the colonial period when the Danes theoretically were the European "owners" of the Nicobar Islands. However, during this period, the islands were occupied technically briefly by the Austro-Hungarians from 1778 to 1783, and later by the British from 1807 to 1814, the time when Denmark and Britain were at war with each other. Neither the Austrians nor the British undertook any substantial activities on the Nicobars during their period of occupation. The Danish declared these islands as their property on January 1, 1756, and they were re-named "New Denmark". They remained nominally Danish till the British took over in 1851.

As already brought out, the Moravian Missionaries, however, could not maintain the colony by themselves. The problem was the climate and diseases like malaria which caused many deaths. In a period of less than 20 years, it was reported that of the 25 missionaries who had arrived on the Nicobars, 11 had died on the islands while another 13 died after returning to Tranquebar on the Indian mainland.[5] The situation became even more difficult for them when the only ship they had possessed in the preceding years was stolen by a pirate. The missionaries moved from one island to another over time. Originally they set themselves up in Nancowry-Kamorta but tried out Teressa, Bambooka and Car Nicobar Islands.

A number of attempts were made to establish a settlement but all failed. At one time on return of the missionaries eight soldiers were sent to keep the flag flying. A new plan was formulated to make better use of the islands. The Danish Government in Copenhagen offered four years' of help—in the form of supplies—to those who would voluntarily go to the Nicobars as part of the Danish establishment. By now, aware of the death-trap, the offer was received without any enthusiasm in Tranquebar and nothing came of it.

Two scientific expeditions were mounted by the Danes in 1755 and later in 1768 at a heavy expenditure to the government. The investments on the Nicobars seemed unprofitable in the short term at least. Consequently, the Danish company started to withdraw from these activities and the Danish Government started to take over their activities. At the same time, by the mid-1770s, the Company's activities in general declined at Tranquebar in the Coromandel Coast of India as compared to the trade in Bengal. In 1777, the crown's decision to take over all the colonies in India, among them the Nicobars, relieved the Company of a financial burden, and it was left to concentrate on trade, in particular with China.

The British Period: The Trading World of the Nicobars 1851-47 (except for the Japanese Occupation 1942-45)

The Danish Missionaries left the Nicobars in 1851 and the British took over. The idea of setting up a penal settlement by the British came in late 18th Century. In 1869 the British formally took over the Nicobar group of islands with permission of the Danish Authorities who had nominal control over them. It was also felt that Nancowry-Kamorta harbour, which is one of the finest natural harbours in the world, could be developed into a penal colony in addition to the one already existing at Port Blair in the Andamans. The penal settlement at Nancowry was developed by the British Government and lasted from 1869 to 1888, a period of 19 years. The convict labour were used for construction of the settlement, planting of vegetables, production of coconut oil, fruits pineapples, yams, mangoes etc. However, it was closed down in favour of Port Blair in the Andamans.

Even after closure of the Nancowry penal settlement the British continued their hold over the Nicobar Islands. By 1897 the British appointed Rev. Solomon, a missionary in Car Nicobar as Government Agent. A school was established by the Anglican Mission in 1896. With the establishment of an Agent and a school in Car Nicobar by 1900 Nicobar was well established as a British territory. By 1918 an Assistant Commissioner post was established in Car Nicobar followed by a post of Tahsildar in Nancowry. The first British officer to be posted as Agent was Mr. Hart in 1918 followed by Bishop Richardson, a famous local tribal, as an interim arrangement for a year. This was followed by another British officer Mr Scott in 1929. Mr. Scott continued for many years till 1942 when the Japanese took over these islands and again came back after they left. His personal popularity amongst the tribals was very high.

The British period, as we will see, was far more dynamic than the preceding Danish one. This was so because the British posted or designated their nationals in positions of administrative power. Starting with 1869 in Nancowry the British administration had much more success in establishing a system of control and enforcing regulations throughout the islands. The penal settlement established in 1869 lasted for 19 years till 1888. This supplemented the one existing in Port Blair at Andaman Islands. One can say that the British actually governed these islands, and in this sense, for the first time the Nicobars were incorporated into a system of statehood. The occupation of the Nicobarese tribals also had a direct connection with trade as they supplied the coconuts for export-the main produce of these islands.

The occasional acts of piracy in these waters were a matter of concern to the British who decided to bring greater control over these waters. In order to bring greater order to the region the British decided to tighten the administration further by regulating trade and stay in the islands. This they achieved by setting up a permanent administration over these islands. It was customary for vessels sailing to Rangoon (now Yangon) from the Straits of Malacca to visit the Nicobars for a cargo of coconuts which the traders bartered at most advantageous rates for goods and rum. Trade picked up once the British established a Penal Settlement at Nancowry and maintained a close surveillance on the trading activities in the region. In only a short time, it was discovered that most of the cases of violence or so-called piracy were the result of provocation on the part of the traders. Stringent laws were established to ensure a certain level of control over the traders, "some of whom have habitually acted in an over-bearing manner towards the Nicobarese, as if imagining themselves to be well-nigh beyond the reach of law".

Regulation of 1882—Permission to Reside in Nancowry Penal Settlement by Traders

Introduction of copra making technology was a game changer. Instead of only export of coconut the British found it practical to allow traders to set up and stay in Nancowry Settlement Area as copra making required a longer stay. This technology shift was mainly due to the Nicobar Trading Company Limited based at Penang who also obtained permission to reside and trade at Nancowry. This shift in trading practice took place as it was found that coconut meat scooped from the shell and dried (called copra) could be exported instead of coconut oil thereby saving on transportation costs. On arrival, the oil could be extracted in Europe for use in many industrial products, while the residue served as valuable cattle feed. This innovation laid the foundations for the copra industry in the

Nicobars. The tropical climate of the Nicobars allowed copra production only during the dry period of the northeast winds when sunshine was abundant. At first, copra comprised only a small part of the exported cargo in relation to coconuts. Over time, this pattern changed and most of the coconuts bartered in the Nicobars began to be converted to copra. Furthermore, the Nicobars were gaining prominence as an important source for coconuts which induced the traders to establish semi-permanent bases on the islands. Residing on the islands had its own advantages: a good rapport with the Nicobarese and favourable negotiating conditions, in which the traders invariably had the upper hand.

By 1882, the British authorities introduced better control over these traders making it possible. From 1889 the agents at Car Nicobar and Nancowry would make five to six visits each year followed by officers of the British administration stationed at Port Blair. During these visits, the administration invariably fined those vessels that were caught trading without a permit or were engaged in any form of illicit trade. It was the objective of the British administration to foster trade in the islands, yet keep control over it. The success of the policy was seen by the growth of trade that took place through this control mechanism. This mechanism was also appreciated by traders as safety of trade also improved. It also brought in some revenue to the British.

By 1883 it was made mandatory for traders to acquire a trading permit on payment thereby permitting them to trade in the islands. This permit could be bought either at Nancowry (and later at Car Nicobar as well) or at Port Blair and had to be renewed annually. Every vessel, before its departure from the islands, was expected to obtain a port clearance from the local officer or agent and to declare the quantity of goods being exported. A register was maintained to ensure control, and to keep a record of the traders and their activities in the islands. This again brought better order and more revenue to the British.

The Nicobarese were friendly but reserved. They were also not keen that traders should settle in the Islands. The Nicobarese of Car Nicobar were for some years opposed to traders establishing their shops and houses in the villages. Traders had been customarily restricted to the Elpanam (community space at the beach) where they could live and trade, and at the end of the season, were expected to leave. However, this changed in the late 1890s with the arrival of Rev. Solomon as catechist and agent who, through his influence over the Nicobarese, gained allowance for the traders to establish shops and houses in the villages and live there for as long as they desired.

Mr. A. de Roepstorff was a British officer posted at the Nancowry Penal Settlement for some years until he was murdered by some convicts in October 1883. Roepstorff holds the distinction of being the first to carry out a near-systematic population survey of the Nicobar Islands in 1883, shortly before his death.

Over time, Car Nicobar became the most important island. Most of the resident traders on these islands came to concentrate on the island of Car Nicobar because of its high density of coconut plantation. Traders came from all around and their profile kept changing. Around 1900, the majority of the traders residing on the islands were from Myanmar while a small number of them came from Laccadives, China, Maldives and the Indian sub-continent. Of the 201 traders in 1901, 154 were Buddhists, 32 Muslims, four were Hindus, and 11 were Christians. However, by the 1920s, the Myanmarese population of traders had decreased from 75 per cent to 25 per cent of the trader's resident on the island. The majority were then a mix of traders from the Maldives, Laccadives, Ceylon and Madras. On average, there was one trader to every 30 inhabitants, with several competing shops in each village. Most of these shops did not function as independent enterprises but were actually "collecting stations" of bigger firms based in India or Myanmar. The more prosperous were the Indian shops that had their company headquarters in Calcutta, Bombay or Colombo. They transported their produce in chartered vessels whereas the Myanmarese firms were much smaller and freighted their goods on boats of other firms. The goods that these shops sold were rice, Chinese tobacco, a variety of cloth and clothes, cutting tools such as choppers (dahs) and axes, soup-ladles, table-spoons, forks, cups, tumblers, enameled soup-plates, salt and sugar, condensed milk, coarse biscuits, matches, kerosene oil and many such items. A decade later, the Muslim traders from the island of Minicoy in the Laccadives came to be the dominant group among all. According to the survey in 1931, of the 3,632 Nicobarese on Car Nicobar, 559 could converse in Hindi and 157 of them Myanmarese. The situation in the central and southern islands was different. These had more interaction with Malays and hence of the 2,531 Nicobarese there, 793 spoke Malay.

There was a lot of traditional festivity amongst the tribals. Roepstorff has shown that most of the goods the Nicobarese imported were "wasted" in feasts and rituals. Roepstorff exemplified his argument by a series of calculations on imports and exports. He began by listing out the needs of the Nicobarese and then multiplying them by population. He calculated that a population of 5,500 Nicobarese would need to export the following number of coconuts annually to meet their requirements for commodities considered most essential, that is, iron, cloth, tobacco and rice. Of course, his biased value judgment was not acceptable to the tribals.

However, calculations and recorded statistics revealed that the number of coconuts that were exported from the Nicobars in 1880-81 amounted to at least six million coconuts. In this sense, five million coconuts were "wasted" on buying goods they did not really utilise. Illustrating his point via another calculation, Roepstorff showed that most of the surplus coconuts went into buying unnecessary things. The export statistics of 1880-81 record 5,534,546 coconuts and Roepstorff rounds this figure to six million to account for some of the unreported trade. According to him, six million coconuts was still a low estimate.

The Village Organisation in Nicobars: The villages had their own headmen called "Captains." The system of "captainship" was not only kept in place but, with the growing necessity of trade and foreign goods, the position became more privileged than before. The British administration further empowered these headmen or "captains" with privileges and presents to the extent that they came to exert a certain influence not only on trade-related matters, but within the society as well. The Captains became the link between the Nicobarese and the outside world, a link that increasingly became central to their lives.

1915: Export Royalty Introduced

In 1915, the British Government introduced payment of royalty for all that was exported from the islands as a means of contribution to the cost of the administration. The royalty initially at five per cent was later increased to 10 per cent in 1919.This was accepted as it also provided for a greater organised trade and some security. The British administration, therefore, introduced revenue generation by taxing the tribals.

1915-20: Abolition of Nicobarese Indebtedness to Traders

The British had an indulgent and paternalistic view of the tribals. An upsetting part of the growth in trade was the increasing indebtedness of Nicobarese to the traders. Nicobarese were simple, easygoing and uneducated. In their desire to buy things available in traders' shops they had no concept or control over their desire. Consequently, the traders were extracting a very high price in terms of coconuts and if a Nicobarese did not have sufficient number of coconuts, the trader would take a mortgage of his future crop. The Nicobarese being simple in nature often found themselves heavily indebted to these traders. The British were not able to contain the increasing indebtedness of the Nicobarese towards the traders. Over time, business relations between traders and the Nicobarese developed on a regular basis and once formed, were rarely severed. Vessels visited the same islands or villages to barter coconuts as they had done in the preceding years, and depending on the success of the last season, new vessels were attracted to the islands. In almost all the cases, bartering had been to the profit of the traders. In 1914, a statistical survey revealed that the Nicobarese owed the traders 7.5 million coconuts; a debt that would take them 10 years to settle. Rev. George Whitehead, in charge of the mission on Car Nicobar for some years, explained how the Nicobarese were induced into debt by the traders:

> '... The trader would invite to his shop someone whom he knew to be fairly rich—that is, to be the owner of a tolerably large number of coco-palms—and would treat him hospitably, giving him tobacco and lemonade and other slight presents. He would then show him goods he had which he thought

> might appeal to the man's acquisitive proclivities—cloth and spoons for display, rice and tobacco for consumption, or choppers (dahs) and plates for use. If the Nicobarese saw anything that he would like to have, as he generally did, the trader would urge him to take it, even though the man told him that he had no nuts in hand, and the ones now ripening on his tree were promised to some other trader for goods which had been received some time ago. If the Nicobarese did not come to the shop, the trader would take the goods round to the man's house and persuade him to take them. Occasionally in this way a Nicobarese man or woman would somewhat lightly take a quantity of goods of the supposed value of thousand (pairs of) nuts; which debt he would be paying off for many years to come. As there was no Nicobarese writing, the trader would give the Nicobarese man a tally-stick on which were cut a number of notches showing how many thousands, hundreds and tens of (pairs of) nuts the man was owing; and when he made any payment of nuts, or bought any more goods, the tally-stick was corrected by the tradesman and returned to the Nicobarese.

The matter of debt was taken up by the administration, at which the traders expressed their anxiety to compromise with their Nicobarese debtors rather than accept official intervention. The initial focus was more on Car Nicobar than Nancowry, since the problem of indebtedness was found to be greater in the former than the latter. Consequently, a decision was taken wherein the administration asked the traders to settle their debts with Car Nicobar within a period of five years, that is, by April 1, 1920. An agreement to this effect was signed by the traders. Credit sales ceased and in only a year, the debt fell from 7.5 million to 1.7 million nuts in Car Nicobar. Efforts in this direction included the introduction of currency and doing away with the barter system. This, however, did not find favour with the Nicobarese, since they were not used to nor did they have any use of currency in their island.

Trader's misbehaviour towards Nicobarese:

> As the number of traders grew, reports of misbehaviour by them also grew. The British Government attitude towards Nicobarese was of benevolence, guardianship and protection. Consequently, the traders were never too happy with the administration. On the other hand the relationship between the traders and the Nicobarese was one of constant arguments that sometimes ended up in severe forms of violence. Each time a court was held on the islands on the occasion of visits by officers, some three or four so-called criminal cases were brought to court and the accused punished by way of fines or imprisonment or both. The Annual Reports reveal that most of the criminal cases concerned Chinese traders in dispute with the Nicobarese. On the other hand, the trade related quarrels were common to all. There have been cases of violence against the traders resulting in murder due to their exploitative nature. While Nicobarese were fined in terms of coconuts, the trading license was cancelled in many cases.

Bishop Richardson's account of the Japanese occupation reflects the traders in an extremely bad light. As soon as news of the Japanese occupation reached Car Nicobars, the question of repayment of debt that had been cancelled by the British administration 25 years earlier was raised once again. The traders approached Richardson in December 1942 and demanded the payment of the old outstanding debt that was now illegal. They threatened to report the matter to the Japanese authorities whom everyone feared. The Nicobarese felt compelled to pay half of the outstanding amount to resolve the dispute.[6] Richardson's remarks on the traders when they were compelled to leave after the war are worth citing:

> "Most of the traders found lives quite easy with good income. The average income each got was from Rs. 144/- to Rs. 180/- per month, including food and clothing. Many of them got married to Nicobarese girls but would also abandon them and their children. Someone will marry the divorced, once again. In this way half castes children were born; left behind and uncared for. Because their religion forbids them to live with none other than their own religion relatives they became vagabonds. Moreover, they look down on their fellow Nicobarese. During the Japanese occupation the traders were all fed free of charge by the Nicobarese; yet they were too proud to say 'Thank You' for everything received from our people; whom they compared to beasts. Well we have done our duty; expecting no reward from the ungrateful friends. We have seen rewarded evil for good. In all their lives here, they have not done a single charitable work; but grabbing..."

1880 Regulation Prohibiting Import of Alcohol, Arms and Ammunition into Nicobars

Another aspect of the traders' activity was the inducement of Nicobarese men through liquor. While the Nicobarese were fond of liquor and they had plenty as each coconut tree would provide a mild alcoholic drink, the traders would induce them by importing cheap hard liquor (arrack) and selling it at a high price. The British administration was actively engaged in fostering trade in the islands but wanted to ensure the establishment of cordial and non-exploitative relations between the traders and the Nicobarese. The administration was extremely sensitive to the behaviour of the traders towards the Nicobarese in their trade negotiations. For example, the administrators noted that the traders took advantage of the Nicobarese addiction to liquor. Once the Nicobarese were drunk, the traders could sell them anything at prices they dictated. Consequently, in November 1880, the administration passed a Regulation prohibiting the import of alcohol, arms and ammunition to the Nicobars without a license.

The Story of R. Akoojee Jadwet & Company

One of the companies that frequently traded with these islands since the turn of the last century was R. Akoojee Jadwet & Company, a partnership firm between two Gujarati families, the Akoojee and the Jadwets. We do not know when the company was first established, but by the early 1900s, the company had their headquarters in Moulmein (Myanmar) and ran a flourishing trade between Gujarat and Myanmar. Their vessels regularly frequented the Nicobar Islands to obtain a cargo of coconuts and areca nuts to be sold in Myanmar. The influence of the company in the coconut trade can be gauged from the fact that they were the only successful enterprise among several competitors to obtain a 30-year lease over the produce of Great and Little Coco islands of the Andaman group of islands from the British Government in the early 1930s. Akoojee Jadwet & Co. had apparently established good relations with Edward Kutchat, chief captain of Car Nicobar Island and the tribals of Nicobar who considered their trade practices fair.[7]

The Interregnum: The Japanese Occupation 1942-45: The Dark Years

The Japanese occupied the Andaman & Nicobar islands during World War II for three and a half years from 1942 to 45. This was a dark period for the islanders as they suffered heavy, brutal treatment and shortages. They took over all the islands without resistance or firing of a single bullet on March 23, 1942 as the British gave up because of their meagre force. Besides the usual difficulties of war time the Japanese were harsh, unsympathetic and highly suspicious of anyone who spoke English. A few Nicobarese of Car Nicobar had good knowledge of English and therefore, the Japanese considered them as British spies. Besides this they abused Nicobarese labour in Nicobar and took them to Port Blair to build huge infrastructure. Two airports at Car Nicobar and one in Port Blair were built mainly by Nicobarese labour. The islands were fortified by cement bunkers and canons. A lot of roads, ports and other war related infrastructure were developed in these three and a half years. The misuse and killing of Nicobarese by the Japanese had put tremendous pressure on the people of Nicobar. The Japanese left a huge stockpile of trucks, weapons, aircrafts and ships when they suddenly left the islands after their defeat in the Second World War.

As already stated the role of the traders at Car Nicobar was most odd. On arrival of the Japanese they greeted them with the hope that since the British Administration had been harsh with them they would get sympathy and 'justice' from the Japanese. As war had made travel impossible for many and they could not go back to their homes, they continued to live in the Nicobars but they had nothing to sell and their business had collapsed. As a result they approached the Nicobarese for revival of their dues which were cancelled in 1920 by a British Government order. They threatened to complain to the Japanese. The Nicobarese held a council and decided to review their so called debt in a settlement by giving them half their dues. On top of this the Nicobarese also arranged to feed them during the occupation. The behaviour of the traders had totally antagonised the Nicobarese. However, the Japanese killed many and only a few managed to flee the islands. According to Richardson, "that was the only benefit we got out of the war".

The Japanese interest in the islands was known for several years even before the war. Since the 1930s, it is reported that the Japanese had already done a detailed survey of the islands and its inhabitants through a Japanese resident of these islands. As World War II kept the British busy in other parts of the world, Japan which had declared war on England at the end of 1941, found it expedient to take over these island without any resistance. With the fall of Singapore in 1942 followed by the occupation of the Philippines, Borneo, Sumatra, Java, Malaya and Myanmar by the Japanese forces, taking over these islands was natural and after losses in Myanmar they wanted to prepare Andaman and Nicobars for an aerial assault on India.[8] With hardly any forces of the British in the islands it was a cake walk and the British officers actually abandoned these islands. Immediately thereafter, a Japanese administration was set up with the army commander assuming the position of governor of the civilian population.

The Japanese had a grand plan for these islands as they realised its strategic significance. With the tip of Great Nicobar controlling the Straits of Malacca and isolation of these islands in the Bay of Bengal, the Japanese were quick to realise its potential from both maritime and aviation aspects. Even the local population was favourably inclined towards them initially but not after they started using the local population for their labour requirements and treating them very harshly. They fortified all the islands with cement bunkers and canons, started Japanese schools for children and wanted the islands to become self-sufficient in food. The Government High School originally run by the British was re-opened and an additional Japanese school was opened as well. In the course of their three and a half years on these islands the Japanese fortified them, built one airstrip in Port Blair, two in Car Nicobar and placed many ships and aircrafts in the various islands, especially in Port Blair and Car Nicobar for an attack on India.

However, there was retaliation by the British later. Ships bringing in supplies were becoming the target of British air-raids and were being sunk just as they entered the harbour. By 1944, the Allied forces had sunk more than 750 commercial ships. Fearing that the news of vessels arriving into the harbour must be given out by the islanders themselves, the Japanese became suspicious of anyone who spoke English. Several such persons were tortured and put to death. When the food situation further worsened in June 1945, the Japanese "dealt" with the crisis with a massacre of hundreds of local people, either rounding them up and throwing them into the sea, or shooting them in the forests.[9] More than a thousand people had to die in this way before the news of the Japanese surrender reached the islands on August 15, 1945. The re-occupation forces arrived on October 7,

1945 and the islands changed hands once again without the firing of a single bullet. The actual proclamation to the public was made by the Governor only on August 21, 1945.

The situation in the Nicobars had been no different. Before the Japanese arrived at Port Blair in March 1942, the British administration, in late February 1942, sent a small vessel to Car Nicobar to evacuate the Assistant Commissioner, Mr. Scott, and the wireless operator, Mr. Ghosh. Four months later, on July 4, the Japanese arrived at Car Nicobar and surveyed the island for any weapons or hidden English troops. Satisfied that there were none, they returned the same day, after installing a post with an inscription in Japanese to mark the day of the occupation of the island. Again, at the end of the year, on December 24, the Japanese arrived at Car Nicobar and took with them 500 Nicobarese as labourers who were needed for building the airstrip at Port Blair. Three months later, in March 1943, again 500 labourers were taken away for work at Port Blair with a promise to return the first batch upon the completion of a six-month stay. At the same time, Car Nicobar was surveyed as a possible base to be used during an attack on India.

Apparently, the impact of war in the Nicobars was mainly limited to Car Nicobar which included aerial bombings while Nancowry and other islands were affected to a much smaller extent.

The key source of information on events that took place at Car Nicobar during the Japanese occupation is the unpublished manuscript of John Richardson, a former student of Solomon and by then a key figure among the Nicobarese. Writing in 1947, Richardson provides a vivid description of the wartime situation on Car Nicobar and of the atrocities committed by the Japanese as he saw and experienced them.

The name of Richardson was eventually placed on top of the list for execution. When he was to be taken away, however, one headman warned the officer, "If you kill him there will be general rising on the island." The plan was dropped, but interrogations continued. Finally, the Japanese decided to get rid of Richardson but just at that time the news of their surrender arrived and Richardson escaped the death penalty. The General in charge told him:

> "This is good news to you. Our Emperor is a lover of peace. He has stopped the war by his own effort, for he cannot bear to see any more sufferings to go on in the world. We can carry on the war for another one hundred years more. As you see here our weapons are all intact. But the sole wishes of our Emperor are peace."[10]

To mend their reputation, the Japanese offered the Nicobarese compensation for the losses of their trees and poultry. The account that was settled was for 120,000 coconut trees, 5,000 pigs, 305,363 coconuts, 18,610 bananas, 2,491 chickens, and 1,535 cattle. Richardson writes that the account settled was far below the actual damage, since the Nicobarese had stopped keeping account of losses after a while. The loss of life was much mourned, as it amounted to 105 Nicobarese, all of them educated. Of these, 90 were killed on Car Nicobar alone, while 12 were killed at Port Blair, two at Teressa, and one at Nancowry.

The Return of the British

On October, 1945, the British re-occupation forces landed at Car Nicobar. Among them was Mr. Scott, the former Assistant Commissioner who now took up the position of Deputy Commissioner. Mr. Scott's landing on Car Nicobar was accompanied by deep emotions as described by Richardson:

> "Mr. R.W. Scott stepped out and walked on the jetty. He made straight for me; for a few seconds no word could be uttered by either of us; instead tears were rolling down. There was joy for being liberated; mingled with the deep sorrow for those no longer with us... Here I could find a friend in need and deed in the person of Mr. Scott, the lost friend whom I did not expect to see alive on this world of woe. To him I could now freely open my ear, for I knew he understood us thoroughly well and could also feel sympathy for us. He was hated by the traders for being in their way. I could feel myself on my feet again."

The return of the British and the last minute stopping of the execution of Bishop Richardson by the Japanese had a profound impact on all. The Nicobarese realised the statesmanship of Bishop Richardson and he became their true leader. Not many Nicobarese had converted to Christianity but after the Japanese departure nearly the whole island of Car Nicobar became Christian and Christianity also spread to other islands. Secondly, the hatred for the traders intensified.

Post War in February 1946, 10 Nicobarese (six from Car Nicobar including Richardson, and four from Nancowry) were taken to Singapore as witnesses of the Japanese atrocities at the War Crimes Tribunal. The court in Singapore sentenced six Japanese officers to death while nine of them were imprisoned for various terms. The Japanese occupation of the Nicobars provided the islands with the first real introduction to violence, cruelty and to modern technology. Never in the past had the islands seen such a massive display and use of weaponry as during these two years. The destruction of existing British infrastructure and records, the torturing and killing of all educated Nicobarese with any knowledge of English, the introduction of trucks, tanks, and guns onto the islands could not but have shaken the Nicobarese out of their long-held security. Two air strips, and 60 km of road encircling the entire island were constructed with local labour, and in two years, the whole landscape was changed with electrical installations, buzzing trucks and soaring aircraft. After the Japanese left the islands on their defeat, they left behind a large number of vehicles and fuel amongst other things. The Nicobarese learnt driving and used these vehicles to their advantage.

THE CREDIBILITY OF R. AKOOJEE JADWET & COMPANY

Akoojee Jadwet & Co. had apparently established good relations with Edward Kuchat, chief of Car Nicobar, by providing space to some enterprising Nicobarese who wished to export their produce directly to Myanmar. During World War II when the Japanese occupied Myanmar, members of the company had to flee back to Gujarat.[11] The company further won the admiration of the Nicobarese when their vessel returned after the war to deliver articles promised in exchange for the produce that had been purchased and shipped to Myanmar prior to the war. Just a few days before the outbreak of World War II, Akoojee Jadwet & Co. vessels carried coconuts from Car Nicobar to Myanmar but before it could reach the shore, war broke out and it somehow managed to reach shore with great hardships. During the war contact could not be established between the firm and the Nicobarese. But it was a surprise to the Nicobarese that the value of the stock the company carried prior to the war was paid to the concerned persons after the war. The fact that the Jadwets came back after the war and paid the Nicobarese all their dues prior to the start of war kept them in high esteem with the Nicobarese.

With the war over, the British planned the re-occupation of the Nicobar Islands. Part of the planning was to re-organise trade and the distribution of food and commodities in the Nicobars. The Government of British India invited the directors of R. Akoojee Jadwet & Co., Ebrahim and Yusuf Jadwet, to Delhi for negotiations. Major R.D. Scott was the last Deputy Commissioner of Nicobars prior to the Japanese takeover and was instrumental in inviting the Jadwets back to Nicobars. In September 1945, a contract was signed between the company and the Government of British India by which the former received the sole license to trade in the Nicobars on a certain royalty payable on exports. The company was also made responsible for distributing food and essentials to the Nicobarese. Following the agreement, the Jadwets arrived at Car Nicobar with the re-occupation forces in late 1945 and established their headquarters at Chuckchuka village.[12] Thus, post reoccupation the stranglehold of petty traders was broken and the Jadwets were made sole trade agents of the government with an obligation to open shops in all inhabited islands of Nicobars.The Nicobarese welcomed the Jadwets with whom they had trust and good relations and who had been found to be fair in trade. The Jadwets arrived in Car Nicobar and were welcomed by Chief Captain Kuchat and Bishop Richardson.

Photo 2: The Author with Chief Captain Kuchat in Car Nicobar in 1975-77

At that time, the trade on Nancowry Islands (or the central group) was run by a Muslim trader, Ilias Malim (also known as Illias Yacoob) Illias, from Gujarat in India, who plied his business between Myanmar and Nancowry islands. He bought coconuts and areca nuts from the natives and in exchange gave them articles that were in demand. The then chief of Nancowry known as Rani Ishlon allowed him to erect a small shop and a copra kiln on which he made copra. The goods were transported to and from Myanmar on a small yatch that he owned. According to Fatima, the granddaughter of Rani Ishlon, "Ilias used to bring full loads of rice, sugar, cloth and kerosene oil and then stay at Nancowry till the goods were finished". Just before the war, Illias married Rani Lachmi, the daughter of Rani Ishlon. However, during the period of the war, Illias remained mostly ill from malaria. After the war, sometime between 1947-48, contact was established between Ilias and Casim Jadwet, a partner in R. Akoojee Jadwet & Co. According to Fatima, Illas brought Casim Jadwet to Rani Ishlon and advocated the transfer of his shop and business activities to the Company. Following the approval of Rani Ishlon, the company established their business at Champin village in Nancowry. Illias returned to Myanmar for treatment but never returned. In the succeeding decades, the company became a formidable force in the lives of the Nicobarese that took different forms and triggered new dynamics in the trading relationship.

1947: India Becomes Independent

On August 15, 1947 India gained independence from British colonial rule. There was no impact on the Nicobars as the policies of benign patronage towards the Nicobarese continued and were further strengthened. Bishop Richardson emerged as a leader of the Nicobar group after the Japanese persecution of him, killing of his son and his near escape from being killed by the Japanese. India acknowledged this fact by nominating him to the first Parliament of India in 1950 in the Rajya Sabha. The tribal policies followed by the British to prohibit exploitation continued. Andaman & Nicobar Islands become a Union Territory directly under the Federal Government as it was earlier.

Development of Modern Trade Practices in Car Nicobars: The Role of John Richardson and the Jadwets in the Cooperative Movement in Nicobars

Bishop Richardson and the story of Car Nicobar have a special strategic importance in the Indian context. Given the historical context these islands require a special mention. It was the British missionaries of the Anglican Church who picked up some tribal boys from Car Nicobar Island during the pre-war days and took them to Mandalay for ecclesiastical education. On completion they were brought back to Car Nicobar and brought up in the church. One of them known as Hachevko later became the Bishop of Andaman & Nicobar Islands and was called Bishop John Richardson. John Richardson was a legendary figure who was sincere and upright. During the Japanese occupation of these islands the Christians who were still few on the island, were suspected by the Japanese to be agents of the British. John Richardson was one of them. They tried to get as much information as they could by various means and in the case of John Richardson it was the ultimate torture as his son was shot dead by the Japanese occupation army in his presence. Post surrender by the Japanese there was tremendous sympathy for John Richardson and under his influence practically all the people on the island became his followers and converted to Christianity (Anglican Church). Car Nicobar got fully converted to Christianity immediately after the Japanese left the islands due to the work done by the missionaries and in particular, Bishop Richardson. The other islands also took to Christianity but to a lesser extent. Bishop Richardson became the undisputed leader not only of the Christians but also of the rest, including some Muslim converts also found in the islands. It may also be pointed out that the Nicobarese joined the Church of North India headquartered in Delhi. Another point to consider is that Bishop Richardson was a proud son of Nicobars who never collected or looked for funds from the Diocese but rather gave contributions to them. The Nicobarese sense of independence and aloofness is amplified by their total self-sufficiency. They rarely demanded anything of the government and accepted the government's presence gracefully. But their most important trait is the high level of cooperative spirit. The person responsible in inculcating these values was Bishop Richardson.

The spirit of cooperation and regard that developed between the Jadwets and the Nicobarese is truly legendary. Bishop Richardson provided the political leadership and the Jadwets the business acumen and together the story of modern Nicobar became famous. The Nicobarese society fully backed both the Bishop and the Jadwets. Following are two excerpts, one on each, which need to be quoted to illustrate the proposition above.

"A Miracle in Paradise"

The Jadwets reversed the years of exploitation by traders in South-East Asia by instructing the Nicobarese in how to do business in Copra and Betel Nut and by helping them set up a steady backbone of co-operatives.

The Jadwets arrived back in Nicobar along with allied forces in 1945. The Japanese had been in occupation of these islands since 1942. The Jadwets mandate was simple: to run a monopolistic but fair trade with the Nicobarese who even in the forties did not know the use of money and relied entirely on barter. They were to take back in their sailing ships Saffena betel nut and copra and provide the islands with essentials. Nicobars seems to have soon cast a benign eye on Jadwets. A monopoly trade became an almost romantic mission to organise the tribals into a profit making co-operative so that the tribals could also put away capital.

The Jadwet firm was converted into Car-Nicobar Trading Company in which 14 co-operatives held 50 per cent share and had representatives on the board. With a similar formula, Nancowry Trading Co. was set up. By 1967, the Jadwets sold their 50 per cent stake in both firms to the Nicobarese and lost the monopoly they had once enjoyed through a decree.

But the link has not been exactly severed. Cassim Jadwet still serves as an advisor to the co-operative. His nephew, Yusuf, is a salaried chief executive Ellon Hinengo.

(Extract from an Article in the Telegraph, December 4, 1988)

Press Report on unveiling of statue of Bishop Richardson in 2010 in Car Nicobar.

"Port Blair, September 18: The Lt. Governor, Lt. Gen. (Retd.) Bhopinder Singh, PVSM, AVSM today unveiled the statue of Rev. Dr. Bishop John Richardson at a function held at St. Thomas Cathedral, Mus village, Car Nicobar. The Lt. Governor also inaugurated a Church mela and interacted with the tribal youth on the occasion. Dr. Purely Lyngdoh, Moderator, CNI, Rev. P.P. Marandih, Deputy Moderator, CNI, Rev. Bishop, Christopher Paul, Bishop of Andaman & Nicobar Islands, Diocese, CNI and Chief Captain, Car Nicobar, Shri Aberdeen Blair were also present on the occasion.

Addressing the function, the Lt. Governor said that it was the greatness of Bishop John Richardson, who had a vision to see that the education of the Nicobari people was the most important priority for development of the community and progress in every walk of life. It is only a great man like him who could carry out this transformation of a primitive tribe to the mainstream by pursuing the policy of literacy and social transformation to catch up with the modern world.

The Lt. Governor said his emphasis was to improve the literacy standard of Nicobari people on priority and for accomplishing the objective, every possible effort was being made to give the Nicobari people good education in the islands as also in the mainland. The large number of Nicobari students studying in higher courses in New Delhi and undergoing various vocational courses in Chandigarh were testimony of the same, he said.

The Lt Governor described Bishop John Richardson as the most revered, popular and distinguished son of Nicobar. He said Bishop John Richardson, the Father of Modern Nicobar and a torch bearer of the Nicobarese community devoted his entire life to spreading the message of Jesus Christ and worked for the overall development of Car Nicobar. "He was a man of culture and saintliness who brought Nicobarese in the mainstream without losing their good old traditions and customs", he said.

Highlighting the achievements and contributions of Bishop John Richardson in the overall development of Nicobar, the Lt. Governor said after completing his higher education from Myanmar, Bishop John Richardson preferred to stay back in Nicobar and worked for the all- round development of Nicobari people and with a missionary zeal, he established schools in villages and prepared the Nicobari language dictionary and Nicobari Primer. The starting of cooperative movement in 1947, the Nicobarese Athletic Association, the Captain System, Village Council and Tribal Council were among the major steps taken by Bishop John Richardson for the benefit of Nicobari people, he said.

He also translated the holy bible into Nicobari language which was printed in Bangalore in 1970.

The Lt Governor noted with appreciation that the magnificent Church, which was the first Church in Nicobar and destroyed by the 2004 earthquake had been re-erected by the Nicobari people themselves.

The re-erection of the Church had instilled a sense of self-sufficiency and confidence amongst all, he added.

The Lt. Governor was all praises that a number of Nicobari students were also pursuing higher courses like MBBS and engineering in various educational institutions in the mainland. He urged the Nicobari youth to work hard, make the community proud and bring name and fame to Nicobar by excelling in every walk of life. Later, interacting with the Tribal Captains, he directed the head of the departments to attend to the problems of the people on priority."

Out of the total tribal population in the Andaman & Nicobar Islands, the Nicobarese are only tribe which showed drastic changes in their life style within a span of two decades. From a primitive lifestyle they had started to move close to full integration. While the Moravian Missionaries of Denmark were unsuccessful in establishing their mission, the Missionaries of the Anglican Church were able to achieve much more. This was mainly because in mid 19th Century, they took with them about a dozen boys from Car Nicobar to Mandalay in Myanmar (erstwhile Burma) where these boys were given full instructions in

Bible studies and also taught English. On return one of them became the Bishop of the island and also their political leader. Rev. John Richardson, as he was called later was instrumental in modernising the entire island and the outlook of the tribals. When India became independent of the British in 1947 John Richardson was nominated to the Rajya Sabha, the upper house of the Indian Parliament. Bishop Richardson combined the qualities of a preacher with a moderniser and brought modernisation to the islands.

Nicobarese Start their Own Business

The private traders from different parts of Asia operated in Car Nicobar before World War II. The main attraction of these islands was coconuts and copra. The private traders would come in their sailboats and offer goods on barter. Often the terms were harsh and Nicobarese being innocent were easily taken for a ride. They also did not allow the Nicobarese to do business on their own by instructing the sailors not to provide any space in the ships. Messers R. Akoojee Jadwet & Co., stand out as their behaviour was much better. They realised the difficulties faced by the Nicobarese while conducting business of their own produce, encouraged them by providing space in their vessels to export their produce to Myanmar. Thus, the Nicobarese started businesses of their own with their local produce with the help of Jadwets.

From Barter to Monetary System

Earlier the barter system prevailed when the business was managed by the traders. The Nicobarese never had the opportunity for use of money as coconut was their currency. The traders were also able to exploit them more with coconut as an instrument of barter.

On appointment of Jadwets as sole traders in Nicobars, money transaction and weights and measurement system was introduced. It took quite a while for Nicobarese to accept currency as they did not know the value of money. As their wants were limited, they did not feel the need for currency. Their produce was sold for purchase of necessary requirements. They rather preferred to have barter system. Whenever the company paid the surplus money in the form of coins with which they were not acquainted, they had a practice to keep the coins in the holes in the side of the walls. At times they even left them behind in the shop. The company's employees were taking pains to trace out the concerned person to handover the coins. In the process the company developed a cordial and amicable relation with Nicobarese and became their trusted friend and helped them in all walks of life.

Introduction of Cooperative Movement

Bishop John Richardson in consultation with the then Chief Commissioner of Andaman & Nicobar Islands and Jadwets thought out a plan to introduce the cooperative movement in the Nicobars so that the Tribals get empowered. The then Chief Commissioner of Andaman & Nicobar Islands Mr. L.A. Majeed, I.C.S and the Assistant Commissioner Car Nicobar, Mr. Sharma, actively encouraged the proposal of the Bishop in empowering the tribals and making them owners of their trade.

As a first step, following encouragement from all quarters, the first cooperative society was organised in Kinmai village in the year 1948 with a meagre share capital of Rs.45/- . Later the cooperative movement extended to other villages of Car Nicobar and all the Primary Cooperative Societies locally named as Panam Hinengo in Car Nicobar were organised between the years 1945-51. Later, this movement was extended to all islands of Nicobars.

The Jadwets were fully cooperative and supportive. Their company was rendering help to the maximum extent to maintain records and accounts of the Panam Hinengos. The introduction of cooperative movement in Car Nicobar Island had strengthened the democratic character among the inhabitants. Panam Hinengos also started playing a pivotal role in the day to day affairs of the villages. They not only acted as business units but also helped in establishment of discipline. The financial structure of the Panam Hinengos showed a remarkable growth year by year.

The success of economic ventures through village cooperatives or Panam Hinengos created a change in outlook of the tribal society as owners of an enterprise and slowly led them to reap the benefits of modern business without disturbing the tribal social values. This change was peaceful and fully controlled by the tribal society and there was no conflict as was happening with the traders earlier.

The Panam Hinengos in Car Nicobar originally established with membership of 279 contributed by a share capital of Rs. 13,275/- has shown remarkable progress in the decade. *M/s.* R.Akoojee Jadwet & Co., besides its business also contributed towards the upliftment of the Nicobarese tribes in all walks of life. The Nicobarese were slow to understand and needed proper guidance.

The company personnel and many non-tribals were also well wishers of the tribals as part of the philosophy of the company. They also helped in utilising various schemes of the government by providing help in understanding and drafting. The day to day contact with the company personnel and government officials paved their way to learn several things necessary for their daily routine life. It was also the policy of the company to employ more and more tribals as they became educationally eligible.

1956: Nicobarese Become Partners

Another important change in the business model of Nicobars took place in 1956. With the growth of trade and the village cooperatives or Penam Henengos becoming mature with tribal management, the Jadwets in consultation with Bishop Richardson and other leaders of the community decided to convert their company Akojee Jadwet & Co into "Car Nicobar Trading Co." This was done with effect from January 1, 1956 with 50 per cent share held by the 14 Panam Hinengoes or Car Nicobar. The Partnership consisted of 19 partners of which five belonged to the erstwhile trading company of the Jadwets plus presidents of 14 Panam Hinengos. Thus, the local people were not only members of their village cooperative but also part owners of the apex company called "Car Nicobar Trading Company."

Thus, Nicobarese were given ample scope to learn business methods and management despite their low but rising educational qualifications. The introduction of cooperative movement in Nicobar Islands gave a new shape and meaning to the life of Nicobarese.

1967: Nicobarese Become Full Owners of Their Company

Another major change took place after a decade. This was regarding handing over trade to the tribals. Car Nicobar Trading Company decided to hand over the entire trade to the tribals. This was done by converting Car Nicobar Trading Company which had 50 per cent shares held by Akoojee Jadwets to Nicobarese Trading Company with 100 per cent tribal ownership. Thus, Nicobarese became the 100 per cent owners of their business. This was done by formation of *M/s.* Nicobarese Commercial Company in Car Nicobar on July 1, 1967 after taking possession of the liabilities and assets of Car Nicobar Trading Company. The shareholders of the new Company were just the 15 Panam Hinengos (Coop. Societies) of Car Nicobar.

All these years while the cooperative movement gained momentum, the financial position of primary cooperatives also showed a geometrical growth, crossing all the initial teething problems. The profits earned by the company were annually distributed to their member Panama Hinengos. Ultimately, the individual member i.e. the villagers were getting benefits in the shape of dividend and bonus. Here, the advantage of professional management by Jadwets along with training and internship of young Nicobarese kept the society and social structure in good shape.

The Nicobarese Trading Company, new 100 per cent tribal owned, however, continued its partnership with the Jadwets. While Jadwets provided technical and financial staff for supervision, the local people were brought into employment in their cooperative.

In the year 1977 a high power team, headed by the then Managing Director of National Cooperative Development Corporation (NCDC) was sent to the Nicobars to explore the future potential of Nicobar trade. The team visited Andaman & Nicobar Islands from January 10-18, 1977 and after a detailed in depth study suggested certain changes to their business practices. Relevant extracts are as follows:

The Nicobarese Commercial Co., (NCC) has been acting as a central level organisation for marketing of copra and betel nuts and for supply of consumer goods. This company which is a private partnership firm is now entirely owned by the 15 "Panam Hinengos" (Multi-purpose Coop.) of the island, the earlier private firm having completely withdrawn its shares. Although, it is a partnership firm for all practical purposes, it is a cooperative federation of the "Panam Hinengos". The Board of Management is elected by the Panam Hinengos. There is no distinct advantage in continuing it as a partnership firm since the earlier private firm has withdrawn and it is now owned and managed by the primary cooperatives. On the other hand, there are several advantages in converting the NCC into a cooperative. Firstly, the society would be able to obtain financial assistance from the government and NCDC for expansion of its activities on favourable terms. Secondly, concessions in the matter of income tax, stamp duties, etc. would be available.

During the discussions that the team had with the office bearers of Nicobarese Commercial Company and the captains of the villages, there was general agreement to the conversion provided the existing arrangements were not to be disturbed. It was, therefore, recommended that the Nicobarese Commercial Company may be converted into a Central Marketing and Supply Society.

However, NCDC felt that since the existing arrangements for management and procurement/sale of goods seemed to be satisfactory and the local population was not in favour of any major change it was suggested that even after conversion into a cooperative existing arrangements of management etc. may be allowed to continue. "Since, this is a sensitive tribal area, it has to be observed that the local sentiments are not offended and any changes necessary are made with the concurrence of the members of the societies for their larger benefit. In due course of time, changes necessary for further improvement of the service may be made through persuasion and education. The existing arrangements for remuneration to the office bearers may also be continued until the members require changes. Likewise, the present staff of the society who have gained experience may not be changed. The present arrangement for sale/procurement of goods may be continued for sometime till better alternative sources are found and the members convinced of the need for change. Caution needs to be exercised in this regard."

1977: Nicobarese Form an Apex Cooperative Called Ellong Henengo Which Is Wholly Tribal Owned

On the strength of the recommendation of the High Power Team sent by the Government of India headed by Managing Director of NCDC, the Nicobarese readily agreed for the conversion of the private partnership firm i.e. the Nicobarese Commercial Co., to a Central Cooperative Society. Necessary by laws were drafted in consonance with the Cooperative, Regulation No.3 of 1973. The proposed Central Cooperative Marketing Society under the Nicobarese name "Ellon Hinengo Limited" was registered on April 5, 1977 with Registration No.251 by the Registrar of Cooperative Societies, Andaman & Nicobar Islands. The actual functioning of the Central Cooperative Society that is "Ellon Hinengo Limited" started from July 1, 1977, the beginning of the cooperative year. It is not out of place to mention that a legendry ship called Safeena, originally a minesweeper of the British Navy, owned by Ms. R. Akoojee Jadwet & Co. was transferred ultimately to the Central Cooperative Society (Ellon Hinengo Ltd.,) at a token value. Akoojee Jadwet, however, continued to provide support with technical manpower and higher level executives. The CEO of the Jadwet family continued after the transition at the request of the cooperative. Thus, day to day affairs and business of the Nicobarese were brought under the cooperatives' fold. The tribes have earned a reputation and goodwill in cooperative field showing their full fledged participation in cooperative activities following democratic principles.

M/s Ellon Hinengo Ltd. of Car Nicobar played a major role to uplift the social and economic condition of the tribal society without prejudices to the customs and habits of the Nicobarese of Car Nicobar. Within two years of its establishment it could acquire a larger ship capable of going in the ocean for Rs.55,00,000 with a loan from NCDC under the flag of a Company registered under the Companies Act, 1956 as Hinengo Lines Ltd. The ship now carries cargo between Andaman & Nicobar Islands and Mainland India. The Merchant shipping Act was amended enabling a cooperative society to own ships and Hinengo Lines Ltd. was liquidated. With the financed support from NCDC of India the society could acquire four more cargo vessels and the total cargo carrying capacity now is 5360 DWT. The tribal cooperative of Car Nicobar is now a shipping concern also and one of its ships does not come to Car Nicobar at all but carries cargo between other destinations.

As part of social obligation to society Ellon Hinengo Ltd., has taken another step in connection with the encouragement of culture and entertainment and constructed a hall in Car Nicobar at a cost of about Rs.7,00,000 with a seating capacity of 600. This hall is used mainly for showing cinema but can be used for other purposes as well.

The society has made another leap forward by establishing an engineering division to undertake civil construction works on contract from defence and civil departments of the government.

There is a plan to establish a copra drying unit to maintain the quality of copra and to shift from the present traditional practice of drying the copra by the heat of the firewood. This project will be of great help to the Nicobarese to fetch profit for good quality of copra. The NCDC has come forward with financial assistance for the project.

The society has yet another scheme to establish cold storage in Car Nicobar availing the financial assistant from NCDC.

Nicobar group of islands are rich in marine resources. Ellon Hinengo Ltd., is also planning to establish a Deep Sea Fishing Project and the scheme is under active consideration of NCDC.

Establishment of an Oil Industry (coconut oil) is also taking shape in view of its potential in availability of raw materials. This project would meet the local demands for this territory and the marketable surplus will be exported to the mainland.

Another noteworthy feature is that the government and financing agencies are happily coming forward to provide finances required. It is perhaps a matter of pride for all to see the development that has shaped the Nicobarese tribes due to their cooperative movement, in particular, encompassing economic activities, and democratic management within a short span of little over 30 years. This has transformed the tribal society to embrace the benefits of modern civilisation and the country needs to be proud of it, especially as it has happened in the remotest part of the country and even the World.

Former Prime Minister of India late Mrs. Indira Gandhi, who visited the society in Car Nicobar on March 7, 1981 had recorded her appreciation on the working of the society as under:

> 'I am glad to hear of the excellent work of the *Car* Nicobar Central Cooperative Society. I give my best wishes to the Society and to the people of this beautiful Island. We want to help them towards a better life, while keeping their own personality and culture.'

2004 Tsunami and the Nicobar Islands: Role of Ellon Henongo

On December 26, 2004 a tsunami hit the Nicobar Islands. The earthquake's epicentre was 163 km away from Great Nicobar, the southernmost island from the archipelago. It was strongly felt in the entire Andaman Nicobar group of islands and the seismic intensity was enough to cause major damage to many civil infrastructures. The total duration of the shaking has been reported by many to be 600 seconds.

The tsunami generated from the Sumatra earthquake caused most damage to the low lying coastal regions of the Nicobar group of islands. The sea rose to about 4.25 m above the high tide line in Great Nicobar. The sea water surged at nearly 700 km per hour and flattened whatever came in its way. It flooded the villages, breached the shore protection walls, certain sections of the low level roads, impaired some bridge and harbour structures and inundated the vast stretches of the shore line. It broke homes and hearts.

The statistics of severity of human loss does not indicate the level of the tragedy. 3400 people died or were missing. The Indian Air Force (IAF) station at Car Nicobar alone lost 116 personnel and the airfield was damaged.

A large number of coconut trees got ripped off and the basic infrastructure was severally damaged.

Social and economic infrastructure in these islands was severely damaged. 68 schools were fully damaged, 40 Anganwadi (women and child centres) became non-operational. Most of the health sub-centres were washed away. A total of 84 fair price shops and 13 storage godowns were also lost to the surging waves.

The power supply system in all the islands were badly damaged. The 2,400 KVA capacity main power house at Malacca, Car Nicobar was washed away. 85 km of transmission line and 12 distribution transformers were lost. Extensive damage was caused to the power houses, DG sets, T&D systems, transmission towers, power distribution transformers, buildings etc. in most of the islands.

24 jetties were severely ruined. In Car Nicobar, the approach to the Mus wharf was partly damaged while the Malacca jetty was totally destroyed. In Campbell Bay, the approach to the jetty collapsed completely. The jetties at Chowra, Teressa, Katchal were submerged in water and washed away. Cracks developed in jetties at Kamorta and Nancowry.

Seven shipping vessels were damaged and two vessels sunk in the sweep of tidal waves. Propellers, hulls, shaft, superstructure etc. were damaged in the above vessels. 38 boats were lost. A forty 40 ton diesel storage tank was uprooted in Car Nicobar.

Road network in most of the affected islands was badly affected. In some places, the roads were washed out while in other cracks developed. The ring road which passes through the entire island of Car Nicobar was completely sunk in and is irretrievable. In Great Nicobar, the main trunk road connecting Indira Point became unserviceable thereby disconnecting all villages which were situated across it.

There was extensive damage in the water supply network. Wells in the flat lands were flooded with seawater. IAF wells which were catering to around 1,700 people got saline. Almost the whole water supply network became non-operational barring the area near the administrative headquarters in Car Nicobar. As a result of the killer tsunami, the economy of these islands was severely affected. The business community suffered losses by way of damages to stock, loss of revenue, and losses to property and infrastructure particularly in Great Nicobars. The whole market at Campbell Bay was flooded with water.

The Directorate of Shipping Services of the Andaman & Nicobar Administration, which controls and runs the entire government owned fleet of ships for the Andaman & Nicobar Group of islands, was helpless in providing ships to the southern Islands. With no ships plying to the island for more than a fortnight, the situation of the residents went from bad to worse. Power supply based on imported diesel was restricted to four hours a day, private and public transport had stopped, and scarcity of food loomed large over the residents.

The last ship that reached Car Nicobar was on November 28, 2011. After that it was mere assurance by the Directorate of Shipping Service.

Acting as a messiah, Ellon Hinengo Limited (EHL) decided to sail its ship 'MV Nicotrade', with 1,700 tonnes of cargo. The ship sailed on December 28, 2011. EHL knew well that the amount of cargo transported was just a relief for the residents. To support the islanders, EHL had decided to do its maximum with whatever minimum infrastructure available with the cooperative.

The Ellon Hinengo Ltd., which had nearly completed 30 years of existence, had also been very badly hit by the severe earth quake and Tsunami killer waves. The society's retail shops in all the 15 villages of Car Nicobar along with stock in trade, records, account books, cars and vehicles go downs at jetties etc. got washed away and nothing remained.

The total loss suffered by the society due to the tsunami was estimated at Rs 100 million. The entire infrastructure for the society had to be rebuilt, apart from the need for the working capital for the revival of its retail outlet branches.

The society had also lost 14 staff members and three family members. However, the society pulled up its socks and is again back fully functioning.

Conclusion

The transformation of a tribal society from a position of exploitation by traders due to their innocence and lack of education to running their own business successfully and running their own shipping line with four ocean going ships is a remarkable achievement, especially considering the remote location of the island.

It may further be stated that in many parts of the world both developed and developing tribals have been exploited by the outsiders. It is to the good luck of the Nicobarese that the British Government restricted land ownership to tribals and also regulated trade by foreign traders since mid 19th Century. The successor Government of India continued this enlightened policy. It is also a matter of luck that the combination of enlightened tribal leadership of Bishop John

Richardson and the business acumen of the Jadwets was able to transform the Jadwet monopoly into a cooperative movement. Further, the NCDC was also impressed by the working of the cooperative and agreed to sanction funds in sufficient quantity to purchase ships.

There is a still brighter future for the Nicobars. This is because the true potential of these islands have not been realised. As the tribal society matures with education it will be able to get the advantages of the next phase of development which can be high end tourism. The strategic location of these islands is to be understood and leveraged. The last island is barely 100 km from Sumatra. Direct flights to Car Nicobar airport from Singapore or Phuket will not be even an hour away. Additionally, if small sea planes are deployed then all the islands can be covered from these areas.

The coral reefs and fishing are both outstanding. The Government of India's protective policy towards Nicobar which prohibits foreigners and restricts even Indians needs to be liberalised. With proximity from South-East Asia there should be leveraging of this advantage. Today, even to visit Andaman Islands tourists have to come first to Chennai or Kolkata and then go to Port Blair. Once direct flights start from Phuket or Singapore or Bali or any other tourist point in that region, things are going to change dramatically for these islands. Mass tourism can be destructive.

Besides the strategic location, these islands present a paradise for environmentalists. With their excellent tropical forests and coral reefs they offer one of the best options for eco-tourism. It has 96 wildlife sanctuaries, nine national parks and one bio-sphere reserve all well protected.

NOTES

1. For a full review of the historical background including the freedom struggle, see B.R. Tamta, *Andaman & Nicobar Islands,* National Book Trust, New Delhi, 1992.
2. R.V.R. Murty, *Andaman & Nicobar Islands: a Geopolitical Perspective,* Northern Book Centre, New Delhi, p. 27.
3. Ibid, p. 82.
4. Ibid, p. 114.
5. Ibid.
6. Rev. Canon John Richardson, *Car Nicobar under Japanese Occupation: 1943 to 1945,* June 1947 unpublished, p. 4.
7. C.M. Jadwet, *Jadwet Saga,* Private Publication, 2004.
8. See n. 1, p. 40.
9. Ibid., p. 65.
10. See n. 6, p. 27.
11. See n. 7.
12. Ibid.

CHAPTER 3

Importance of Straits of Malacca

"Peace, Stability and Freedom of Navigation in the Pacific Ocean are inseparable from Peace, Stability and Freedom of Navigation in the Indian Ocean – Shinzo Abe, Prime Minister of Japan".[1]

WHY STRAITS OF MALACCA IS THE PREFERRED OPTION?

Strait of Malacca being 900 km in length is the longest international navigational route through a strait, as it connects the Indian Ocean via Andaman Sea on the west with South China Sea on the east via the Strait of Singapore. The strait provides the shortest route for ships to reach between East Asia and Europe. With the narrowest point being 11 miles and width between 11 to 200 nautical miles (nm), the seaway in this strait is not always wide as at certain parts of the strait, the navigable route is less than one nm and a certain part of its navigable area is less than 30 metres deep. At a particular point on the strait, the maximum draught recommended by the International Maritime Organisation (IMO) for passing ships is 19.8 metres. However, even with such limiting navigational constraints in the Strait of Malacca, the Strait is still an attractive and preferred navigational route for international shippers compared to other alternative routes like Sunda or Lombok-Makassar Straits in the Indonesian archipelago.[2]

The first alternative is the 80 km long Sunda Straits. It is 15 miles wide on its north-eastern entrance but the strong currents and limited depth has prevented deep-draft ships of over 100,000 Dead Weight Tons (DWT) from transiting this strait. Moreover, the Sunda Strait is unsuitable as it has highly irregular bottom topography of the Straits and the presence of rip tides render it unsuitable for vessels drawing over 18 metres of water to use the Straits. In addition, there are hazards posed by the numerous oil drilling platforms to the north of Western Java. The Sunda Straits has yet no available detailed navigational map.

The second alternative is the Lombok Strait. With a minimum passage width of 18.5 km and depth of more than 150 metres, the Lombok Strait, on the other hand, is the safest route for supertankers because it is wider, deeper and less congested than the Strait of Malacca. Lombok Strait does not feature serious

Map 7: Oil Transit Chokepoints

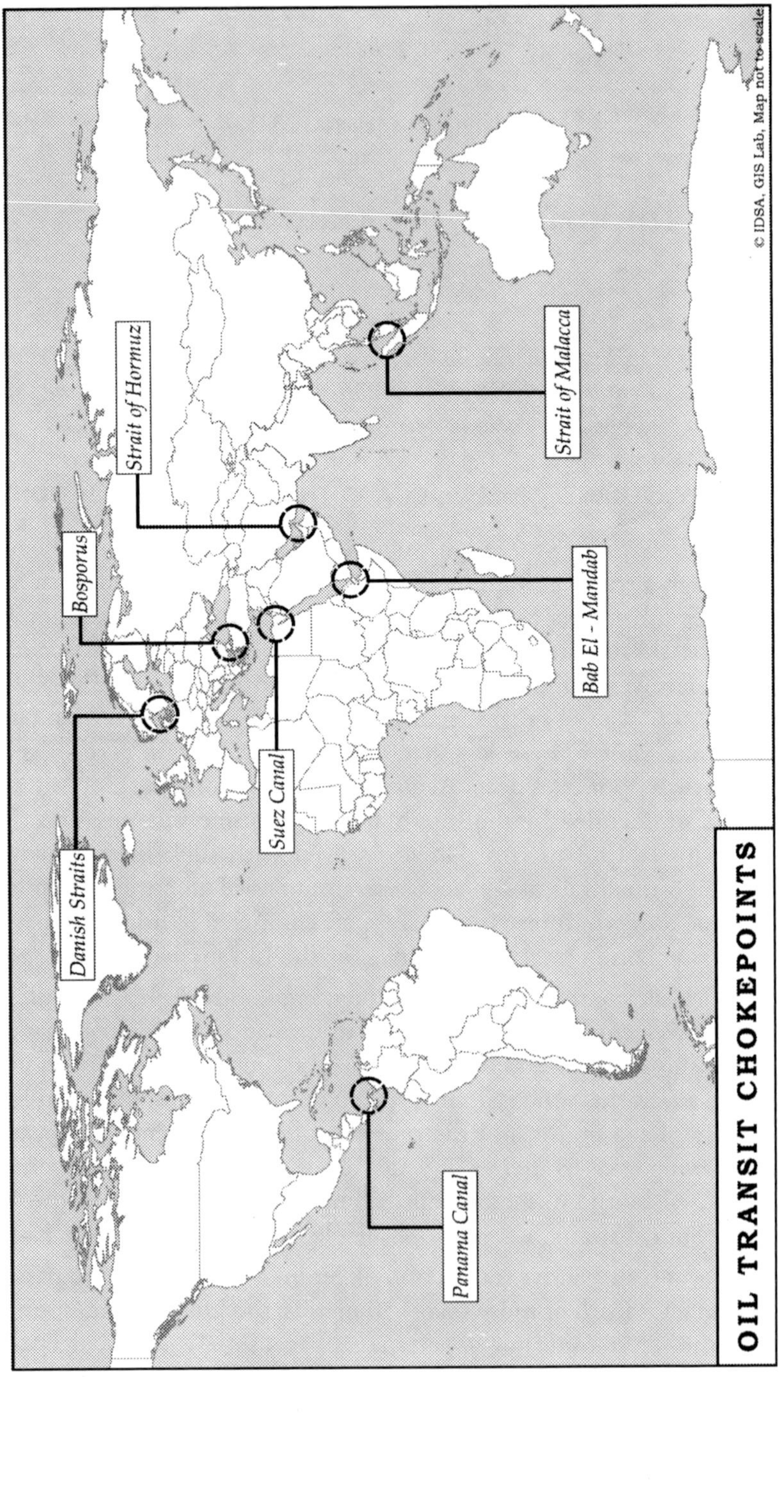

navigational hazards along the navigational channel but the routes require an additional three and a half days navigating at full commercial speed of 14-16 knots, an extra mileage of 1,600 nm, which add to transportation cost where in the long term operation it is not profitable to the tanker operators.

Closure of Straits of Malacca will cause a major economic disaster. The blockage and bombing of the Suez Canal in 1956 was a crisis of international dimensions. It was done when President Nasser of Egypt nationalised the Suez Canal Company after the refusal of US and Britain to finance the construction of Aswan High Dam in Egypt. He felt that tolls from Suez Canal could help build the dam. This was then a major international economic crisis as the Suez Canal was closed with 46 ship wrecks after its bombing by the British. Suez Canal was also a major choke point like Straits of Malacca when at that time 10 per cent of global oil passed through it. The blockage of Suez Canal in 1956 is a reminder of what could happen to Straits of Malacca. The present Iranian threat of blocking the Strait of Hormuz, through which one fifth of world's traded oil passes, could become a reality if US and Iran are not able to come to an understanding over the Iranian Nuclear Programme.

During World War II, the Malacca and Singapore Strait were mined. The battle of Malacca Strait led to sinking of the Japanese ship Hugaro around the end of the war. Currently, the three states of Singapore, Indonesia and Malaysia maintain submarines in the straits. India and Thailand are not known to have deployed submarines in this region. According to Michal Jarocki, no nation can control the traffic through the strait relying on military strength alone. Developing and maintaining a dominant position in the region also requires strong and positive relations with the regional straits.[3]

Based on these facts and fears, a concern has been raised by the international community that would immediately raise freight rates. Freight rates around the world would be affected, thus adding costs to many nations' imports and exports. The closure of the Strait of Malacca is not such a big problem because there are alternative routes like Sunda Straits or Lombok-Makasar Straits. In reality, however, the cost of re-routing maritime traffic, especially oil tankers, can be expensive. To divert the tankers on the Middle East-Japan route from Malacca to the Lombok Strait would cost more than US$ 340 million per year to the Japanese petroleum industry. The Straits of Malacca is, therefore, a critical chokepoint of world oil trade because a huge quantity of oil passes through it, and this number is expected to increase significantly in the next coming decades.

PIRACY AND ITS IMPLICATIONS FOR ANDAMAN & NICOBAR ISLANDS AND STRAITS OF MALACCA

The 900 km long Straits of Malacca has Malaysia and Thailand on its north and Indonesia in the south, with Singapore in the east and India in the west

(Great Nicobar Island). Piracy in the Straits of Malaccas has been known for many centuries and is a historic fact. The strait is narrow, contains thousands of islets and is an outlet for many rivers making it an ideal location for piracy as the pirates can easily hide at a very large number of places. Traditionally, piracy was practically state sponsored or an important political tool of the adjoining state. It is said that in 14th century Parmeshwara, a Palembang prince used pirates to protect his kingdom from other kings and which later led to founding of the Sultanate of Malacca. In 18th and 19th Century as European colonisers arrived piracy picked up. Even Chinese pirates were found to be operating in these waters. In 1830s, the British and the Dutch agreed to curb the rampant menace of piracy in the Straits of Malacca. They even drew a line of demarcation of the strait between themselves and took up the job of fighting piracy on their side of the demarcation. Their success in curbing piracy was substantial in those days.

The present scenario regarding piracy in Straits of Malaccas is that piracy has been reduced and is coming under control. The International Maritime Bureau (IMB) reports on piracy worldwide. In 2004, Straits of Malacca accounted for 40 per cent of the worldwide piracy. According to their report of 2006 piracy in the Straits of Malacca fell for the third year. Attacks on ships in the Straits of Malacca fell from 79 in 2005 to 50 in 2006. However, IMB reports that as late as 2007 Indonesia continued to be one of the worst pirate infested regions with 37 attacks since January 2007, though still an improvement over the previous year. Only one hijacking and two kidnappings were reported in 2009. Although, the number of attacks have dropped substantially due to increase and aggressive patrolling by the littoral states, ships are still advised to continue making a strict anti-piracy/robbery watch when they are transiting the straits.

Solving the menace of piracy: In 2004, the three countries on the Straits of Malacca, namely, Indonesia, Thailand and Singapore, increased their efforts to patrol. While Singapore was in favour of international support, Indonesia and Malaysia were opposed to it. Indonesia had expressed that it does not have the financial means to provide full anti-piracy support. There are two other countries that are directly involved and they are Thailand and India. Royal Thai Navy based in Cape Panwa in east of Phuket is coordinating with other armed forces from Singapore, Malaysia and Indonesia to combat pirates in the Straits of Malacca. India has also joined the effort and the Indian Navy and the Indian Coast Guards have finally joined the multi-national piracy patrol in the Straits of Malacca in 2006.India is also reportedly building a Un-manned Aerial Vehicle (UAV)-patrol base in the Andaman & Nicobar Islands.[4]

Use of technology in meeting the piracy menace is important. According to IMB's 2006 report all large ships of over 500 gross tons now have to have a security alert system on board which includes real time ship location devices. There is also a system information system—a 14 nation pact to combat piracy.

Map 8: Location of Attacks in the Malacca and Singapore Straits 2000-05

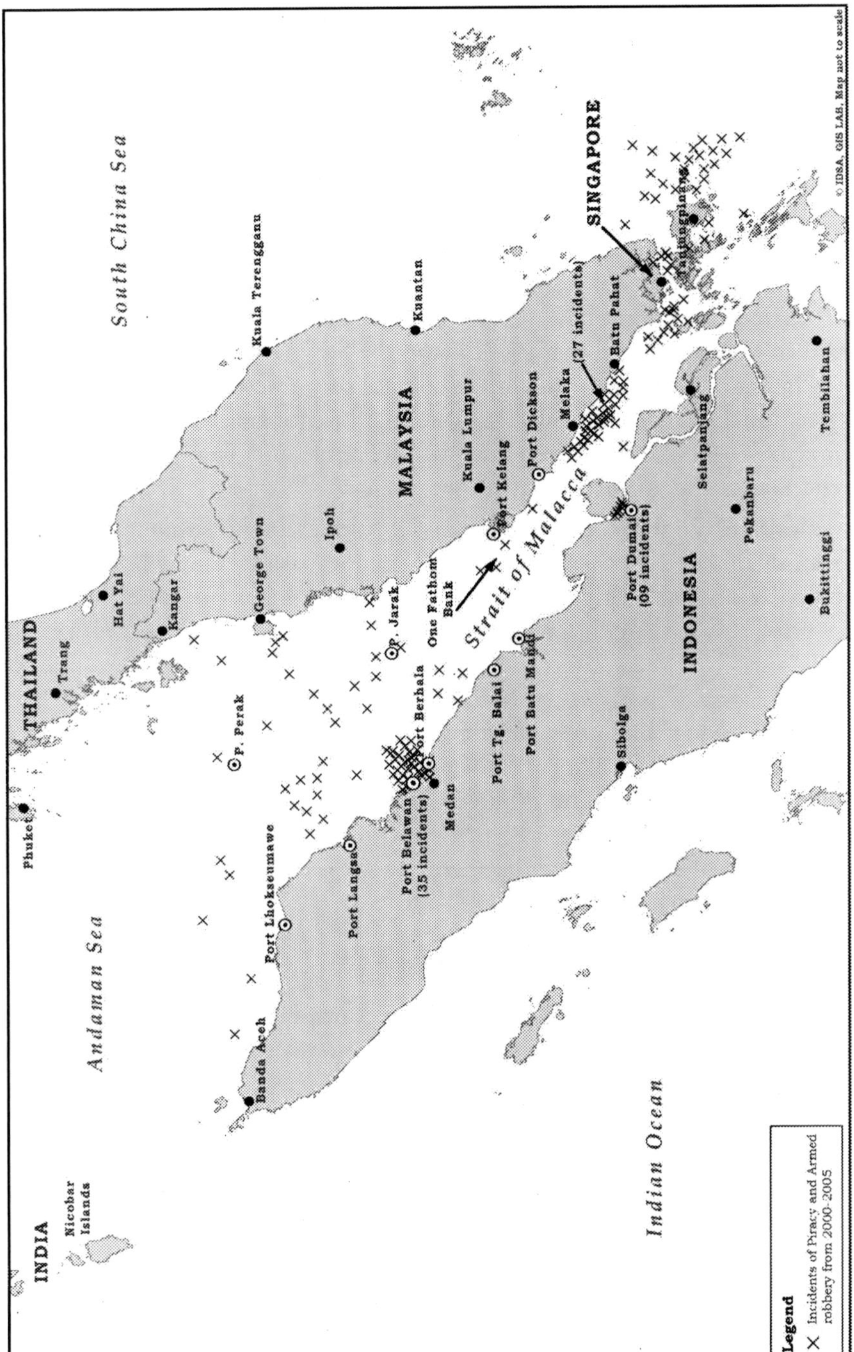

This is perhaps the first time that an international body has been set up to deal solely with the problem of piracy in Asia.

IMB as an additional effort has also opened free of charge, a 24 hour Piracy Reporting Centre (PRC) based in Kuala Lumpur in Malaysia. The main purpose of PRC is to make the shipping industry aware of the risk involved in the Straits of Malacca and make it a single point of contact for ship Masters anywhere in the world who are under pirate or armed attack. Further, information so received is immediately broadcasted to various governments and law enforcement agencies without delay. Such a service to ships under attack is a great service being provided that too free. Donations, however, are accepted by PRC for its efficient functioning. Straits of Malacca Patrol (MSP), "Eyes in the Sky" (EIS) Air Patrol are two more government organisations helping to control the piracy menace. The other is the International Exchange Group (IEG) set up for cooperative security measures by four states namely Indonesia, Malaysia, Singapore and Thailand to ensure safety of the Straits and to further cut down piracy.[5]

Lloyds of England, the famous and world leading insurance company, had previously declared the Straits of Malacca as a war- risk area for insurance purposes. Such a declaration of high war risk leads to high insurance premium. By 2006 they lifted this advisory after Singapore and Indonesia launched their sea and air patrols, just two years after Singapore and Indonesia started their joint effort. Therefore, piracy in Straits of Malacca is on the mend. Piracy in other parts of the Indian Ocean like Gulf of Aden, Yemen and Somalia is another story. Yet passage of billions of dollars of trade does not discount the fact that piracy in this region can start again. The isolated Nicobar Islands can become safe heavens unless full surveillance is kept by the Indian Coast Guard and Navy. In addition, threat of illegal migration and control of the vast EEZ of India around these Islands is also an issue to be looked into.[6]

Piracy in Indian Ocean Region (IOR)

While piracy in Straits of Malacca is under control there is an increasing menace of Piracy in the Indian Ocean. On the Arabian Sea side there is piracy going on in Yemen, the Red Sea and Somali coast. It is because of this that Straits of Malacca also remains vulnerable. So far the situation is under control in this region but there is a need to maintain and reinforce the existing set up.

The area of operation of pirates in the Indian Ocean is now considered to be about 2.5 million square nm. While Somalia has been the epicentre of this activity it is spreading to other areas also. Further, ransom payments by private shippers has gone up and according to some estimates in 2010 alone about 1,181 people and 53 ships were hijacked and ransoms averaging US$ 5.4 million per ship were paid. It is also estimated that 30 per cent of the ransoms paid reach terror groups. The concept of 'sea jihad' is now being talked of. Further insurer Lloyds have now stopped paying if ship owners paid ransom to pirates with terrorist group links.[7] While Andaman & Nicobar Islands are free of piracy with increasing piracy along Somali coast and spreading towards Arabian Sea, it could well spread towards Bay of Bengal and Andaman & Nicobar Islands. It will, therefore, not be prudent to assume that piracy in Straits of Malacca is over and proper surveillance is still required as there is every possibility of piracy getting revived in the Straits.

Small Arms and Drug Trafficking in the IOR

According to Prof. Aparajit Biswas of Centre of African Studies, University of Mumbai,[8] Andaman & Nicobar Islands Group is also very insecure. This is so because the waters around it are routes for Chinese gun-running to Bangladesh, from where arms reach North-East India. According to her this was the main reason why the government of India upgraded security structures of the island in 1998 and established a high service command to combat smuggling of arms and narcotics in the region. She further states that "Andaman & Nicobar Islands provide the key to the eventual success of India's 'look east policy' enunciated by Prime Minister Narsimha Rao in 1990s." It is the close proximity of these islands with South-East Asia that makes India a part of this region as South Asia. It is evident that spread of illegal arms and drugs in IOR is alarming. Regional associations like ASEAN, ASEAN-ARC, Bengal Initiative for Multi Sectoral Technical and Economic Cooperation (BIMSTEC), Mekong Ganga Cooperation (MGC) Project have a great deal of potential. It may also be stated that except for Laos all other countries are maritime countries. Under such a scenario Andaman & Nicobar Islands of India provide the most ideal and logical base from where sea power could extend its reach.

The defence minister has announced some measures to revamp the Coast Guard setup as piracy is creeping closer to Indian waters. Radar coverage of India's coast is increasing by addition of 46 coastal radars by 2012, Coast Guard stations are going up from 22 to 42 and 12 more Dornier aircrafts are being acquired along with construction of a large number of ships at Indian shipyards. Along with this the manpower of the Coast Guards is also being increased by 50 per cent. The minister has also proposed a joint command under the aegis of UN.[9] On January 25, 2011 India's permanent representative at the UN made the observation that it was disturbing to see piracy increasing further and further from the coast of Somalia. The shift of attacks in south and east of Indian Ocean reflects the pirate's ability to shift out of the traditional security corridor established by naval forces and extend their reach to approximately 1,000 to 2,000 miles from Somalia. The UNSC has anti-piracy provisions which need to assess and deploy the international maritime fund. It may also be pointed out that about six per cent of international seafarers engaged in international companies are Indian Nationals and therefore high-jacking of ships with Indian crew also becomes a problem of the Indian Government.

China's Malacca Dilemma

The Chinese have referred to the Straits of Malacca as their "Malacca dilemma". This is so because this strait is perhaps the world's most important waterway linking the Persian Gulf with South China with about 40 per cent of world trade passing through it. It is the shortest route between India and the Pacific Ocean and carries a very large part of the gulf oil. Between the straits of Hormuz and Malacca there is a huge value of the world trade flowing. In so far as the Chinese are concerned their oil imports from the Middle East are about 50 per cent of their total import and will become 75 per cent by 2015. More than 80 per cent of China's oil imports are carried by tanker ships through the Straits of Malacca. Any blockage of this route will derail their economic growth. The Strait is about 900 km long but around Singapore where it is called Philips Strait, it is barely 2.4 km wide. Daily nearly 12 million barrels of oil in super tankers pass through it. In a war scenario the Straits of Malacca can easily be a target and blocked. Further, the question being raised is whether the Straits of Malacca is getting congested and over used with over hundred thousand ships passing through annually. The most pressing problem for China is the over reliance on oil from Middle East sources which comes through Straits of Malacca. China would like to have a say in the administration of the Straits of Malacca. They presently feel that while piracy in the Straits can be controlled the saturation of this sea lane is going to cause deep problems for trade especially for them.

While China seeks to have a greater say in the administration of this sea lane, the littoral countries do not want its participation, especially in view of its dubious claims and show of force in South China Sea. Further, US as it is claimed, has managed to get a foothold with an airbase at Banda Ache, the Sultan Sikander Muda Air Force Base, on the northern most tip of Indonesia. In the meantime China has stepped up its engagement with Myanmar with millions of dollars of military assistance, has made the Myanmar Army the second largest army after Vietnam in South East Asia from 180,000 to 450,000 men and vastly more technologically sophisticated.[10]

Andaman & Nicobar Islands: Strategic Reach

About 30 per cent of India's EEZ is a result of its sovereignty over these Islands. This issue is not fully appreciated by Indian policy makers. There is a need to leverage this great asset and the locational advantage of these islands. It may also be emphasised that Indian borders do not end with Indian peninsula but go right up to Sumatra with these maritime assets deep in the Bay of Bengal. With declaration of Port Blair as a major port in 2010 and extension of the naval airport by the civil administration to 11,000 feet along with its declaration as an international airport, a fresh impetus has been given to this island for promotion of trade and tourism. However, with no international ships or airline arriving in Port Blair so far this is a meaningless gesture. There has been little visible effort made in offshore oil exploration. With a huge EEZ the canvas of India's strategic region of planning becomes stretched. Indian Navy and Air Force have a much wider area to cover after United Nations Commission on the Limits of Continental Shelf (UNCLOS) III gave an additional 0.66 million sq km of EEZ in Andaman & Nicobar Islands. Consequently, the defence forces formed its first joint Tri-Command in 2001 in Andaman & Nicobar. This is a positive step, as was necessary at this stage to complement the vast responsibility of EEZ.

The Andaman & Nicobar Islands stretch from south of Myanmar to Sumatra. As a result India's maritime border also gets stretched. India has five countries with which it has a maritime border on the eastern side in the Bay of Bengal, namely Myanmar, Thailand, Malaysia, Indonesia and Bangladesh. Though, Bangladesh is quite far away from these islands. As under-sea surface wealth becomes extractable the value of the Economic Zone gains importance. Then there is also the issue of Continental Shelf. The limits of the continental shelf as required by the UNCLOS are still to be determined.

India's Malacca Advantage

According to Robert D. Kaplan in his book *Monsoon: The Indian Occean and the Future of American Power* "Hemmed in on land by a combination of Himalayan Mountains and failing states of Pakistan, Nepal, Bangladesh and Myanmar, India can best project power at sea. India stands sentinel astride the major sea lanes from the Strait of Hormuz to Strait of Malacca, where the threat of naval containerised terrorism is very real.... India can play the role of chief balancer vis-à-vis China."[11]

It is to India's advantage that the Great Nicobar Island is only 90 km from the western tip of Straits of Malacca. India's serious land border issues with China including the unfortunate acceptance of Tibet as a region of China in 1954 without a quid pro quo, the Chinese meddling in the disputed Kashmir issue with Pakistan, and the string of pearls policy adopted by China can only be countered by using the strategic advantage that India has in the Bay of Bengal. As strategic depth of world powers shifts to Indian Ocean and growth in international trade, the importance of Straits of Malaccas increases, especially for China. India's most strategic asset in Andaman & Nicobar Islands is the Great Nicobar Island (GNI). The fact that the ASEAN members are wary of Chinese designs is an advantage to India to be leveraged. While China is a much bigger economy and a more powerful military nation, it always looks to seek an advantage over other countries not so wealthy or powerful. The Chinese South China Sea claims are an example of how China is bullying its neighbours to settle its claims however irrational they may be. Chinese always look for a tactical advantage. Chinese attack on India in October 1962 was during the period of Cuban missile crisis when the attention of the then two super powers USSR and USA was diverted. The terrain was in their favour and they preferred to go to war on October 20, 1962 when the cold weather sets in and Indian troops were not prepared for the weather. The war lasted a month when on November 20, 1962 Chinese declared ceasefire and withdrew because of Cuban crisis getting resolved.

China Factor in South China Seas

China is upsetting all its littoral countries by claiming sovereignty over South China Sea and East China Sea. As a matter of fact China is already in deep dispute over Paracel and Spratly Islands as well as over Mischief Reef and Scarborough Shoal and other locations with Taiwan, Vietnam, Philippines, Malaysia and Brunei. Further, Indonesia's claims of EEZ overlap with China's claims. Vietnam has rejected China's historical explanation and claim over these islands. Historical claims do not have much legal standing.[12] In such a background India needs to take all its littoral neighbours into confidence and come to a mutually acceptable arrangement. At present Cambodia, Laos and Thailand do not have any boundary dispute with China and therefore, do not have a problem with China. Luckily, India's relations with all its littoral neighbours in the east is excellent and it is necessary that this is maintained and improved.

India's Unsettled Land Borders

It is unfortunate that India's land borders are entangled in disputes with Pakistan and China. Problems in Kashmir arose in October 1947 with Pakistan sending irregulars into the Kashmir Valley through the city of Baramula and India's appeal to the UN for a resolution backfired on India. As a result India now has an ongoing dispute for the last 60 years without a solution in sight. To compound this issue is the issue of border with China. The Chinese Premier Chou En-Lai visited India thrice in six months in 1960-61 presumably to settle the border dispute but his suggestions were rebuffed by the Indian Premier Nehru leading to the 1962 border war which India lost. Meanwhile, China settled its border with Myanmar (then Burma) in 1961 mainly along McMahon line which otherwise they do not accept (but Myanmar broke its diplomatic relations with China later in 1967-70 because of Beijing's support to Communist Party of Myanmar. China had also invaded North Myanmar in 1956). With Nepal they settled their 1,414 km border based on customary traditional boundary line in 1960 and with Pakistan in 1963 in which the latter gave away a portion of Kashmir under its occupation to China. China accepted this with a proviso in the Agreement. India has no border dispute with Myanmar. However, the control of the Myanmarese Government north of Mandalay is very weak. Various underground armies like Kachin/Shan armies do operate and control the region which makes India's borders with them vulnerable. This is more so as Indian insurgent groups like Naga underground outfits seek shelter in north Myanmar.

And even United Liberation Front of Assam (ULFA) operates across the border in Myanmar and seeks help of China and Pakistan through their outfits.

It may be recalled that over the last 60 years or so two countries broke off diplomatic relations in 1967 with China i.e., Myanmar and Indonesia. In both cases it was interference in internal affairs of the country. It is also ironic that China tried its best in 1971 to stop the birth of Bangladesh and then tried to deny it membership of the UN.[13]

A Report called 'Non-Alignment 2.0" issued by an Independent Group of 'Eminent' Experts states:

> 'China will, for the foreseeable future, remain a significant foreign policy and security challenge for India. Skirmishes and incidents have occurred along the LAC. The Strategy of India should be to "hold the line" on the Sino-Indian land frontier but maintain and, if possible, enlarge India's current edge in the maritime south. This strategy takes into account both the superiority of current Chinese deployment and the posture on the land boundary, and the unlikelihood of the border issue being resolved in the near future.'[14]

Malacca Dilemma: Finding Alternatives to Straits of Malacca

The Straits of Malacca carry 600,000 to 100,000 ships every year and any blockage or disturbance in the Straits of Malacca will harm the interest of all countries including India but more so China as a majority of its oil import passes through it. Since China does not have good petroleum reserve, they have been thinking of bypassing the Straits of Malacca to avoid a possible blockage. The following are the four alternatives which China is considering, some under implementation and some under planning:

The Alternatives to Straits of Malacca

Will the alternatives to the Straits of Malacca mentioned below work? According to Chen Shafeng of Peking University[15] in spite of the below mentioned measures the dependence of China on Straits of Malacca will continue. According to him China is going to rely on foreign fuels, particularly oil from Middle East. Crude Oil from Africa has also risen. Saudi Arabia, Angola, Iran and Russia remain its principal suppliers. Most of the crude imports from Middle East and Africa pass through Straits of Malacca. Threat of piracy, maritime terrorism and US active presence in the Asia-Pacific waters are the three main critical issues for China. While piracy and terrorism are issues which are of minor nature, the US involvement in Asia-Pacific is of concern to China. The US presence is, capable of blocking all, though it would be a costly proposition. While China's attempt at conserving energy is very much on the cards, bypassing the Malacca dilemma is certainly a very necessary objective. China has three alternative strategies and Malaysia and Thailand have one each. These are explained below.

1. Pipeline from Myanmar to Kunming along with road transportation.
2. The Kra Canal.
3. A pipeline from Gwadar in Pakistan to Shanghai via Xinjiang.
4. Malaysian Alternative.
5. Dawei project.

ALTERNATIVE 1
THE MYANMAR ALTERNATIVE

The isolation of Myanmar due to sanctions by the West forced Myanmar into improving relations with the PRC who exploited the situation and maintained strong economic and military relations. In spite of Myanmar adopting democracy

Map 9: The Myanmar Alternative

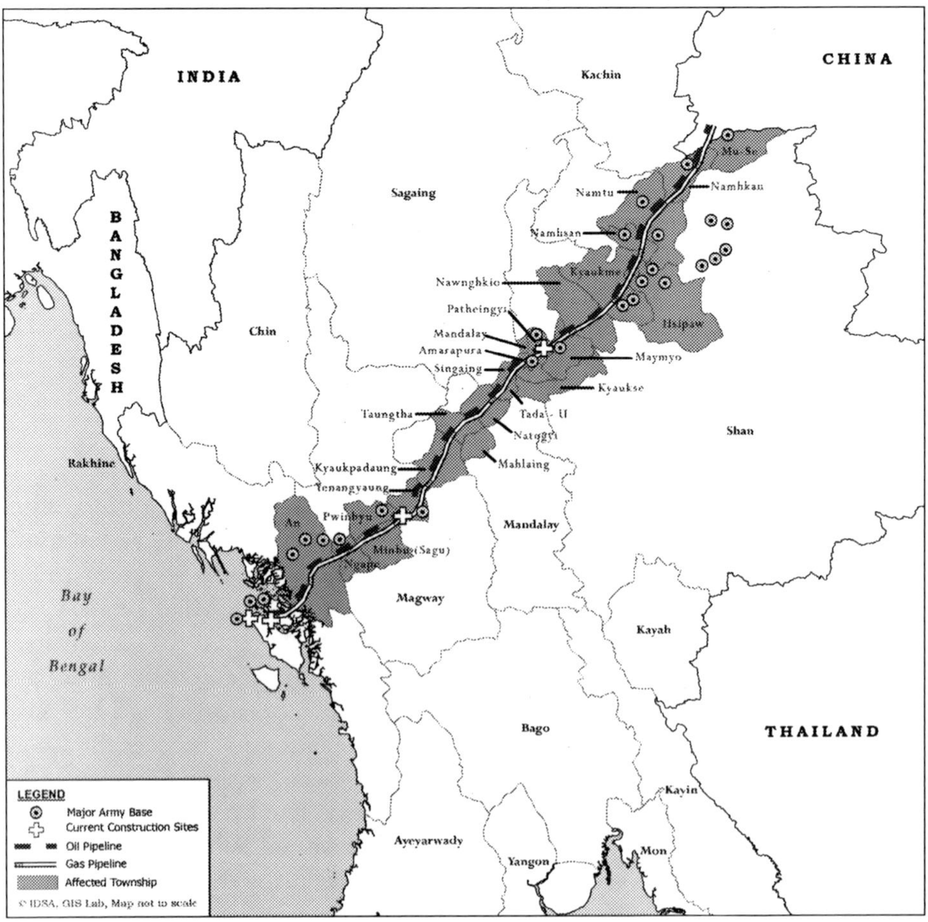

and relations with China getting diluted, the Chinese investment both in civil and military spheres will continue to have a stranglehold over it. It also appears that Myanmar is looking to get out of China's embrace and stranglehold as more alternatives open up. However, as Myanmar moves towards democracy, distancing itself from China, Chinese co-operation with Myanmar is in trouble. Already Myanmar has called off the construction of a huge dam in the north Kachin state due to local protests. This hydel project would have benefitted Yunan province of China with electricity. India, which was very close to Myanmar in Nehru's days became indifferent to the Military Junta and lost out to China. When most of the world was not talking to Myanmar it was China that consolidated its hold over Myanmar. It may be recalled that it was India's Nehru who requested Chinese Premier Chow En Lai to finalise the border with Myanmar, which they did along the McMahon line in 1961. But now India's diplomacy has to work harder to make up for the lost time.

Although, bilateral trade between China and Myanmar exceeds US$ 1.4 billion, Chinese exports to Myanmar are typically manufactured goods like steel and textile products and imports from Myanmar include raw materials like natural rubber, raw wood and now oil and gas. China's main interest is in Myanmar's extensive oil and natural gas reserves and setting up a pipeline from Bay of Bengal to Kunming in China. It is, therefore, one of the chief partners of the Myanmarese regime in the project to renovate and expand the Sittwe seaport in the Bay of Bengal and has received rights to develop and exploit natural gas reserves in the Arakan region. China extensively aided the construction of strategic roads along the Irrawaddy River trade route linking Yunnan province to the Bay of Bengal. China has already signed up with Myanmar for construction of two pipelines from Sittwe in Myanmar to Kunming in Yunnan Province with an estimated cost of around US$ two billion. Such a pipeline from Myanmar to Yunnan is very appealing to China because oil tankers from Middle East and Africa would be able to bypass the Straits of Malacca.

Chinese firms have been involved in the construction of oil and gas pipelines stretching 2,380 km from Kyankphyu Deep Sea Port in Myanmar's Arakan coast to Kunming in China's Yunnan Province. China National Offshore Oil Corporation (CNOOC) and the China National Petroleum Corporation (CNPC) hold important contracts on upgrading Myanmarese oilfields and refineries and sharing of production. Petro China has completed the gas pipeline from the Shwe oil field off the coast of the Rakhine State leading to Yunnan, accessing and exploiting an estimated 2.88 to 3.56 trillion cubic feet of natural gas. The project is expected to deliver US$ 30-50 billion to the Myanmar Government in 30 years. Initially this deal was offered to India with a pipeline through Bangladesh but since India and Bangladesh could not agree to the pipeline, China got the better of it.[16] A parallel pipeline is also part of the project–designed with an annual capacity of 22 million tonnes of oil and 12 million cubic metres of gas when completed. The pipeline will therefore provide both gas and oil from Myanmarese wells as well as pump up oil from ships coming into Myanmarese ports to Kunming in Yunan, bypassing the Straits of Malacca.[17]

China is also the most important supplier of military aid to Myanmar and maintains extensive strategic and military cooperation. Since 1989, when no other country was prepared to supply anything to China due to sanctions, China exploited the isolation of Myanmar and supplied Myanmar with jet fighters, armoured vehicles and naval vessels and trained Myanmarese Army, Air Force and Naval personnel. Access to Myanmar's ports and naval installations provides China with strategic influence in the Bay of Bengal, in the wider IOR and in Southeast Asia. China has developed a deep-water port in Kyaukpyu in the Bay of Bengal. It has also reportedly built an 85-metre jetty, naval facilities and major reconnaissance and Electronic Intelligence (ELINT) systems on the Great Coco Island, located 18 km from the northern most islands in the Andaman group, giving China capabilities to monitor India's military activities, including missile tests. China has been assisting in constructing a naval base in Sittwe, a strategically important sea port close to eastern India's largest city and port, Kolkata. China also funds road construction linking Yangon and Sittwe, providing the shortest route to the Indian Ocean from southern China.

China and Russia also vetoed a UNSC resolution designed to punish Myanmar. In recent years, however, China has shown a lack of willingness to back the Myanmar Government and has attempted to destabilise the political situation in Northern Myanmar. This is an indication of strained relations between the two countries.

Post the democracy movement in recent years, Myanmar has moved to develop strategic and commercial relations with India, with whom it shares a very old relationship, having been a part of India under the British. Increasing trade and military cooperation with India, developing bilateral relations with Japan and with ASEAN shows a desire in Myanmar's foreign policy to avoid excessive dependence on China. Myanmar joined ASEAN as a member in 1997.

After the Kokang incident in northern Shan state of Myanmar in August 2009 which attracted international media interest, relations between Myanmar and China have soured. It is clear that Myanmar was prioritising internal conflicts over its ties with China; however some Chinese analysts, such as Shi Yinhong,[18] played down the relationship between Myanmar and China, saying "They're not great friends. They don't listen to what China says." China had urged Myanmar to ensure the stability of the border area and protect the interests of its citizens in Myanmar. The Myanmarese Foreign Ministry later apologised to China about the incident, but also ran a story on the Dalai Lama in the government newspaper the *Myanmar Times*, the first mention of him in the state controlled Myanmarese media for 20 years. Chinese officials were said to be "furious" and "extremely upset" over not being forewarned about the offensive on the border. It may be recalled that while Myanmar was first to recognise communist China in 1959, it broke its diplomatic relations in 1967 when it suspected it interfering in its internal affairs and encouraging a communist movement in Myanmar.

It is in India's interest to ensure that the traditional close relationship with Myanmar is restored and the Chinese influence which grew due to sanctions imposed by rest of the world, are nullified. This means that Indian diplomacy has to work hard to convince the US to lift all the sanctions against Myanmar. They also have to work hard to ensure decline of Chinese influence over Myanmar and bring back India as a favoured neighbour.

ALTERNATIVE 2
KRA CANAL

Even though distance saved by the Kra Canal in comparison with the present route of Straits of Malacca, is not so significant, nevertheless according to a computerised picture, ships could save some 28 to 40 hours when travelling through the Kra Canal.

Straits of Malacca

Traffic Estimates
(Ships Over 1,000 DWT)

1972	15,000	(MAX. 20,000) - TAMS
1993	42,000	(Inter-Reg. only) U.S. CNA
1997	92,000	U.S. CNA, Lloyds
1999	103,000	U.S. CNA, Lloyds

Note that the kra canal capacity at 80 per cent of allowable density is 110,000 ships per year per lane.

China's second alternative to bypass the Straits of Malacca is to help build an alternative canal to Straits of Malacca. This can be done by reviving the old project of Kra Canal in Thailand. This proposed canal which will cut through Kra Isthmus of southern Thailand will be about 44 km long and will link directly to the Indian Ocean avoiding the Straits of Malacca and also cutting distance to Chinese Ports. However, with rocky land of up to 75 metres above the sea level the engineering and labour requirements will be huge. The project was approved by the Thai Senate in 2007 but is stalled due to environment concerns. The Singapore Government is concerned as they would lose their pre-eminent position. The US had also shown its concern amid the growing influence of the Chinese

Map 10: Straits of Malacca

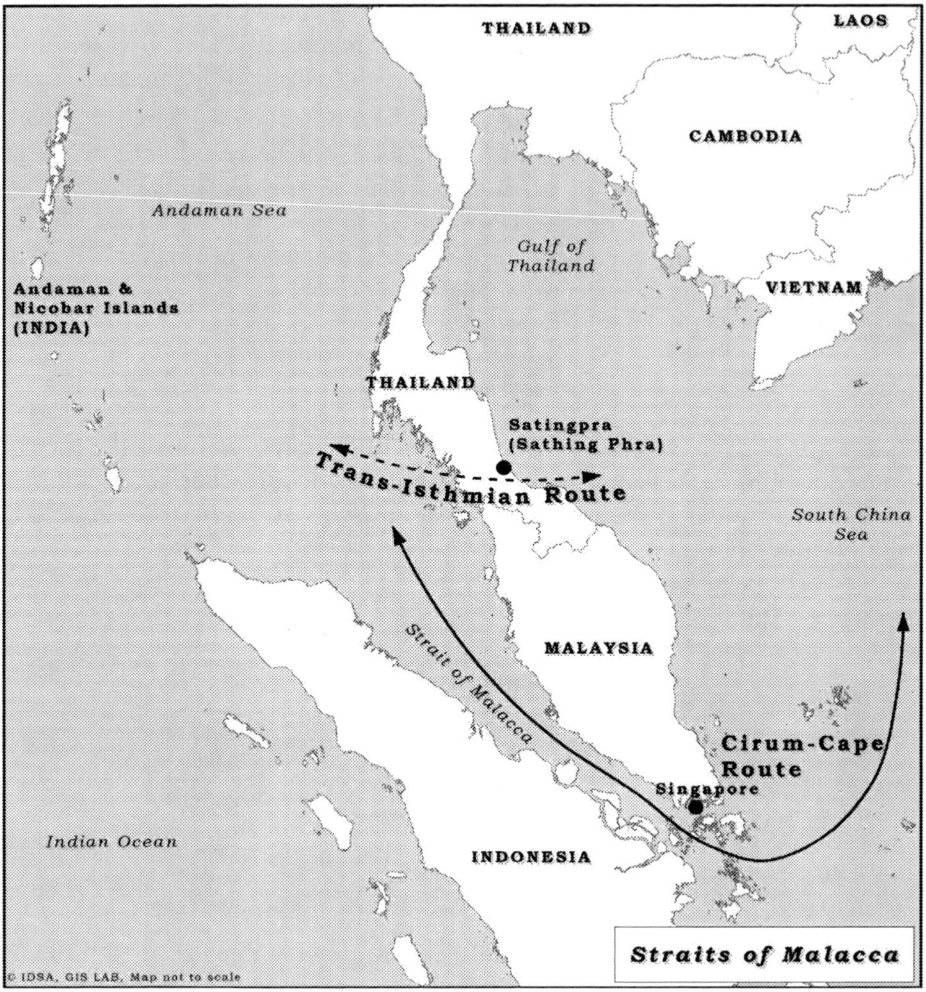

in the region. The estimated cost of such a canal would be around US$ 20 billion with about 30,000 workers involved and a time period of 10 years.

Thailand-China and Kra Canal

The idea of building a canal across the peninsula of Thailand-Malaysia which will bypass Straits of Malacca is very old. However, due to its high financial costs it was always shelved. Currently, China is again taking interest as this could be a means to bypass the Straits of Malacca.

Based on a report prepared appearing in *Washington Times*, China's strategy of underwriting construction of the canal across the Kra Isthmus, complete with Chinese port facilities and refineries, is part of its "string of pearls" strategy of forward bases and energy security. The Chinese plan called for construction over 10 years, employing roughly 30,000 workers and costing between US$ 20 to 25 billion.

In so far as India is concerned the distance from Great Nicobar Islands to the western tip of Kra canal would be about the same and the shipping route will still go past Nicobars. However, India should take up diplomatically with Thailand their concern as Chinese involvement would be detrimental to Indian interest. India should have no objection if Indian engineering companies and labour is involved. It may be pointed out that Suez Canal opened in 1869 and is 193 km long while Panama Canal opened in 1914 and is about 82 km long. A 44 km long canal as an alternative to Malacca is well within the realm of possibility. The cost benefit analysis and its use has not been worked out in detail but even if 25 per cent of the existing traffic of ships that use the Straits of Malacca use this and pay for it, it can become self-sustaining and economically viable.

Thailand has also proposed an alternative to Straits of Malacca. Instead of Kra Canal, it has proposed a pipeline running underground across the Isthmus. Such a pipeline will benefit not only China but other countries like Japan, South Korea etc. However, high costs and political issues have not made it possible for this pipeline to see the light of day yet.[19]

ALTERNATIVE 3
GWADAR PORT

Chinese alternative to Straits of Malaccas: Gwadar Port in Pakistan

The last and third alternative by China to bypass the Straits of Malacca is to build a pipeline and a road from Gwadar Port in Balochistan in Pakistan all the way up to Kashgar in Xingjiang, China.

In August 2001, the Chinese and Pakistan Governments signed a financing agreement for building the Gwadar Port with US$ 198 million, a preferential loan while Pakistan raise a US$ 50 million. Gwadar Port built by China is about 460 km west of Karachi and only 75 km east of its border with Iran and next to the busy Straits of Hormuz. The first phase was completed in 1999 but it became operational only in 2008 with the first ship to dock being from Canada. A second phase is on the anvil.

The port was being run by Singapore's Port Authority (PSA) International which won a contract for 30 years in which China did not take part. However, the project was not making money and PSA has got out of it. China has now taken over the running of the port through one of its Public Sector Undertakings (PSU's), the Chinese Overseas Port Holdings Company (COPHC). China has

Map 11: Gwadar to China Pipeline

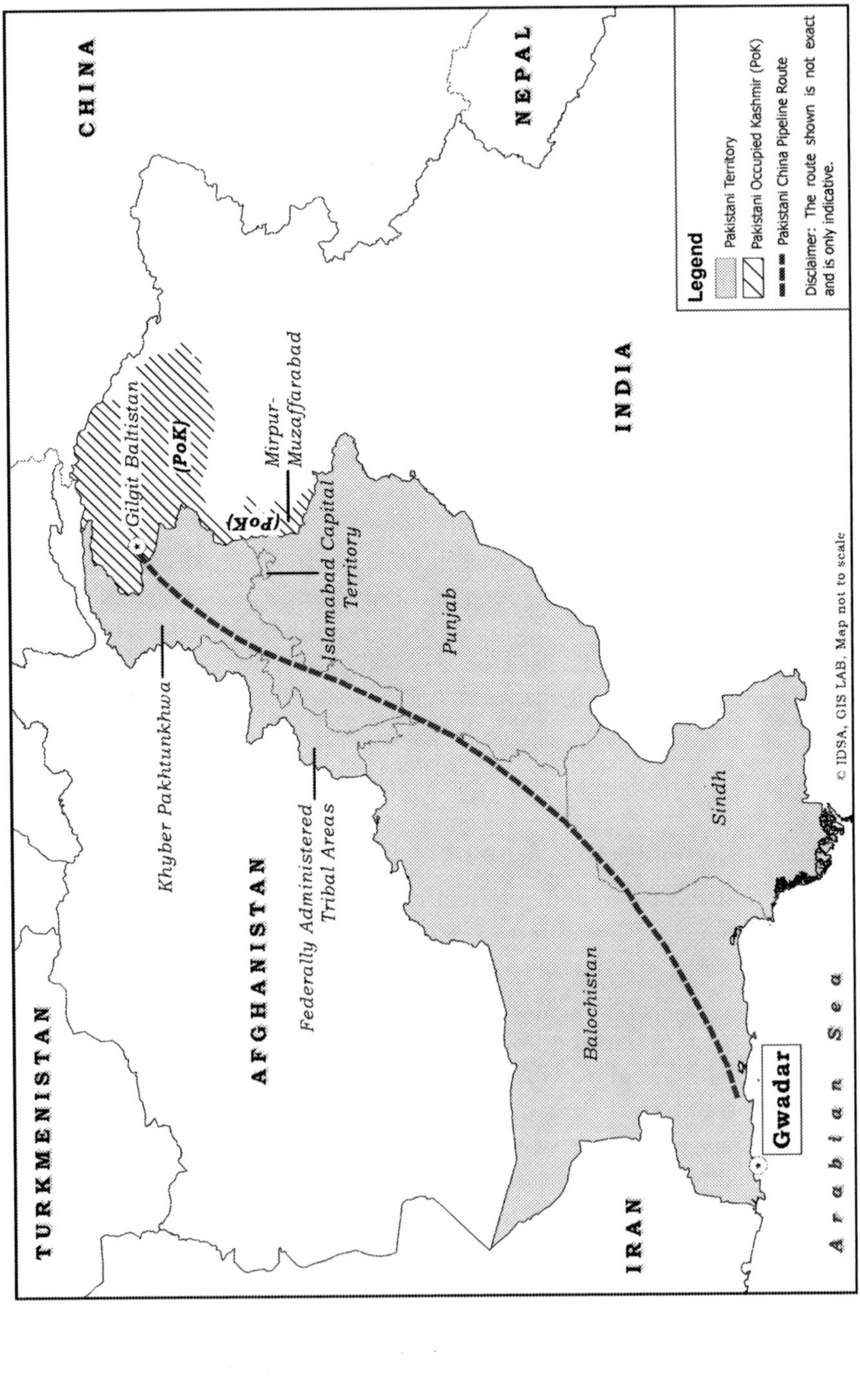

also been wanting to build a pipeline from Gwadar Port to Xingjiang along the 1,300 km Karakoram Highway built by them through Kashmir, Hunza valley and Gilgit which is under occupation of Pakistan. This pipeline can carry the crude oil from Gulf and African States all the way to China. The COPHC has taken over and has assured to invest US$ 750 million immediately to further improve the infrastructure.[20] This may also perhaps become a Chinese naval port as it has strategic importance. 60 per cent of China's crude supply comes from the Gulf countries.

With special relations between China and Pakistan, India can expect a pipeline and a tunnel from Gwadar to Xingjiang to come up which will help bypass Malacca for their oil shipment. During the visit of Prime Minister of Pakistan Mr. Nawaz Sharif in 2012, an agreement was signed between the two governments to provide a Pakistan-China Economic Corridor with a 200 mile long tunnel connecting Pakistan Gwadar Port with Kashgar in Xinjiang in North West China. The corridor will pass through Pakistan Occupied Kashmir (POK). It is not clear whether the Government of India has lodged a protest with China on using the part of Kashmir with Pakistan.[21]

Once again India has watched helplessly as China walks away by constructing a pipeline over territory in Gilgit. This is similar to Pakistan giving away a piece of Kashmir to China in its border settlement in 1963 (a fact which is mentioned in the Sino-Pakistan Agreement of 1963). But the pipeline has technical and security issues and will take time to come up.

ALTERNATIVE 4
MALAYSIAN ALTERNATIVE

A fourth alternative has also come up with the announcement by Malaysia of constructing a pipeline across northern Malaysia for about US$ seven billion between Bay of Bengal and South China Sea. This 300 km or 185 miles long pipeline will allow ships to divert a third of all oil now being carried through Straits of Malacca. Rahim Kamil Sulaiman, Chairman of the project, announced in May 2007, that the work on it will commence in 2008 and finish by 2014. Trans-peninsula Petroleum signed an agreement with a Malaysian company Ranhill Engineers and Constructors for design and construction in presence of the Malaysian Prime Minister Abdullah Ahmed Badawi and the Indonesian President Susilo Bambang Yudhoyono. It was also proposed to have two refineries at Kedah where the crude oil from Gulf would be refined. Refined oil will then be loaded on to ships bound for China and Japan with a combined refining capacity of 450,000 barrels a day.

So far nothing further has been heard of this project. If it comes up it will impact Singapore which is also a political and economic rival of Malaysia. If the scheme is successful it will carry about 20 per cent of the oil that passes through the Straits.[22]

ALTERNATIVE 5

Dawei Project is a proposal coming from Thai Prime Minister Yingluch Shinawatra to develop a Chennai-Dawei corridor which was discussed during a visit to India. This is another alternative to Straits of Malacca and is proposed with Thailand in collaboration with Myanmar as Dawei is on the shores of Andaman Sea in southern Myanmar close to the Thai border. The project is not based on cutting a canal but building a land based transport corridor running across Myanmar and Thailand. This project will create an overland system of logistics along with a massive industrial complex. Dawai Development Corporation has already been set up with controlling stake of an Italian company called Ital-Thai. An agreement has already been signed between the Military Government of Myanmar for development of the complex in 2010. However, the new Democratic Government of Myanmar has already overruled the Ital-Thai plans to build a coal fired plant on environmental grounds. India has also signalled its interest in the project.[23]

The Chinese Malacca dilemma is causing the government of China to find alternatives. While the Myanmar alternative is secure, the other two alternatives of Kra Canal and a pipeline through Pakistan are still not clear. The Gwadar alternative faces many technical problems although Pakistan and China have signed up for a 200 mile long tunnel at a cost of US$ 18 billion. All these alternatives will mitigate a part of the Chinese Malacca dilemma. In addition, China is also building oil and gas pipelines across Russia. However, the Chinese export dependence is also mainly ship based and Straits of Malacca take a very large share of it (China has already started railway based exports to Europe up to Germany). Any impact on this will impact Chinese economy adversely.

All these projects raise tremendous technological challenges and viability issues. The gas and oil pipeline from Myanmar to Kunming is already operational. Since the Government of Myanmar has already signed an agreement on March 27, 2007 on the issue of oil and gas pipelines, with a planned expenditure of US$ 1.5 billion and one billion respectively, of which one of the pipelines has already started and the other is expected to be completed shortly. China National Petroleum Corporation (CNPC) holds 50.9 per cent stake while the rest is owned by Myanmar Oil and Gas Enterprise.

Taking into account the China-Myanmar oil and gas pipelines, China-Pakistan oil pipeline and also China-Russia and China-Kazakstan oil pipeline with their capacities, Chen Shaofeng,[24] has come to the conclusion that even if all these operate at full capacity, they will meet China's requirement by 26 per cent only and, therefore, China will still need to depend heavily on the Straits of Malacca.

Chen Shaofeng goes on further to state that the Malacca Dilemma for China makes it go in for a naval build up to preserve its SLOC. Further, as China's trade and imports grow it needs a globally capable navy to keep its trade protected. At the same time, Chen concedes that China's military build up is likely to lead to an arms race as other countries in the Asia-Pacific are not willing to see the power balance being broken and lack of transparency by China may appear to be like a threat to world security. US in particular will not allow it and other countries will follow. For example, Japan has already embarked on its quasi aircraft carrier as the Japanese constitution does not allow owning of an aircraft carrier. US might use the threat of denial i.e. denying China access to its crucial SLOCS, especially its imports of oil through South China Sea.

In so far as India is concerned, the Gwadar Port and pipeline project of Pakistan and China are most disturbing. This is because close relations of Pakistan and China in military matters makes Gwadar Port a near certain Chinese naval facility. Also, use of POK by China for purposes of a pipeline, even against the wishes of local population, is unfortunate. India's protest for use of POK is so mild that it is not even felt. The Myanmar pipeline to China is already a reality. As long as Myanmar does not offer to the Chinese navy port facilities, there is little harm to India. The other three proposals of Kra Canal, the Malaysian and Dawei-Chennai proposal are vague and at this stage cannot be taken seriously.

The fact that China is seeking alternatives to the Straits of Malacca confirms that China has realised that its rise is being looked at with fear, doubt and hostility. Further, its major claim to the South China Sea followed by military action is making countries in South East Asia hostile to it. Its crude methods of use of force to seek what it might perceive to be its rightful due, but is not accepted otherwise is reminiscent of its military occupation of Tibet and is not paying dividends. India needs to leverage this opportunity with use of hard and soft power in the Andaman Sea/Bay of Bengal/South China Sea.

NOTES

1. Shinzo Abe, *Mint,* January 01, 2012.
2. Sam Bateman, Catherine Zara Raymond and Joshua Ho, "Safety and Security in Malacca & Singapore Straits", Policy Paper, Maritime Security Programme, Institute of Defence & Strategic Studies, Singapore, 2006.
3. Michael Jarocki, "India's Strategy Towards Strait of Malacca", *Global Strategies*, April, 1, 2012.
4. "Piracy and Armed Robbery in Straits of Malaccas: A Problem Solved?" *National War College Review,* at www.humansecuritygateway.com/documents/nwrc/piracy&robbery.
5. R. Pulugan, "Taking on Regional Piracy Calls for New Directions in Straits of Malaccas", January 01, 2010.
6. See Air Marshal Dhiraj Kukreja, "Security Challenges of India: Andaman & Nicobar Islands", *Indian Defence Review*, January–March, 2013.
7. Nirmala Sitharaman, *Asian Age*, June 26, 2011.
8. Aparajit Biswas: "Small Arms & Drug Trafficking in Indian Ocean Region", Working Paper No. 4, Centre of African Studies, University of Mumbai.
9. See *Asian Age*, September 28, 2011.

10. Wo Kong, "China's quest for energy security," Energy Resources Environment Programme, SAIS, Johns Hopkins University; Georgia Institute of Technology.
11. Robert D. Kaplan, *Monsoon: The Indian Ocean and the Future of American Power*, Random House, New York, p. 125.
12. *China-South East Asian Relations: Trends, Issues and Implementation for the United States*, Congressional Research Services, Library of the Congress, April, 2006.
13. Brahma Chellaney, *Asian Juggernaut: The Rise of China, India and Japan,* HarperCollins, 2006, p.145.
14. *Non Alignment 2.0* is a product of collective deliberations, debate and report writing involving an independent group of analysts and policy makers namely Sunil Khilnani, Rajiv Kumar, Pratap Bhanu Mehta, Lt. Gen Prakash Menon (Retd), Nandan Nilekani, Srinath Raghavan, Shyam Saran and Siddharth Varadarajan.
15. *International Journal of Chinese Studies*, 1(1), January 2010, pp. 1-24.
16. C. Raja Mohan *Samudra Manthan: Sino-Indian Rivalry in the Indo-Pacific*, CEIP, Washington D.C., 2012, pp. 121-123.
17. *Economic Times*, July 30, 2013, p. 13.
18. Shi Yinhong, Professor of International Relations, Centre for American Studies, Renmin University of China.
19. C. Raja Mohan, no. 16,
20. *Hindustan Times*, February 02, 2013, p. 17.
21. *Indian Express*, July 06, 2013.
22. *International Herald Tribune*, May 29, 2007.
23. C. Raja Mohan: *Indian Express*, January 26, 2012.
24. Chen Shaofeng, "China's Self-Extrication from the Malacca Dilemma", *International Journal of China Studies*, 1, January 2010, pp. 1-24.

CHAPTER 4

The International Law of the Sea and India's Maritime Legislative History

India is fortunate in having all its legislation with regard to maritime issues and boundaries in place except for with Pakistan and Bangladesh. With Bangladesh the maritime boundaries are being settled in arbitration and hopefully will be resolved soon. With other countries India has settled all the maritime boundaries. The following gives a detailed description of India's maritime issues:

DEVELOPMENTS TILL 1965

Traditionally, the international law of the sea had come to be based on the basic principle of "freedom of the seas". Beyond the narrow coastal strip of territorial waters, the seas could be freely used by all nations for fishing and for navigation. Coastal states used to be content with exclusive rights in their narrow belt of territorial waters.

US was the first to extend its jurisdiction over coastal seas. With improved technology, the discovery of petroleum and natural gas in the shallow waters of the continental shelf led the US to issue the Truman Proclamation in 1945, which claimed sovereign rights over the resources of the continental shelf adjacent to its coast. Around the same time, coastal states found that the fishing areas near their coasts were being poached by larger and better equipped fishing ships of distant foreign states. Both these developments, combined with the emergence of newly independent states after the decolonisation of Asia and Africa, led to a spate of unilateral claims by the coastal states to extend national jurisdiction over large adjacent sea areas to protect their fishery resources.

POST-INDEPENDENCE INDIA

On attaining independence in 1947, India was quick enough to realise the importance of the sea and proclaimed the traditional territorial sea of three miles. But by 1955, in view of the international developments, India issued four presidential notifications to safeguard its maritime interests:

Map 12: Bangladesh's Low Water Baseline Perceived by India and Myanmar

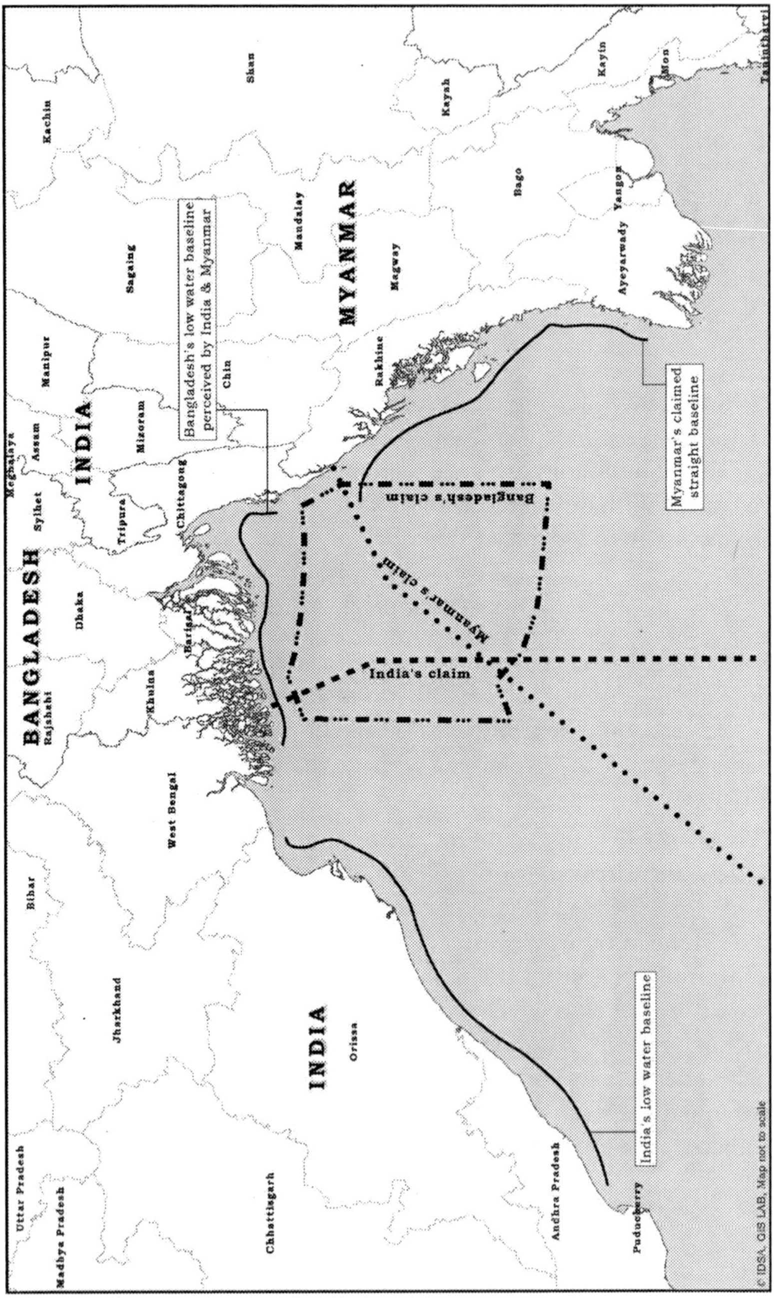

(a) On August 30, 1955, India claimed full and exclusive sovereign rights over the seabed and subsoil of the continental shelf adjoining the coast but beyond territorial waters. Neither the depth nor the distance from the coastline was indicated.
(b) On March 22, 1956, India claimed territorial waters of six miles from appropriate baselines.
(c) On November 29, 1956, India claimed a conservation zone for fisheries up to a distance of one hundred miles from the outer limit of territorial waters.
(d) On December 3, 1956, India claimed a contiguous zone.

Several other developments were also taking place. The USA and the Soviet Union were unable to agree on the width of territorial waters—the Soviet Union wanted 12 miles whilst the USA wanted only three miles. Technological developments in the industrialised West began to make it possible to extract oil and gas from the seabed. The newly independent nations of Asia and Africa began to feel that the International Law of the Sea would be exploited to their disadvantage. To sort out all these matters, the first UNCLOS I was convened in 1958.

UNCLOS I—1958

UNCLOS I was able to codify the traditional law. It adopted what came to be known as the Geneva Conventions on the Law of the Sea. Its principles were:

- The freedom of the seas as long conceived.
- The sovereignty of coastal states in the territorial sea.
- The ancillary physical, customs, sanitary and immigration rights of coastal states in a contiguous zone.
- The acceptance by UNCLOS I of the Continental Shelf Convention.

This enabled the countries bordering the North Sea to divide the sea area for extracting oil and gas.

The UNCLOS I participants remained divided on several issues:

- The rights of coalitions of coastal states, land locked states and archipelagic states.
- Certain states contested the rights of passage through straits used for international navigation like the Straits of Gibraltar, Hormuz and Malacca.
- Land based mineral producers tried to carve out for themselves as much as they could of the newly found seabed mineral resources.

UNCLOS I completely failed to agree on:

- The precise width of the Territorial Sea (three miles or 12 miles) and the extent of the Exclusive Fisheries Zone (EFZ).
- The prior authorisation and/or notification of the passage of foreign warships through the territorial sea of a coastal state.

The Second Conference, UNCLOS II, was therefore convened in 1960 to resolve these issues.

UNCLOS II—1960

UNCLOS II attempted to extend the jurisdiction of coastal states over territorial waters to six miles, with an additional six miles as an EFZ. This failed to gain the required two thirds majorities for its acceptance.

After UNCLOS II failed to achieve agreement on the width of the territorial sea, many countries unilaterally extended their offshore jurisdiction. The South American countries reaffirmed their earlier claim of their territorial waters extending 200 miles from the coast. African states like Nigeria, Congo, Mauritius and Ghana also extended their territorial sea to distances much beyond 12 miles.

Passage of Warships through the Territorial Sea

At UNCLOS I, India had proposed that the passage of foreign warships through the territorial sea of a coastal state should be subject to prior authorisation and notification to the coastal state. As this requirement was not accepted and therefore not included in the 1958 conventions on the territorial sea and the contiguous zone, India declined to ratify all four Geneva Conventions. In subsequent years, India resiled from this position. As a growing maritime nation interested in the freedom of navigation both for itself and the international community, India sought only prior notification for the innocent passage of foreign warships through territorial waters.

Developments After 1965

India's Extension of Territorial Waters

On September 12, 1967, India extended its territorial waters to 12 miles. This was largely a reaction to Pakistan's extension of her territorial waters from three to 12 miles, rather than an act of maritime policy.

The Seabed Committee

During the 1960s political, technological, economic and naval developments began to change the situation. Advances in seabed exploitation technology made it possible to exploit the seabed much beyond a depth of two hundred metres, thereby rendering the 1958 Conventions outmoded. The deployment of Submarine Launched Ballistic Missiles and worldwide apprehensions of a competitive scramble to achieve predominant control over the seabed led the UN to discuss the need to evolve means for the peaceful use of the oceans. In 1968, the UN General Assembly constituted a 42 member "Seabed Committee" on the peaceful use of the seabed.

In December 1970, the General Assembly adopted the "Declaration of Principles" governing the Seabed, the ocean floor and the subsoil thereof, beyond the limits of national jurisdiction. The Declaration stated that these areas and their resources are the *common heritage of mankind* and shall be subject to an international regime as established by an international treaty.

Seabed Mining

India's interest in the mining of polymetalic nodules from the seabed derived from its long term strategy for metals like nickel, cobalt, copper and manganese. In the early 1970, the Government of India had initiated a programme of scientific investigation and evaluation of the manganese nodule resources in the Indian Ocean.

Offshore Oil and Gas

By the early 1970's, India had discovered oil and gas in Bombay High and promising fields were being forecasted in the Godavari, Krishna and Palk Bay basins, as also gas in the Andaman Offshore.

India has been quite meticulous in taking care of its maritime border, especially in the east. India's maritime legislative history is as follows:

MARITIME ACT, 1976

On August 25, 1976 India passed the Maritime Zones Act which claimed a 12 mile territorial sea, a 24 mile contiguous zone, a 200 mile EEZ and a continental shelf up to 200 miles or the outer edge of the continental margin, whichever is greater.

Soon after this Act, a committee was set up to consider the type of force that should be created to enforce compliance with its provisions. Three options emerged:

I. To entrust this responsibility to the marine wing of the MoF. This option was not pursued as the functions were too onerous.
II. To set up a separate Coastal Command, as a part of the navy, to oversee these functions. This option was seriously considered since it would avoid the expenditure of raising and maintaining a separate armed force. The MEA however felt that patrolling of the EEZ and protection of national

assets was a peace time role for which defence assets should not be used.

III. To set up a separate armed force of the Union, along the lines of the US Coast Guard. This option was finally chosen, as it avoided the navy being distracted from its primary role of preparing for hostilities.

An interim Coast Guard was constituted on February 1, 1977, which operated under the aegis of the navy until August 18, 1978. A permanent Coast Guard was constituted as an armed force of the Union on August 19, 1978. The Coast Guard Act 1978 requires the Coast Guard to:

(a) Ensure the safety and protection of offshore terminals, installations and other structures and devices.
(b) Provide protection to fishermen, including assisting them when in distress at sea.
(c) Protect the marine environment by preventing and controlling marine pollution.
(d) Assist the customs in anti-smuggling activities when patrolling the seas beyond Indian territorial waters.
(e) Enforce the Maritime Zones Act of 1976.
(f) Take measures for the safety of life and property at sea.
(g) Collect scientific data.

The Coast Guard thus became the principal agency for enforcing all national legislation in the Maritime Zones of India, working in close liaison with other Government authorities to avoid duplication of effort.

During hostilities, India's Coast Guard would function under the overall operational command of the navy as is done by other Coast Guards of the world.

UNCLOS III—1973-82

With a view to establishing an equitable international regime for the exploitation of seabed resources, the UN General Assembly (GA) convened the third conference, UNCLOS III in 1973.

It took UNCLOS III nine years of discussions to finally adopt the Convention on April 30, 1982. However, this convention took 12 years to formally come into force on November 16, 1984. UNCLOS III aimed to define an agreed set of rules to govern the use of the seas which would strike a fair balance between:

(a) Those who considered that a coastal state should have no right whatsoever over the living resources of the seas beyond a territorial sea of 12 miles; and
(b) Others who maintained that a coastal state should have full or limited sovereignty over the sea and its resources out to an (EEZ) of 200 nm

The acceptance of this concept of the EEZ was a landmark contribution of UNCLOS III.

At UNCLOS III, India's stand was that as a developing country centrally located in the Indian Ocean, with a coastline of over 64,000 km, its basic national interests were:

(a) To obtain assurance of smooth and free navigation though traditionally used waters and straits used for international navigation.
(b) To achieve archipelagic status for the Andaman & Nicobar Island group and the Lakshadweep Island group which between them, comprised over 1,280 islands and islets.
(c) To protect essential strategic and security interests in the waters around its coast.
(d) To secure the free mobility of naval war ships.
(e) To preserve the marine environment in the sea areas adjacent to its coast, because the channels of navigation passed near its long coastline.
(f) To regulate within its EEZ, the conduct of marine scientific research by foreign research agencies.

India advocated from the baselines, a territorial sea of 12 miles, an EEZ of 200 miles and a continental shelf to the outer edge of the geological continental margin. India also made specific proposals on the requirement of prior notification for warships passing through the territorial sea, enlargement of safety zones around offshore oil rigs, designation of special areas for the protection of the resources located therein (as for example the coral lagoons in the Lakshadweep where tankers could run aground) and several other proposals.

THE OUTCOME OF UNCLOS III—THE 1982 CONVENTION ON THE LAW OF THE SEA

The 1982 Convention on the Law of the Sea met most of India's interests. It adopted:

- 12 miles as the uniform limit for the width of the territorial sea.
- A 200 miles EEZ, within which the coastal state exercises sovereign rights and jurisdiction for certain specified economic activities.
- A continental shelf extending to the outer edge of the continental margin, to be delimited with reference to either 350 miles from the baselines of territorial waters or 100 miles from the 2,500 metre isobaths.
- Regimes for the abatement and control of marine pollution, for marine scientific research, for the international seabed area and for unimpeded transit passage through straits used for international navigation.
- The 1982 Convention included India as one of the four states named as 'pioneer investor' for seabed mining. On August 17, 1987, India

became the first state to be so registered, after having fulfilled the criteria stipulated in the convention.

There were several areas where India's stand was not accepted. The major ones were:

Passage of Warships through the Territorial Sea

There was vehement opposition from the US and the Soviet Union to prior notification before warships transited through territorial waters, on the grounds that it would seriously jeopardise their strategic and security interests. There is therefore no provision in the 1982 UNCLOS requiring prior notification or authorisation for the passage of foreign warships through the territorial waters of a coastal state. By 1977, Pakistan, Bangladesh, Sri Lanka and Myanmar had all unilaterally promulgated that prior authorisation and notification was required for the passage of foreign warships through their respective territorial seas.

India's Maritime Zones Act 1976 also requires foreign warships to give prior notification for passing through India's territorial waters and enjoins all submarines and other underwater vehicles to navigate on the surface and show their flag while passing through these waters.

Archipelagic Status for the Andaman & Nicobar Islands

The convention granted the status of an archipelago only to those groups of islands that were political entities by themselves as for example Indonesia, the Philippines and the Maldives. This was because of fear of interference with the freedom of navigation through archipelagic waters that might be created if the off-lying islands of continental coastal states were to be granted archipelagic status. For example, the distance between the Andaman group and the Nicobar group of islands is 76 miles. If archipelagic status had been granted to these groups of islands, India would have had full regulatory control over the navigation of ships passing through the 10 Degree Channel, which would then have been part of India's archipelagic waters, and therefore subject to the restricted regimes of archipelagic sea lanes passage.

Enlarged Safety Zones for Offshore Installations

The UNCLOS I Continental Shelf Convention had provided for a safety zone of 500 metres around artificial islands, installations or structures on the continental shelf. India's view at UNCLOS III was that this zone was inadequate, considering the time that a huge super tanker takes to come to a stop. India therefore advocated enlarged safety zones. The suggestion did not receive adequate support. A provision was, however, incorporated in the 1982 Convention that if authorised by generally accepted international standards or as recommended by the competent international organisation, then a coastal state may promulgate safety zones larger than 500 metres.

India's gains after the 1982 UNCLOS—Apart from the benefits of an agreed Law of the Sea, India gained in the following significant areas:

(a) India's EEZ became the 12th largest in the world. The extension of the EEZ to 350 miles or 100 miles beyond the 2500-metre isobath added two million square km to India's jurisdiction.
(b) As a result of UNCLOS III India was able to gain 0.66 sq km of EEZ which is about of 1/3rd of India's EEZ. According to Swaminathan Anklesaria Aiyer, India has been known to have massive deposits of methane hydrates. An Indo-US Scientific Joint Venture of 2006 explored four areas Kerala-Konkan Basin, Krishna-Godavari Basin, the Mahanadi Basin and the Seas of Andaman Islands. The Andaman achieved thickest ever deposits at 600 meters below the sea bed. The potential of finding hydro-carbons in the EEZ of these islands seems possible and needs greater exploration.[1]
(c) Pursuant to the 'pioneer investor' status, the International Seabed Authority (ISA) allotted to India a 150,000 square km mine site in the central Indian Ocean for the seabed mining of poly-metalic nodules. The richest area at this site has a density of 21 kilograms of nodules per square metre.

Chinese have also been allotted 10,000 sq km in the Indian Ocean by the ISA to explore seabed for ore for a period of 15 years.

MARITIME BOUNDARIES

India has maritime boundaries with five states located opposite to it (Sri Lanka, the Maldives, Myanmar, Indonesia, Thailand) and two adjacent states (Pakistan and Bangladesh).

Maritime boundary agreements were amicably concluded with:

(a) Sri Lanka in 1974 and 1976.
(b) Indonesia in 1974.
(c) The Maldives in 1976.
(d) Thailand and Indonesia, on the tri-junction point, in 1977.
(e) Myanmar in 1982.

Maritime boundary agreements with the adjacent states of Pakistan and Bangladesh have yet to be concluded. Meetings have been held with Bangladesh since 1976 and with Pakistan since 1986.

India's Maritime Border with its Neighbours

Except for Bangladesh, India has settled its maritime boundaries in the Bay of Bengal with Indonesia, Thailand, Malaysia, Myanmar and Sri Lanka. Following is a brief description of its maritime borders in the Bay of Bengal. India has nine boundary agreements with its neighbours.

There was a lot more bonhomie between India and Indonesia in the Sukarno days when India had become very close to Indonesia but the goodwill got dissipated over time. There were differences between India and Indonesia over Andaman & Nicobar Islands which is now a settled issue. Indonesia claimed archipelagic status and adopted archipelagic baselines that were accepted by the Third UN Law of the Sea Conference. Thus, the Indonesian territorial sea, EEZ and continental shelf are all measured from archipelagic baseline and therefore the two countries' claims on the continental shelf overlapped in the Andaman Sea and the Bay of Bengal. However, India was able to settle its continental shelf boundary with Indonesia by two separate agreements—the first in 1974 on delineation of the area between Great Nicobar and Sumatra and the other in 1977. While the first agreement settled the issue of the continental shelf on modified equidistant principle, the second agreement of 1977 was concerning the EEZ and also determined a tri-junction point following which India, Indonesia and Thailand signed a boundary treaty to determine a common tri-junction point in the Andaman Sea. An agreement between the Government of the Republic of India and the Government of the Republic of Indonesia relating to the delimitation of the continental shelf boundary between the two countries was signed on August 8, 1974 and came into force on December 17, 1974.

This was a major difference between the Indonesian perception of their maritime boundaries and that of India which was reconciled. The 1974 Agreement between the Government of the Republic of India and the Government of the Republic of Indonesia on the extension of the 1974 continental shelf boundary between the two countries in the Andaman Sea and the Indian Ocean came into force on December 22, 1980.

India and Thailand

In 1978 the Government of India and the Kingdom of Thailand signed an Agreement delimiting the seabed boundary. This was based on the determination of the tri-junction point between India, Thailand and Indonesia on the basis of the UNCLOS III Agreement between the Government of the Kingdom of Thailand and the Government of the Republic of India on the delimitation of sea-bed boundary between the two countries in the Andaman Sea signed on June 22, 1978 and which came into force in December 15, 1978.

India-Myanmar

Post India-Thailand Agreement of 1978 India started negotiations with Burma (now Myanmar) and after considering their national legislation on December 23, 1986 India reached an Agreement with Myanmar delimiting the boundary in the Coco Channel, the Andaman Sea and the Bay of Bengal based on provisions of UNCLOS.

India and Bangladesh

Indo-Bangladesh maritime issues are little more complicated. The two adjacent countries have an adjacent coastline but the disputed basin covers 4,500 square miles of area. According to the Indian version, the entire area falls within India's EEZ based on the principle of equidistant line used in delimitation of maritime boundaries. Bangladesh has used a different method which follows a ten-fathom isobath and declared its 10 nm and 200 nm EEZ should be measured from the straight baselines. This has led to a large variation. Besides this, there is also a dispute over an island located in the estuary of Haribhanga River. The issues between Bangladesh and India can be best settled by international arbitration as their award will be neutral and would not cause any heartburn between the two countries. However, the MEA in India had announced that they would try and settle bilaterally. While there may be issues of underwater oil and gas and therefore the differences, India's stakes in making a settlement with Bangladesh are very high. India has finally agreed to international arbitration as demanded by Bangladesh. Incidentally, Bangladesh also had a maritime boundary dispute with Myanmar which has been settled by arbitration.

AGREEMENTS WITH LITTORAL NEIGHBOURS

India and Sri Lanka

An agreement between Sri Lanka and India on the boundary of waters between the two countries and related matters was signed on June 26 and 28, 1974. Further another agreement between Sri Lanka and India on the maritime boundary between the two countries in the Gulf of Mannar and the Bay of Bengal and related matters (with map) was signed on March 23, 1976. A Supplementary Agreement between Sri Lanka and India on the extension of the maritime boundary between the two countries in the Gulf of Mannar from position 13 m to the tri-junction point between Sri Lanka, India and Maldives (point T) was signed on November 22, 1976.

TRI-JUNCTION AGREEMENTS

With Indonesia and Thailand

An agreement between the Government of the Kingdom of Thailand, the Government of the Republic of India and the Government of the Republic of

Map 13: Maritime Borders Between India-Indonesia-Thailand

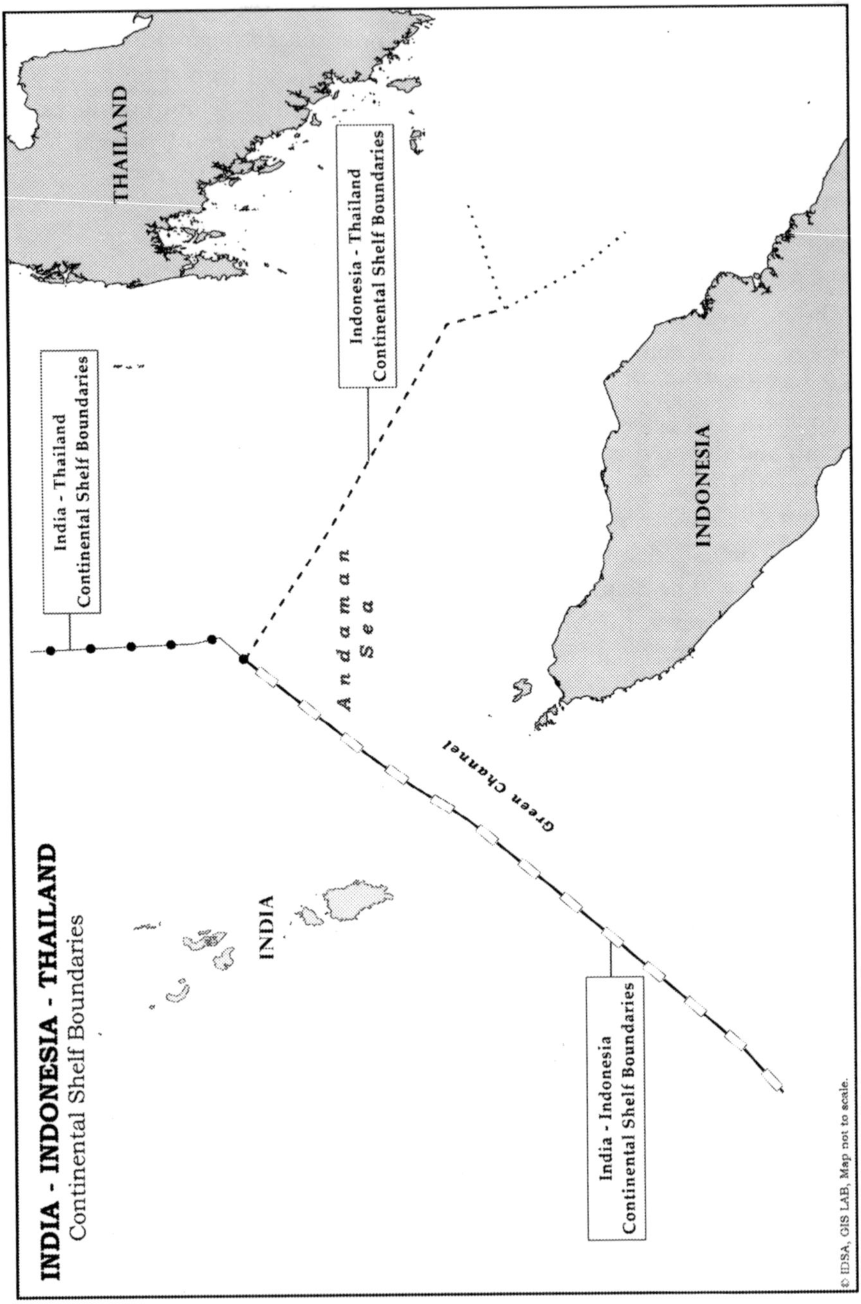

Indonesia concerning the determination of the tri-junction point and the delimitation of the related boundaries of the three countries in the Andaman Sea was signed on June 22, 1978.

With Maldives and Sri Lanka

An agreement between Sri Lanka, India and Maldives concerning the determination of the tri-junction point between the three countries in the Gulf of Mannar was signed on July 23, 24, 31, 1976.

With Myanmar and Thailand

An agreement between the Government of the Union of Myanmar, the Government of the Republic of India and the Government of the Kingdom of Thailand on the determination of the tri-junction point between the three countries in the Andaman Sea was signed on October 27, 1993.

NOTES

1. Swaminathan S. Anklesaria Aiyar, Swaminomics, *Times of India*, March 17, 2013.

CHAPTER 5

South China Sea

"ASEAN'S PALESTINE[1]"

Surin Pituswan, former Secretary General, ASEAN
China, ASEAN and India

CHINESE POLICY OF DECLARING CORE INTEREST AND THE CAMOUFLAGE OF PEACEFUL RISE

China's policy of declaring core interests which are non-negotiable is a psychological tactical move. From Taiwan as a core interest to Tibet and Xingjiang and now South China Sea, it is an increasing list over which China has vague historical claims but is prepared to use its military for securing them. Its first step towards use of military force over Tibet started in the 1950s immediately after the communist party took over defeating Chiang Kai-shek. Taiwan was recognised by Western powers and now is part of China's core interest. The Tibet occupation process took nearly 10 years culminating in the Dalai Lama leaving Lhasa in the middle of night and seeking refuge in India. However, it became a core interest later. China has now built up a formidable navy and is making un-substantive claims over East and South China Seas, annoying Japan, South Korea, Philippines, Brunei, Taiwan, Vietnam and Malaysia. The doctrine of declaring core interest and 'bullying' smaller states is part of China's foreign policy plank of 'Peaceful Rise'.

BASIS OF CHINESE CLAIMS OVER SOUTH CHINA SEA

South China Sea consists of around 250 islands, atolls, cays, shoals and sandbars most of which are uninhabited and some permanently submerged. These are listed as archipelagos. Macclesfield Bank, Scarborough Shoal and Spratly Islands are disputed between Peoples Republic of China and Vietnam with Malaysia, Philippines and Brunei also claiming a part of the archipelago. The Paracel Islands are disputed between Peoples Republic of China (PRC), Republic of China (Taiwan) and Vietnam. The Pratas Islands are disputed between PRC and the

Map 14: Chinese Claims Over South China Sea

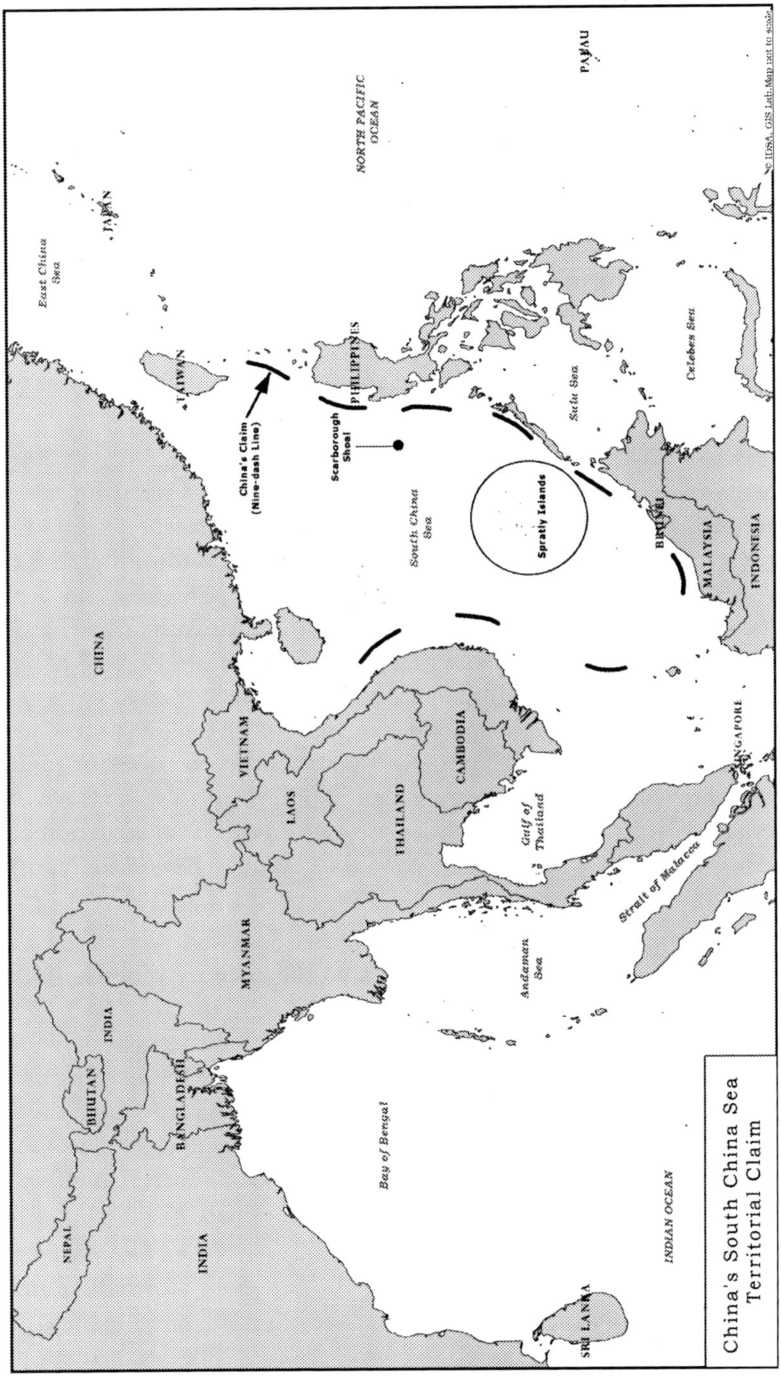

Republic of China. The Macclesfield Bank is disputed between PRC, Republic of China (Taiwan) and Philippines. The Scarborough Shoal is disputed between PRC, Republic of China and Philippines. There are minerals, natural gas and oil deposits in dispute. Estimates and undiscovered oil reserves in South China Sea as mentioned earlier, range as high as 213 billion barrels of oil.[2] Vietnam is already a major producer of oil with production of 24.4 million tons. 26 per cent of its total produce comes from the South China Sea. Petro-Vietnam, a public sector undertaking has already concluded about 60 oil and gas exploration contracts with various foreign countries. However, China is using force to stop this. In May 2011 two maritime surveillance vehicles cut off the exploration cables of a Vietnamese exploration ship.[3] ASEAN wants to present a united approach for a code of conduct in this region. Philippines wants a dispute redressal mechanism but China wants to settle only bilaterally.

China bases its claim on a large part of the South China Sea on 2000 years of history, which it claims gives Beijing a compelling argument for controlling this vast area of sea. Chinese officials argue that the Paracel and Spratly Island chains were once important parts of the Chinese nation and could have rich reserves of fossil fuels. Such arguments of Chinese history are vague, not acceptable to others and legally very difficult to prove. As Santosh Kumar, formerly of the Indian Foreign Service (IFS), points out "Beijing's claim on grounds similar to those for Tibet, and adjoining Indian territory, are based on 2000 years of history during which it says that the islands were regarded as an integral part of China."[4] Moreover, Vietnam and the Philippines strongly refute China's claim. China does not want arbitration or even a multilateral approach to solve it. It wants to do it bilaterally so that it can indulge in arm-twisting of weaker nations. It now considers its claims in South China Sea as it's 'core interests' adding to its list of Tibet[5] and Taiwan.

China's claim over the entire South China Sea (and also East China Sea where it has disputes over islands with Japan) and military action to secure it is reminiscent of the manner in which it took over Tibet in 1950-59. While alternative routes from the Middle East and Africa for energy supply are being worked upon as discussed in chapter 3, the Indian Ocean route is largely unavoidable. China is getting gas and oil from the Central Asian countries and Russia, but there are road blocks. The South China Sea and the East China Sea claims aim to look for various potential hydrocarbon resources. China's sustained development is dependent on energy.

China's cartographic aggression is well established. Based on historical claims it has tied India into knots over Arunachal Pradesh in North East India and Ladakh in the North West. In a similar manner it is now claiming the entire East and South China Sea based on China's mysterious "Nine Dash Lines".[6]

Map 15: China's Claims Over India

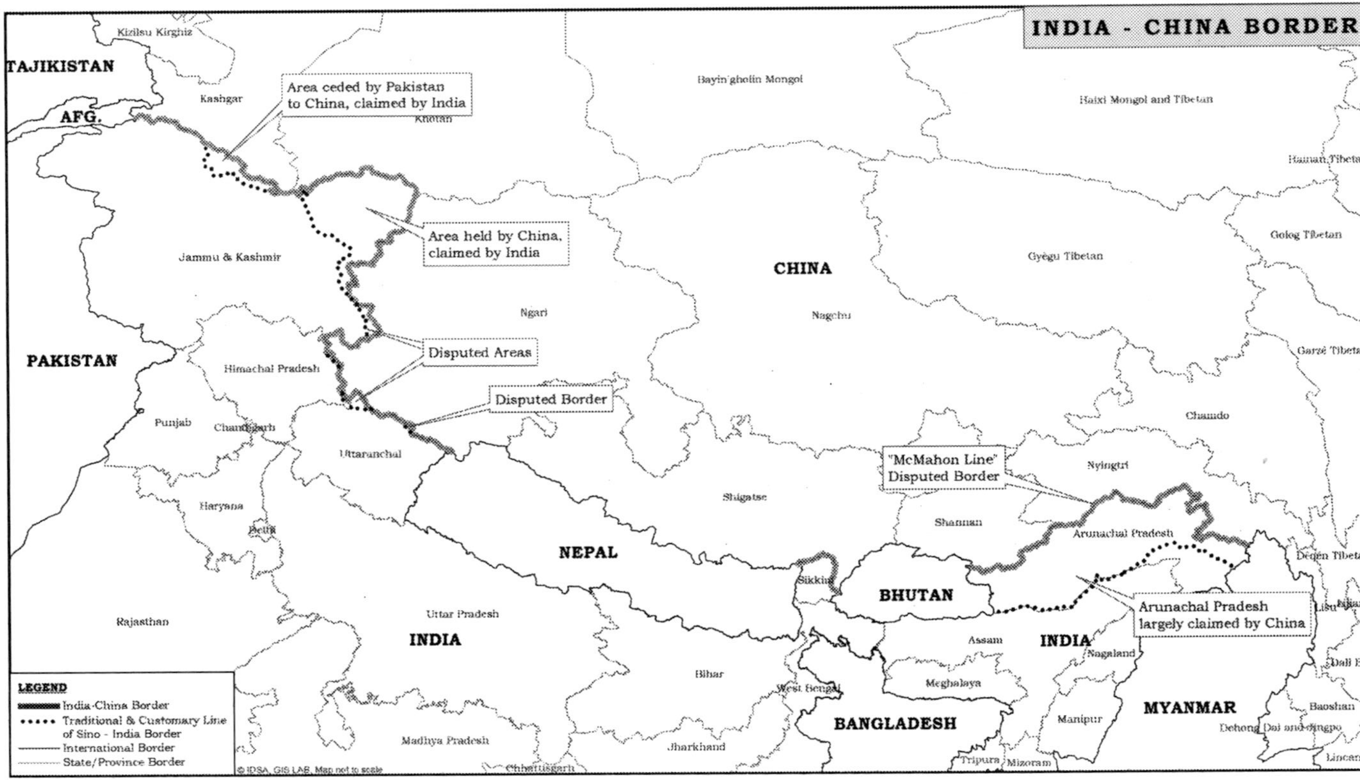

Communist China is essentially a military power from its earliest days starting with 1949. The political approach to sustain China's energy supply is being seen by the PLA as a weakness. The PLA is emphasising military solutions. At the same time it may be said that China has land borders with 14 countries and has successfully used diplomacy and its power to settle 12 of them including Vietnam. Its unresolved border with India and its taking away parts of Kashmir from Pakistan which were under Pakistani occupation is a matter of tension with India. The PLA Navy is in the process of establishing its fourth fleet in San Ya, Hainan Islands. Equipped with at least one aircraft carrier, modern frigates and destroyers, and advanced submarines including SSNs and SSBNs, this fleet will dominate over other countries in the South China Sea.

Oil Rush in South China Sea: According to estimates by the Chinese, the oil deposits in South China Sea could be as high as 213 billion barrels, which are more than Kuwait's reserves. This figure may be disputed by the US Energy Information Administration (EIA) which puts it around only 28 billion barrels but it is still a great deposit. Further, it is estimated that natural gas accumulation in the region may be 25 trillion cu m, which is equal to the proven reserves of Qatar.[7] Be that as it may, China sees great potential in getting hold of this area and has therefore made a claim over the entire South China Sea. This has been done by making a claim of sovereignty over the Paracel and Spratly Islands. How valid is this claim? Paracel Islands were with Vietnam till 1974 when China forcibly wrested control from Vietnam over this island. However, the Chinese claim goes back 2000 years as in the case of Tibet. These islands were regarded as a part of Imperial China when China was comparatively weaker. Chinese claim over these islands is as weak as it was over Tibet.

China's Status under UNCLOS III and Disputes with its Maritime Neighbours

While UNCLOS III does not go into sovereignty issues, once a state becomes a party to UNCLOS III, it is obliged to bring maritime claims and national laws into harmony and conformity with the convention. It is also a principle of International Law that one cannot use its domestic laws as an excuse not to conform to its obligations under International Law. China has however, exercised its right under Article 298 to get out of the compulsory binding dispute settlement regime. It wants to settle disputes with each country bilaterally and dissuaded ASEAN not to even discuss it or even pass a code of conduct for South China Sea.

Under these conditions, the Chinese belligerent attitude is also part of its insecurities. The two main insecurities of China in this context are its inability to have stable control over Tibet and securing the SLOC, particularly in the Straits of Malacca. If it gets control and sovereign rights over South China Sea and is able to pump out oil, the issue of oil supply through Straits of Malacca will become less important.

In the case of India, the Chinese have not only encircled but also taken over 5000 square km of the territory of Kashmir which was under Pakistan's occupation. In 1963, China signed a border agreement with Pakistan under which they accepted that the area is under dispute with India and interestingly, they did mention that this territory is subject to final settlement between India and Pakistan. Now they are investing and working even in the area which is with Pakistan as a disputed territory. India's protests are weak and hardly known in India. They are also building a pipeline from Gwadar Port through this territory into China and have recently signed an agreement with Pakistan of building a pipeline/tunnel through it. Similarly, in South China Sea which has potentially major petroleum deposits, China has laid claim to the entire area, which is not accepted internationally and by half the ASEAN countries like Philippines, Indonesia, Malaysia, Brunei, Vietnam and Taiwan. This has been followed by physical occupation of some islands and use of navies/coast guard to drive away other nationalities from fishing. In the East China Sea, they have also laid claim over Japanese owned Senkaku Islands.

Although it is already facing problems due to maritime territorial disputes with Japan, Vietnam, Philippines, Brunei and Indonesia in South and East China Seas, China has encircled India in a strategic alliance with Pakistan, Myanmar, Sri Lanka and Bangladesh. India is now at the stage of facing the Chinese onslaught as part of their maritime aspirations extending into the Indian Ocean. China also plans to build a fleet of aircraft carriers as part of their naval modernisation. They are now attempting to increase their presence in the Indian Ocean. The first step has been taken by them by setting up a base in Seychelles.[8]

The Chinese Government has got approval from the International Sea Bed Authority (ISA) to explore and mine deposits of poly-metallic sulphide ore, a source of zinc, lead, iron, silver and gold in 10,000 sq km of the seabed in the South-West Indian Ocean. While they have stated that such seabed exploration would serve the common interest of mankind, it should be taken with a pinch of salt. It is not clear why China has been given licence to explore the seabed in Indian Ocean and not in the Pacific. Whether India objected to it or not is also not known. Having claimed the entire South China Sea, China's designs on Indian Ocean need to be watched carefully.

It is necessary for India now to provide a credible projection of its presence, both hard and soft, not only along its maritime borders on the mainland but also in the Bay of Bengal where Andaman & Nicobar Islands are located. Will China claim parts of Indian Ocean as their core interest in their next stage of dominance?

China is the world's largest energy consumer. It receives over 70 per cent of its petroleum imports via the Indian Ocean. An official of the Development

Research Centre (DRC) under their State Council, the Chinese equivalent of a Cabinet, has stated that Government of India should take the initiative to propose a cooperative mechanism on sea lanes in the Indian Ocean. This itself is a major new development where China has pointed out that there is a vacuum in the Indian Ocean which needs to be filled. This refers in particular to the Strait of Malacca. India, therefore, needs to take an urgent initiative of making these islands its real frontier in the context of maritime activities like it did for North-East India in the fifties by forming NEFA (after taking it out of Assam and putting in under (MEA) through the Governor of Assam acting as Agent of The President of India. This proposal has been elaborated in chapters 9 & 10.

China-India-Vietnam and South China Sea: Chinese Strategy of Denial

The *Chinese Defence White Paper* of January 2008 points out the struggle for cornering strategic resources, dominating vital areas and strategic locations. The Chinese point out that they are implementing the military strategy of "active defence" which implies development of Advanced Assault Capabilities. They have developed this into the doctrine of "Access Denial". This involves developing capabilities of modernisation of weaponry of all types: cyber war fare, anti-ships, anti-carriers, SSBN capability etc. This also implies protecting and securing maritime interest which is implemented both in terms of direct military action in South China Sea and the String of Pearls Strategy.[9] With declared core interests increasing, starting with Taiwan then Tibet, Xinjiang and now South China Sea, the Chinese intolerance of other countries sovereign claims is increasing and is being reflected in military terms.

India's cooperative oil exploration in South China Sea with Vietnam is a critical test of Chinese doublespeak, its overbearing tactics and its ability to arrogate to itself certain positions only on the strength of its ability to speak strongly, which, to its credit it has been doing even when it was a poor and weak nation. While China wants India to be a non-player beyond South East Asia, it does not stop itself from meddling in India's neighbourhood of Pakistan, Myanmar, Bangladesh, and Sri Lanka. There is absolutely no justification for China to object to India's participating in joint exploration with Vietnam in the oil and gas rich South China Sea. It may be pointed out that India's trade with East Asia exceeds that with EU or US.[10]

The Chinese have opted to use strong arm tactics by small acts like stopping BP and Exxon Mobil from drilling off Vietnam in 2007-08, challenging a US Navy ship 75 miles from Hainan Island in 2009 or challenging Indian naval vessels and India's ONGC vessels around Vietnam. They are objecting to India undertaking cooperative oil exploration with Vietnam. China's claim in South China Sea is not acceptable to other littoral countries as it is not based on law. However, it is felt that if China is not able to secure sovereignty of these areas by making vague historical claims it would settle for joint exploration of oil with these countries bilaterally.

Chinese Insistence on Bilateralism Instead of Arbitration under UNCLOS

Chinese claims in the South China Sea have been analysed by Leszek Buszynski[11] of the Australian National University (ANU). According to him, China and Vietnam claim the entire South China Sea, while Malaysia, Philippines, Indonesia and Brunei have laid claim to contiguous areas. The two principles that govern claim, work against Chinese claims to the entire area. One is effective occupation and the other is the second principle of UNCLOS which lays down the rules to claim resources based on the EEZ and the continental shelf. The effective occupation principle has made China occupy by force Paracel Islands—an archipelago of 30 islands nearly equi-distant from Chinese and Vietnamese coasts and the Spratly Islands—an archipelago off the Philippines and Malaysian coasts. The Chinese claim is based on history but does not carry much weight. Vietnam's parliament has already passed a maritime law that reasserts claims to Spratly and Paracel Islands. Simultaneously China National Offshore Oil Corporation (CNOOC), a Chinese state owned company has opened nine blocks to international bids for oil and gas exploration which reach within 37 nm of Vietnam's coasts. According to the *Economist Magazine* this was probably a political stunt by China in response to Vietnam's new law.[12] UNCLOS came into being in 1982 and the Chinese do not want to use UNCLOS which has an arbitration clause. While China has opted out of arbitration under Article 298, the Philippines have gone to UNCLOS in spite of it. The Philippines case may not be hopeless on the grounds that Chinese claim over South China Sea is not really a sea boundary delimitation. If Philippines gets over the jurisdictional issue, it has a good chance of winning.[13] Although, technically speaking, UNCLOS has no provision about how to deal with sovereignty, however, the provision of UNCLOS on baseline, the regime of islands, low tide elevations, the EEZ, the continental shelf; maritime boundary delimitation and dispute settlement are all applicable to South China Sea. The ASEAN countries since 2009 have taken measures to clarify their claims and bring them to conformity with UNCLOS. Even though China has opted out of the system of compulsory dispute settlement for disputes relating to maritime boundary delimitation and historic waters, some legal disputes pertaining to interpretation or application of provisions of UNLCOS are subject to *Compulsory Binding Dispute Settlement* under part XV of UNLCOS. In addition, it may be possible for ASEAN countries to seek advisory opinion from International Tribunal for the Law of the Sea (ITLOS) on one or more legal issues relating to the South China Sea Dispute.

In a commemorative summit to mark the 20th Anniversary of India's Look East Policy held in Delhi with ASEAN in 2012, ASEAN sought intensification of Maritime Security Cooperation with India, calling for freedom of navigation and safety of sea lanes for unfettered trade in accordance with International Law.[14] Vietnam also offered the port of Nha Trang on South China Sea for the use of the Indian Navy. A Vietnamese delegation led by its Naval Chief, Vice Admiral Ngyuyen Van Hien visited India in 2011 for this purpose.[15]

According to Lowy Institute for International Policy of Sydney, all states of South China Sea including China are legally bound by provision of UNCLOS III. It has been established that the legal framework of settling rights and obligations with respect to use of portions under UNCLOS also sets out maritime zones that the coastal states can claim including 12 nm of territorial sea, and an EEZ of 200 nm. However, in South China Sea there is a major dispute with Philippines, Vietnam, Brunei, Taiwan on one end and China on the other leading to use of force by China. China's claims to most of South China Sea cannot be reconciled with claims of other states as its claims are based on history.

Michael Wesley, former Executive Director, Lowy Institute for International Policy says the disputes could have global implications. "The first level is a set of territorial disputes between China and several Southeast Asian countries." He further stated that "The second level is a dispute between China and the US over the conditions under which ships pass through this waterway, which convey about a third of all global shipping. And, I feel that there is a real chance that conflict could break out because of inexperienced maritime forces, with little or no mutual understanding of how to manage maritime incidents." Wesley is calling on Australia, which has strong military ties to the US and an entrenched economic relationship with China, to do more to broker a deal in the South China Sea. "Look, Australia really needs to be more concerned about this issue," he said. "About 54 per cent of Australia's trade passes through the South China Sea, and really what is at stake for Australia here is the outcome of the standoff between China and the US could have a real effect on the strategic balance of the Pacific Ocean. So we have really big interests in this." According to Wesley maritime tensions pit communist China and Vietnam against one another, unite usual enemies China and Taiwan, and draw the US back into partnership with Vietnam.

China-US Rivalry in the Straits of Malacca and South China Sea

Middle East is the biggest supplier of oil to China, Japan and Korea. China has established a strategic oil reserve and by 2020 it should have a reserve capacity of 90 day's crude oil imports. The first phase of its reserve has been completed in 2009 with about 100 million barrels or over 20 days of oil imports. The reserve is about three times that of India. While China is incapable of stabilising the Middle East tensions, it wants to keep South East Asia including the South China Sea lane under its influence. The US presence in South China Sea and in the Straits of Malacca is not to their liking. However, with their aggressive maritime claims in the South China Sea they have lost a lot of goodwill and will have to depend upon their military strength alone. China had already deployed in 1988 PLAN troops for a garrison to guard the disputed islands claimed by them and Vietnam in South China Sea in order to reinforce their claim. In the conflict, Vietnam lost three vessels that were set on fire and three men died, some were wounded and 70 were missing.[16] The Chinese have also elected 45 legislators to govern 1,100 people who live in the Islands of Spratly and the Paracel to prove their jurisdiction. Similarly, China and Philippines are also fighting over Scarborough Shoal near the coast of Philippines but claimed by China. The recent debate in the ASEAN meeting in Cambodia in 2011 where ASEAN as a group was not able to pass a resolution on a Code of Conduct because of arm twisting of Cambodia by China is a reflection of the present state of affairs. In fact, this was the first time that such an ASEAN meeting was not able to issue a joint communique.[17] This also shows the extent of different views over China in the 10 country group of ASEAN and how China is able to exploit it. The differences have since then been resolved in 2013 after Brunei took over the chairmanship of ASEAN.

The US also has interests in Malacca and South China Sea. The first is to deter a threat of attack and therefore control the Straits of Malacca and second is to use the South China Sea route undeterred. The Chinese feel that this amounts to "certain power share". As a result they have started both defensive and offensive naval strategies. The US, on the other hand, wants to prevent the rise of a hegemonic state and therefore, wants to build up allies and partners. It has allies in Japan and South Korea. There is no doubt that as of present the US is the biggest stakeholder in the Straits of Malacca followed by China. The South China Sea has now become an issue of US-China strategic rivalry. As China deploys new naval capabilities and strategies, it is no more a complimentary relationship. China would like to settle for a favourable regional arrangement in which territorial claims would be adjusted and oil reserves would be shared. The ASEAN is not agreeable and the US has openly sided with the ASEAN at the Hanoi Regional Forum meeting. In July 2010, the US Secretary of State, Hillary Clinton backed the ASEAN countries' claim and stated clearly that claims in South China Sea should be pursued on the basis of UNCLOS and land features.[18] US has also lifted the ban on ties with Indonesian Special Forces in July 2010 and the Philippines continues to be a major non-NATO ally of US.

While the US Navy may be on the decline, it is certainly increasing its presence in the South China Sea.[19] US has proposed to station ships in Singapore and Philippines. Both countries are likely to accept the request. The purpose of the move is to keep the sea lanes open. In addition, the US military is also increasing its presence in Australia. Japan, in any case remains a close ally.

China-Japan rivalry over Senkaku Islands (called Diaoyu by the Chinese) in North China Seas is leading to yet another major tension. While US is an ally of Japan, so far it is keeping a neutral position. With the purchase of Senkaku

Islands by the Japanese Government the long simmering rivalry between China and Japan is now a major issue. According to Greg Nancy,[20] US must take a decisive step and insist on international mediation. Since both nations use history selectively and international law to justify their claims, it is leading to protest in China where Chinese have vandalised and looted Japanese companies like Panasonic and Toyota which suspended operations in China.

ASEAN–China: Code of Conduct in South China Sea

ASEAN consists of 10 countries of which at least five have definite maritime problems with China i.e. Vietnam, Philippines, Indonesia, Malaysia and Brunei. The other members of ASEAN namely, Cambodia, Myanmar, Singapore have no problem with China. Myanmar and Cambodia have huge Chinese interests and investment in their country but it can be noticed that Myanmar is trying to cool off its relations with China. Singapore would welcome an alternative power like India to counterbalance China while Cambodia's present dependence on China with no territorial dispute would continue to back China. Japan, not a member of ASEAN but being in the same predicament as Vietnam, Philippines, Brunei and Indonesia would be happy to back the anti-China group within ASEAN. Taiwan has similar problems as the countries mentioned above.

The issue of evolving a Code of Conduct in South China Sea has been a matter of tension between the two. While ASEAN countries especially those impacted by China's claims are keen for a formal Code of Conduct between various countries so that they do not come into conflict, China has been evading the subject and would like to settle maritime border claims bilaterally only. There was little progress in the last Summit held under the chairmanship of Cambodia. However, foreign ministers of ASEAN and China have now agreed to hold a special meeting to speed up the progress on a Code of Conduct in South China Sea.[21] This proposal has come from China although no date has been fixed. In the meantime, China is opening up some disputed islands to tourism.[22] While in July, 2012, the ASEAN Forum ended without a joint communique, in July, 2013 they issued a communique emphasising the 11-year-old non-binding agreement between China and ASEAN to peacefully handle competing claims in South China Sea.[23]

Vietnam, India and South China Sea

The only country which has given Communist China a hard time is Vietnam. The Chinese forces were able to beat back the US forces in 1950. In 1962, it wanted to teach India a lesson which indeed it did. In 1969 it gave USSR a hard time on the Ussuri River. However, when it came to Vietnam, it bloodied China every time it came down South. In 1979 it gave PLA of China a drubbing killing 25,000 and injuring 75,000 of its 100,000 troops which came down to teach Vietnam a lesson. Vietnam is now seeking India's hand in a partnership with cooperation in joint oil exploration. The Indo-Vietnam agreement over exploration of blocks 127 and 128 off Spratly Islands between ONGC Videsh of India and the Vietnamese authority has provoked China to issue aggressive statements. China issued a demarche to India that its permission was necessary before India could explore in these waters. This is similar to what the Chinese did in the 1950's after they militarily occupied Tibet. By 1954, India gave up its presence in Tibet voluntarily and reached a quid pro quo settlement and called it a region of China by signing the 1954 Panchsheel Agreement.[24] *Global Times*, a party paper of CCP had stated that the Indo-Vietnam deal was a serious provocation to the Chinese Government and urged the Chinese Government to stop this cooperative effort from happening. *China's People's Daily* was a little softer and asked the three countries to come out with specific locations of the concession so that jurisdiction over it could be verified.[25] Although, India has so far not found any oil in block 127 or 128 in spite of having spent over US$ 30 million in exploration, Vietnam does not want India to leave the block. Politically also, India should not leave.

A month after China objected to oil exploration by India in the South China Sea under a contract awarded to the Indian state-owned company ONGC Videsh Ltd. by the Vietnamese and three months after the Chinese Navy warned the Indian naval ship *Airawat*, which was sailing in international waters between the Vietnamese ports of Nha Trang and Hai Phong, to leave Chinese waters—a warning that *INS Airawat* ignored—India and Vietnam signed an agreement on energy cooperation. The agreement was signed during the visit of Vietnamese President Truong Tan Sang to New Delhi to further cement the India-Vietnamese strategic partnership. The two countries also decided to pursue a regular security dialogue, which has further incensed the Chinese.[26]

India has, however, rejected the Chinese objection on grounds that the Vietnamese claims are in accordance with international law. The then Foreign Minister S.M. Krishna had stated that ONGC Videsh will go ahead with the oil and gas exploration.[27] According to Lexzek Buszvnsky, this changes and complicates the situation as India has status and power to resist China.[28] India and Vietnam signed an agreement on energy cooperation during the visit of Vietnamese President Truong Tan Sang to New Delhi. The two countries also decided to pursue a regular security dialogue.[29] Further, at the 14th India-Vietnam Joint Commission meeting on Trade, Economic, Scientific and Technological Cooperation co-chaired by Indian Foreign Minister, Krishna his counterpart Pham Binh Minh, and Krishna stated that with the growth of strategic partnership to the satisfaction of both sides there is a need to add greater content to bilateral relations by adding defence and security among other items.[30]

The Chinese worry is that India is gradually expanding its presence in East Asia where Beijing has been holding influence over small countries. These countries, mostly members of ASEAN are in favour of India playing a role in a big way as a balance. According to Bharat Karnad, Professor at Centre for Policy Research (CPR), New Delhi "Vietnam has offered port of Nha Trang in South China Sea for Indian Navy's use and Indian navy flotilla voyaging frequently between Andaman and Nha Trang, sustained by a parking and provisioning arrangement on the Central Vietnamese Coasts, will amount to a near permanent Indian presence in the South China Sea, signalling Indian intent and forward positioning that can mess up the Chinese naval and strategic calculations and push Beijing planners for once on a back foot. At a minimum, it will be an analogue to the sizable Chinese para-military (Peoples Armed Police) presence in Gilgit and Baltistan regions of POK."[31]

It has also been reported that India has accepted the offer of Vietnam to allow Indian naval warships to drop anchor at its southern port of Nha Trang. It will give India the key to sustainable presence in South China Sea and will enable India a bigger role in the strategic South-East Asian region which overlooks the key shipping lines. It will also make Andaman & Nicobar Islands more relevant as naval ships will be more frequent between Vietnam and Andaman & Nicobar Islands.

According to *Economist*,[32] Vietnam could be India's Pakistan, a loyal ally as Pakistan is to China that exerts indirect debilitating pressure on its strategic rival. Further, it states "India also wants to push back what it sees as a Chinese provocation. Among these is the apparent Chinese stroking of unresolved territorial disputes that led to the 1962 war. In recent years, it has revived its claims to most of Arunachal Pradesh".

However, late B. Raman, a strategic analyst of India and a former Additional Secretary in the Cabinet Secretariat, in his article 'South China Sea'[33] had stated that 'India should avoid rushing in where even US exercises caution'. While Chinese claims in South China Sea had been rejected by the US and the Indian position has been similar to that if the US, it had led into 'inherent seeds of an undesirable military confrontation between India and China in the South China Sea'. He had further stated that it would take India five to 10 years to bring its infrastructure on par with China in Tibet where India can expect retaliation. While this may be true, in case there is a confrontation with China in South China Sea, India expects support from the ASEAN, the US, South Korea and Japan.

Raman's argument need not be accepted. The difference of 5 to 10 years in infrastructure between India and China pointed out by him is something which India cannot easily make up in a short time especially when the terrain is not in its favour. However, instead India needs to develop an Access Denial Strategy in the Bay of Bengal with the aim to deny maritime access to China's military or any other inimical extra regional power in areas which are of core interest to

India. Besides the McMahon line, the Ladakh border, India should also declare parts of Bay of Bengal as its core interest. India's EEZ, while open to ships for navigation, should be under surveillance, especially in Bay of Bengal, to ensure that Chinese naval ships do not roam around freely without a quid pro quo. Therefore, there is a need to not only build up a naval and air presence in the Andaman & Nicobar Islands but go beyond and build up a naval presence in Vietnam in collaboration with their government. In fact, it is necessary for India to strengthen its presence in Great Nicobar Islands and develop a network or defence pacts with ASEAN countries to ensure that if Chinese do anything foolhardy[34] either on India's northern borders or with ASEAN countries, India would in a position to take retaliatory measures in South China Sea/Straits of Malacca. Therefore, Indian efforts at consolidating friends/allies/partners in the Indian Ocean have been in the right direction which is described in chapters 6 and 7.

The regional political bloc ASEAN is continuing to explore new ideas to resolve the dispute. With Brunei taking over the rotational annual chairmanship of ASEAN in 2013 and a new Secretary General, Le Luong Minh, a former Vietnamese diplomat, there may be some new developments in resolution of the issues. Brunei is oil rich and is not dependent on China's largesse like Cambodia, the previous chair of ASEAN was. Vietnam is already suspicious of Chinese intentions in the South China Sea and therefore, the new Secretary General will be tougher on China. At the same time US has deepened its strategic ties with Philippines, Singapore, Indonesia and Vietnam.[35]

What Should Be India's Strategy Towards China in the Maritime Sphere Including South China Sea?

While the Indian Navy is going strong on having a forward policy in strengthening Andaman & Nicobar Islands by opening a new airbase called Baaz at Great Nicobar Island, the MEA, on the other hand, is soft peddling the issue thereby making India look weak. The statement on the other hand by Chief of Naval Staff Admiral D.K. Joshi that the Indian Navy is ready to protect its interest in South China Sea even if it means sending forces to it is strong and reassuring.[36] He also stated that rapid modernisation of the Chinese Navy is a concern to India. His statement found resonance among Asian states and was welcomed by the Vice-President of Philippines. However, the Indian National Security Advisor (NSA) Shivshankar Menon who was at the time in Beijing was unhappy about it. India needs to be more circumspect and pro-active in South China Sea than they were in the Himalayas. During the visit of the Chinese Defence Minister, General Liang Guanglie to India in late 2012, the first such visit since 1976, in a joint communique, the two countries agreed to cooperate in the Asia-Pacific Region. While most of this went unreported and there was silence on both sides, it did raise the question that the Chinese finally noticed India's geopolitical importance in Asia-Pacific which they never bothered to do earlier. In fact, between the Dalai Lama and Straits of Malacca, India has two bargaining points with China. Here, Andaman & Nicobar Islands can play a major role if they are developed as a major naval and air base.

The Chinese are concerned over Indian naval capabilities in the Indian Ocean and their potential alliance with US in blockading China's oil supplies. They have noted with interest the establishment of Andaman Nicobar Joint Command and the naval fleets of US, Japan and India working together. According to C. Raja Mohan, "The mutual distrust between India and China on multilateral issues deepened in 2000s despite the proclaimed desire for cooperation on global and regional issues and hopes for coordination of issues relating to energy and maritime issues". In this connection, he quotes Robert Blackwell who was President George Bush's First Envoy to India during 2001-03: "President George W. Bush based his transformation of US-India relationship on the Core Strategic Principle of Democratic India as a key factor in balancing the rise of China". He further quotes an editorial in China's *Global Times* of June, 2009 which acknowledged India's growing power potential but dismissed New Delhi's ability to leverage it with China by avoiding a closer strategic partnership with the US and goes on to say that if India thinks that fear and gratitude for its restrain will cause China to defer on its territorial disputes then it is mistaken as China will not make any compromise on its border dispute with India.[37] At the same time, Brahma Chellaney feels that "while Hillary Clinton has declared that US-Japan Treaty applies to Senkaku Islands, it does not mean that US would use its military capability to repulse Chinese action." Taking on from here, he feels that while US wants to build up new strategic partnerships with India, Vietnam, Indonesia etc., it is wary of taking sides in Asian territorial disputes and should not be depended upon.[38]

According to Aaron Friedberg,[39] a scholar at Princeton University on Chinese issues, China is building an "Anti-Access Capacity". It is building a defence weapon system that will deny access to areas it believes are in its historical sphere which includes Tibet/Taiwan/Arunachal Pradesh and South China Sea.

The Chinese Naval Maritime Plan of 1982 outlined by then Vice Chairman of the Military Commission, Liu Hauquing laid down a three stage plan. The first stage which ended in 2010 was to establish control of waters within the first island chain which extends from Japan to Okinawa and covers both the East and South China Sea up to Straits of Malacca. The second stage which was to start from 2010 and end in 2020 would be China establishing control of waters within the second island chain linking Ogasawara Island, Guam and Indonesia. During the last and final stage from 2020-40 China would aim to put an end to US Military dominance in the Pacific and Indian Oceans using aircraft carriers. The Chinese have been quietly committed to this policy and have been increasing their naval capability in a very fast manner. The PLA Navy is now focussing on "Sea-Denial" or "Anti-Access" capabilities.[40]

The latest tactical step by the Indian Navy has been the announcement in 2012 of establishment of a forward base in Great Nicobar Island called Baaz—a step in the right direction. This conforms to the concept of Access Denial which should apply to a country like India. Such a strategy will seek to contest and deny regional or extra regional countries their ability to project military power unilaterally to secure their interest either through aggression or through de-stabilising activities.

Therefore, a Maritime Access Denial policy needs to be developed. According to Admiral Vijay Shankar (Retd.) former Commander in Chief, Strategic Forces Command (SFC) of India, there should be a trigger to implement such a policy which he calls "Red Lines". He has defined it in the following manner:

(1) Any large scale attempt to change the status quo in India's territorial configuration.
(2) Large scale military build up at Hambantota in Sri Lanka or Gwadar in Pakistan or Sittwe in Myanmar.
(3) Aggressive deployment that disrupts India's own energy supply and resource traffic or dislocates the network.
(4) Any attempt to provide large scale military support, covert or otherwise, to promote internal warfare against states.
While Admiral Vijay Shankar's "Red Line" may not be easily implementable, what India requires is a definite presence in South China Sea to counter any further move by China in POK, Gilgit or Baltistan. As a result, it is important for India to look towards ASEAN and other littoral countries of Bay of Bengal as well as South and East China Seas and build up a civil and military relationship.

Chapter 6 describes the development of relationships of India in the civil sphere and Chapter 7 in military terms. The role of Andaman & Nicobar Islands in the new Look East Policy by countering China in north and north-west India should be the focus of this policy to meet China from a position of strength. Chapters 9 and 10 will focus on this.

NOTES

1. *The Telegraph*, December, 2012.
2. Based on US Energy Information Administration Report of 2008.
3. Leszek Buzneski, "The South China Seas: Oil, Maritime Claims, and US-China Strategic Rivalry", *The Washington Quarterly*, 2012.
4. Santosh Kumar, "South China Seas Oil Rush", *Economic Times*, November 25, 2011.
5. Chinese claims over Tibet and its armed accession in 1950s is also based on their version of history.
6. "South China Seas: Hang it both ways", E*conomist* July 08, 2012,

7. Santosh Kumar, no. 4.
8. "China to Open its First Military Base Abroad in Indian Ocean" *The Economic Times*, December 12, 2011.
9. Vice Admiral Vinay Shankar (Retd), "Securing Sea Power and the Right to Un-impeded Entrée: The Uncertainty Paradigm", *Defence and Security Alert*, 2012.
10. Binod Singh, "About Supremacy, not sea", *Times of India*, September 25, 2011.
11. Leszek Buzneski, no. 3.
12. www.economist.com/node/215582626?frsc=dg%7ca
13. Julian Ku, "Game Changer? Philippines seeks UCLOS arbitration with China over South China Sea", Opinion at www.juris.org/2013/01/22/game-changer/phillipines-seeks-UNCLOS-arbitration-with-China-over-the-south-china-sea/
14. "India–ASEAN Seek Enhanced Maritime Security Cooperation", *Mint*, December 21, 2012.
15. Bharat Karnad, "Good Morning, 'Nam", *Asian Age*, July 7, 2011
16. B.R. D.E. Lengochy, "Chinese invasion of Spratly Islands in 1988", at www.eyedrd.org/2011/07/chinese/invasion-of-spratly-islands-in-1988.htm.
17. Sana Hashmi, "South China Sea in Imbroglio: An Indian Perspective", *Journal of Air Power & Space Studies*, 8 (1), 2013, p. 156.
18. Leszek Buzneski, no. 3.
19. Reuters December 16, 2012 at www.reuters.com/article12011/12/16us-navy-asia-IDUSTRE7
20. Rodger Baker, "Understanding China-Japan conflict", at www.stratfor.com/weekly/understanding-china-japan-island-conflict#
21. Yahoo news Singapore, at www.sg.news.yahoo.com/ASEAN-China-meet-maritime-code-conduct-16
22. Yahoo news Singapore, at www.sg.news.yahoo.com/china-open-disputed-islands-tourism-0743504
23. Simone Orendain, "China agrees to discuss 'Code of Conduct Rules'", Globalsecurity.org: July 4, 2013.
24. For details see Claude Arpi, *Born in Sin: The Panchsheel Agreement: The Sacrifice of Tibet*, Mittal Publications, New Delhi, 2004.
25. Santosh Kumar, no. 4.
26. "Countering China's Encirclement Plan", *Deccan Herald*, October 31, 2011..
27. *Times of India*, September 17, 2011.
28. Leszek Buzneski, no.3.
29. Gurmeet Kanwal, "Strategic Encirclement by China, Looking East to counter it", *The Tribune*, November 12, 2011.
30. *Times of India*, September 17, 2011.
31. Bharat Karnad, no. 15.
32. Banyan, "Not as close as lips and teeth: China should not fear India's growing friendship with Vietnam", *Economist*, October 27, 2011, p. 42.
33. B. Raman, "South China Sea: India should avoid rushing in where even US exercises caution—analysis," September 18, 2011, *Eurasia Review* at www.eurasiareview.com/18092011/south-china-sea-india
34. While the borders between India and China in the Tibetan Region are not settled, there is an informal Line of Control (LOC). India has complained that Chinese troops constantly violate the LOC. A recent incursion of 18 km by infiltrators into the Indian side of the LOC who pitched tents and remained there for about 20 days has led to a great deal of media attention in India and created tension in India's political system. See "Bold & Brazen China", *The Pioneer*, April 25, 2013; Claude Arpi, "Intrude, Violate and then offer to discuss", Editorial, , *Pioneer*, April 26, 2013; K.C. Singh, "That '62" *Asian Age*, April 25, 2013.

35. *Economist,* February 09, 2013 p. 24.
36. *India Today,* December 03, 2012.
37. C. Raja Mohan, *Samudra Manthan: Sino-Indian Rivalry in the Indo-Pacific,* CEIP, Washington, D.C., 2012, pp. 207, 222, 239 & 246.
38. Brahma Chellaney, "America's Great Asian Dawdle", *The Economic Times,* August 14, 2013.
39. Quoted by Dr. Namrata Goswami, from recent Op. Ed., *New York Times* at Defence Forum India.com/forum/china/151273-chinese-insecurity-indian-concern.html.
40. Rakesh Kaul, "PLA Navy in the 21st Century: Developments and Implications", *Defence & Diplomacy Journal,* I (2) 2012.

CHAPTER 6

Rise of Regional Groupings in Indo-Pacific Region: Civil Initiative

INTRODUCTION

Geo-politically speaking Asia embraces land mass from Israel to Russian Far East. The term Asia-Pacific was coined in World War II and now under the new geo-political situation is gaining popularity as Indo-Pacific. The term encompasses countries on either side of Indian and Pacific Oceans and therefore, is on either side of Straits of Malacca. Hence, the critical importance of Straits of Malacca in terms of Indo-Pacific and within that the position of Andaman & Nicobar Islands.[1]

With the US having budgetary problems reflecting in its reduced defence budget, the unipolar power of the US Navy is on the decline. Further, with increase in shale gas production in the US, its dependence on import of oil amounts to just 10 per cent of its needs and even this figure will decline. The strategic need to patrol the SLOCs will also therefore decline. While US has expressed its desire to maintain its presence in the Indo-Pacific, it is moving towards concepts of shared values, interests and challenges, rather than alliances. Consequently, it considers India a "lynchpin" in its new strategy. Another question that needs to be answered is whether the Indian and Pacific Oceans could be considered a single strategic region. US considers it so. India is also moving towards accepting it. With Myanmar joining ASEAN, the concept of the Indo-Pacific has gained weight.[2]

China is now coming up as a military power but its maritime claim is isolating it in the Indo-Pacific region. As a result, a reluctant India is being seen as a balancing factor by countries of the Pacific. A number of regional groupings have come up in the Indo-Pacific region in the last half a century, these are as under:

ASEAN—A TRUE INDO-PACIFIC REGIONAL GROUP

Established in August 1967, ASEAN has pursued regional economic integration and more in East Asia. Its progress can be compared to the erstwhile EEC which has now emerged as the European Union. It now consists of ten countries and six dialogue partners. India was invited initially to become a member but it is understood that she spurned it and it is now only a strategic partner. ASEAN has had several economic integration initiatives in East Asia like the ASEAN Free Trade Agreement (AFTA), the ASEAN Framework Agreement on Services (AFAS) and the ASEAN Investment Area (AIA). However they now want under ASEAN Vision 2020, to also establish an ASEAN Security Community, ASEAN Economic Community, and ASEAN Socio-Cultural Community by 2020.

The concept of ASEAN Security Community (ASC) is interesting. While the purpose of security community would be to live in peace with each other and the rest of the world at large in a just, democratic and harmonious manner, however, with the developing situation in the South China Sea, ASC would take up a very meaningful role as it embodies the ASEAN aspiration to achieve peace, stability, democracy and prosperity in the region. Already five out of ten ASEAN members are threatened by Chinese aggressive postures in South China Sea after it used its navy to occupy certain islands. China does not want ASEAN to be involved in security of the region and wants to deal with each member bilaterally. In the last meeting of ASEAN Ministers held in Cambodia in 2012, China managed by behind the scenes manoeuvres to scuttle the preparation of an ASEAN Resolution on code of conduct in the South China Sea. However, this has since been corrected in 2013 in a meeting of ASEAN ministers.

The ASEAN Regional Forum (ARF) formed in 1994 comprising 27 countries continues to play a role in enhancing political and security dialogue. China and India are both members of ARF. The ARF will, perhaps provide assistance to ASC to check growth of Chinese influence in this region.

China's dominance the Indo-Pacific region is becoming a great cause of concern for India also. This is so because China has provided military support to all of India's immediate neighbours i.e. Pakistan, Sri Lanka, Myanmar and Bangladesh besides underground Malaysians working in North-East India. It has also set up a naval base in Seychelles. This has been a serious destabilising factor for India. In addition, China's behaviour towards India is also a cause of concern. Not only for historic reasons but for the way China behaved with India. Besides the issue of stapled visa of Arunachal Pradesh to citizens of Arunachal Pradesh of India and non-issue of visa to a serving Indian Army General posted in Kashmir, it also does not want India to join the Security Council as a permanent member with veto power. Considering that India had supported China's entry into the UN when the Taiwanese regime represented China under the influence of the West, there is hardly any quid pro quo from the Chinese side. China in control of the Indo-Pacific region would threaten India's security, especially as it has full control over Pakistan and the Tibetan border. Further, India's rising trade with countries on the east of India and the west coast of the US also goes through Malacca and South China Sea. As a consequence, India has attempted to improve its interaction with Southeast Asia by rebuilding its long lost ties with ASEAN.

Look East Policy of India, 1991

During the prime ministership of P.V. Narasimha Rao in 1991, it was decided by him that India cannot afford to ignore ASEAN and other countries east of India.[3] This was the new "Look East India Policy". This policy was continued by Prime Minister A.B. Vajpayee. At a lecture in Singapore in 2002, he stated, "[The Southeast Asian] region is one of the focal points of India's foreign policy, strategic concerns and economic interests." India then became a sectoral dialogue partner of ASEAN in 1992 and a full dialogue partner in 1995. India then became a member of the ASEAN Regulatory Regional Forum (ARF) in 1996. ASEAN and India have been holding summit level meetings since 2002. In 2009 India signed a Free Trade Agreement (FTA) with ASEAN with some restrictions. Trade with ASEAN is growing but there is an imbalance against India. India has become a strategic partner with ASEAN since 2012. This means that the relationship between the two moves beyond current emphasis on economic into deeper political and security cooperation. Further, the declaration of India-ASEAN Vision 2020 as a roadmap is yet another achievement.

The strategic location of the Andaman & Nicobar Islands places it among the most crucial regions in the world. With Myanmar being included in ASEAN, India now shares a land boundary with ASEAN, apart from sharing maritime frontiers with Indonesia and Thailand and its EEZ with Malaysia. India considers ASEAN to be the nucleus of the East Asian region and believes in laying emphasis on its interaction with ASEAN.

As stated earlier, India's land and maritime borders extend right up to Sumatra with Great Nicobar Island only 80 miles from the tip of Sumatra and entry point of Straits of Malacca. Further, India's EEZ is 30 per cent (post UNCLOS III) in the Bay of Bengal between Myanmar, Thailand and Indonesia due to Andaman & Nicobar Islands. The people of ASEAN countries are not fully aware of this fact as yet as they not fully aware of Andaman & Nicobar Islands. India on its part has kept Andaman & Nicobar Islands largely prohibited to foreigners as part of its "Masterly Inactivity" Policy. The impact of its geographic location needs to be brought into focus by opening these islands to high-end tourism to display India's soft power. With deep concern regarding China's influence in the region, India should look towards ASEAN to carry out a multilateral security order in the Indo-Pacific. At the same time, as explained by Hong, "from the ASEAN and Japan perspectives, India was seen as a possible counterweight to China in Southeast Asia, India has publicly avoided being drawn into such a role. India is, in fact, looking to develop a complementary relationship with China instead of a competitive one. However, for China, India can best be a subordinate friend rather than an equal."

What has not come out in public perception in ASEAN countries is that India does not end with Peninsular India. With Andaman & Nicobar Islands extending right up to Straits of Malacca its EEZ is 30 per cent out of Andaman

& Nicobar Islands. If Myanmar can be a full member of ASEAN so can India as India has greater proximity to the ASEAN region than Myanmar due to these archipelagos. The only thing is that Andaman & Nicobar Islands have been ignored territories of India and people in ASEAN countries as also worldwide are hardly aware of its existence. Only if India decides to extend its *effective* territory up to Straits of Malacca by both opening Andaman & Nicobar Islands for tourism as well as complementing it with tourism of Thailand, Malaysia and Indonesia by direct flights that its existence will be felt and ASEAN countries will appreciate their proximity to India which they still consider a faraway country. An "Incredible Andaman and Nicobar" campaign needs to be carried out by the Ministry of Tourism after announcing a tourism policy in conjunction with the defence forces so that the coverage is not just based on proximity to airports but also strategic locations. An MOU signed between the Lt. Governor of Andaman & Nicobar Islands and the Governor of Phuket in Phuket on June 29, 2005[4] remains on paper with nothing implemented as part of India's Masterly Inactivity policy. More of this will be discussed in Chapter 9.

Would ASEAN like India to join in as a member now?[5] ASEAN and India together constitute a community of 1.8 billion people with a gross turnover of 3.8 trillion as stated by the Indian Prime Minister in his opening remarks at an ASEAN Conference. India and ASEAN have a trade target of US$ 100 billion by 2015 and US$ 200 billion by 2022. A FTA is on the anvil. On security, ASEAN wants a code of conduct in the South China Sea which China opposes and India supports. India is now a declared strategic partner of ASEAN. With South China Sea in such turbulence with China's unacceptable claims on it and India having settled all its maritime issues with all littoral countries except Bangladesh and Pakistan, India is regarded as a peaceful neighbour, sluggish but dependable. Therefore, India would be an outstanding counterweight to China, especially when they know that India has serious political issues with China and will not get friendly with it for many years to come in spite of good trade relations. At a ASEAN–India Commemorative Summit in New Delhi in December 2012 both sides pledged greater cooperation amongst political and security platforms, including greater maritime security and safety. The shift from trade to maritime security between ASEAN and India is a new development. However, according to Admiral Arun Prakash (Retd.), the agreement signed was a farce, as according to him there are similar agreements with China. He further stated that India has a timid foreign policy.[6]

A special relationship with ASEAN at a political level is possible only if Indian diplomacy is quick enough to undertake this task. The ASEAN Security Community line of action adopted in Bali in 1976 holds a lot of promise as it is anticipated that ASEAN may take collective action against China's sovereignty claims over South China Sea.

BIMSTEC

On June 6, 1997, a new sub-regional grouping was formed in Bangkok and given the name Bangladesh, India, Sri Lanka, and Thailand Economic Cooperation (BIMSTEC). Myanmar attended the inaugural June Meeting as an observer and joined the organisation as a full member at a Special Ministerial Meeting held in Bangkok on December 22, 1997, upon which the name of the grouping was changed to BIMST-EC. Nepal was granted observer status by the second Ministerial Meeting in Dhaka in December 1998. Subsequently, full membership has been granted to Nepal and Bhutan in 2003.

In the first Summit on July 31, 2004, leaders of the group agreed that the name of the grouping should be known as BIMSTEC or the Bay of Bengal Initiative for Multi-Sectoral Technical and Economic Cooperation.

Aims and Purposes

According to the Bangkok Declaration on the establishment of BIST-EC, the aims and purposes of BIST-EC/BIMST-EC are to create an enabling environment for rapid economic development, accelerate social progress in the sub-region, promote active collaboration and mutual assistance on matters of common interest, provide assistance to each other in the form of training and research facilities, cooperate more effectively in joint efforts that are supportive of, and complementary to national development plans of member states, maintain close and beneficial cooperation with existing international and regional organisations, and cooperate in projects that can be dealt with most productively on a sub-regional basis and which make best use of available synergies.

BIMSTEC was initiated with the goal to combine the 'Look West' policy of Thailand and ASEAN with the 'Look East' policy of India and South Asia. BIMSTEC could be considered as a link between ASEAN and SAARC. BIMSTEC covers 13 Priority Sectors led by member countries in a voluntary manner namely, Trade & Investment, Technology, Energy, Transport and Communication, Tourism, Fisheries, Agriculture, and Cultural Cooperation.

What makes BIMSTEC different from other organisations would be that BIMSTEC represents one of the most diverse regions of the world, be it by way of life, religion, language, culture, etc. BIMSTEC clearly separates issues of development into 13 Priority Sectors besides focusing only on economic cooperation which make BIMSTEC cover all aspects regarding the word 'developing'.

BIMSTEC provides a unique link between South Asia and Southeast Asia bringing together 1.3 billion people—21 per cent of the world population, a combined GDP of over US$ 1 trillion, and a considerable amount of complementarities. A study shows the potential of US$ 43 to 59 billion trade creation under BIMSTEC FTA.

Cooperation with Asian Development Bank (ADB)

Asian Development Bank (ADB) has become BIMSTEC's development partner since 2005, to undertake a study which is designed to help promote and improve transport infrastructure and logistics among the BIMSTEC countries. ADB has already finished the project BIMSTEC Transport Infrastructure and Logistic Study (BTILS). The final report of the said study from ADB has already been conveyed to all members and feedback is waited.

Membership Criteria

Eligibility: Countries seeking membership should satisfy the conditions of territorial contiguity to, or direct opening into, or primary dependence on the Bay of Bengal for trade and transportation purposes. It may be noted that this organisation is not in a position to include either Pakistan or China.

Institutional Structure and Arrangements

BIMSTEC as a regional organisation can be of great relevance to India as it consists of only seven members all connected with Bay of Bengal (both Nepal and Bhutan have great stakes in Bay of Bengal and a transit route through India). Two of its members, i.e. Thailand and Myanmar are members of ASEAN and therefore, can provide a good link to this association which is important for strategic purposes connecting Bay of Bengal to South China Sea. BIMSTEC has a convention on combating terrorism, transnational crime and illicit drug trafficking.

India could have leveraged its advantage of BIMSTEC membership by offering Port Blair as a possible location for the BIMSTEC Secretariat. While Sri Lanka and Bangladesh offered headquarter facilities, the location of Port Blair in the centre of Bay of Bengal makes the place very attractive. This could have opened up Port Blair as an international destination. Further, Port Blair is a very peaceful area, equidistant for all members of BIMSTEC unlike Sri Lanka which is one corner. However, Bangladesh has now been selected as the Headquarters for BIMSTEC. Nevertheless, India should offer Port Blair as a possible venue for some of its conferences and seminars.[7]

Indian Ocean Rim – Association for Regional Cooperation (IOR-ARC)

The Indian Ocean is the world's third largest Ocean. It carries half of the world's container ships, one third of the bulk cargo traffic, two-thirds of the world's oil shipments. It is a lifeline of international trade and economy. The region is woven together by trade routes and commands control of the major sea-lanes. The IOR constitutes between a quarter and a third of the world's population (close to two billion) which makes it a massive market. It is rich in strategic and precious minerals and metals and other natural resources, valuable marine resources ranging from food fisheries to raw material and energy for industries. It has abundant agricultural wealth in terms of the variety and mass of arable land and has significant human resources and technological capabilities. Many countries of the Rim are becoming globally competitive and are developing new capacities, which can be jointly harnessed through regional co-operation efforts.

Government of Mauritius convened a meeting in March 1995 to discuss the enhancement of economic co-operation among countries of the IOR. Representatives from the governments, business sectors and academia, from Australia, India, Kenya, Mauritius, Oman, Singapore and South Africa, subsequently referred to as the "core group states" or M-7, attended the meeting. In a joint statement issued at the end of the meeting, the participants declared that they had agreed on "principles of open regionalism and inclusivity of membership, with the objectives of trade liberalisation and promoting trade co-operation. Activities would focus on trade facilitation, promotion and liberalisation, investment promotion and economic co-operation."

The IOR-ARC was formally launched at the first Ministerial Meeting in Mauritius on March 6-7, 1997. This meeting adopted the IOR-ARC Charter, and determined a number of administrative and procedural matters. Currently, the membership consists of 19 countries of IOR.

Principles of the IOR-ARC

The Charter declares that the IOR-ARC seeks to build and expand understanding and mutually beneficial co-operation through a consensus based, evolutionary and non-intrusive approach. There are no laws and binding contracts. Compliance with consensus based decisions remains without any rigid institutional structure to specify any rules and regulations. Co-operation is based on principles of sovereignty, equality, territorial integrity, political independence, and non-interference in internal affairs, peaceful coexistence, and mutual benefit.

Membership is open to all sovereign states of the IOR willing to subscribe to the principles and objectives of the Charter. The IOR-ARC is firmly based on the principle of open regionalism, as encouraged by the WTO. Decisions on all matters and issues and at all levels are to be taken on the basis of consensus. The IOR-ARC explicitly excludes bilateral relations and other issues likely to generate controversy and be an impediment to regional co-operation.

Co-operation within the association does not prejudice the rights and obligations of the member states within the framework of other economic and trade co- operation arrangements and will not apply automatically to member states of the association. It does not seek to be a substitute for, but to reinforce, be complementary to and consistent with, the bilateral, plurilateral and multilateral rights and obligations of member states.

IOR-ARC Objectives

The main focus of the IOR-ARC is on economic co-operation and particularly on trade and investment. It is primarily an outward looking forum for economic dialogue and co-operation.

The 11th meeting held in 2012 held at Bengaluru was chaired by India. Seychelles, one of the founding countries re-joined the grouping as its 19th member state after having left the organisation in 2003. India's External Affairs Minister S.M. Krishna inaugurated the meeting after taking over the chair for the next two years from Yemen, the previous chairman. While releasing the Bengaluru communique, he cited India's first Prime Minister, Jawaharlal Nehru, who had envisioned a grouping of countries bordering the Indian Ocean that could help one another in tackling common challenges. In his concluding remarks, Krishna stated that the 19 countries from three continents have decided to work together to realise the full potential of IOR-related institutions that have been established over the years. The Bengaluru declaration, however, focused more on the issue of maritime security keeping in view the challenges posed to international shipping and commerce by the pirates from Somalia. The group discussed ways and means to consolidate cooperation in areas such as maritime security, combating piracy, natural disaster management besides education, fisheries and marine resources management, trade and investment promotion, capacity building and tourism.

The Bengaluru Declaration shared concerns over the prevailing situation regarding maritime security in the Indian Ocean, particularly at the increasing level of piracy off the Horn of Africa, which posed a threat to international and regional navigation, maritime commerce and the safety of sea farers. The declaration fully supported international efforts at the UN and several initiatives at the regional level as well as the Contact Group on piracy off the coast of Somalia, which is coordinating anti-piracy efforts. It pledged to jointly combat the menace through sharing of information and technical assistance. Maritime security impacts strategic security of the nations in the region. Noting that IOR maritime domain is at the crossroads of commerce and its busy energy trade routes pass through vulnerable points, the Bengaluru Communiqué accepted that the menace of piracy has assumed alarming proportions in recent years. Further, it stated that the menace of piracy is increasing the cost of trade directly and insurance premia and human cost indirectly to the shipping industry. The group needs to build upon existing national, regional and multilateral measures to enhance coordination to combat piracy. To enhance the security in the Indian Ocean, India advocated building functional relationships between navies and coast guards.

Diplomatic and Security Challenges

Security and diplomacy go hand in hand. Diplomacy is the ultimate weapon in the search for security. The group noted that stabilisation of Somalia will contribute to dealing with piracy in the region. As members take practical steps consistent with international law to combat piracy, IOR-RIM could serve as an effective vehicle for sharing information, experience and best practices. However, in order to combat piracy in the IOR, this grouping should seriously deal with the Somalia piracy issue by immediate diplomatic recognition to the Republic of Somaliland and promote the democratically elected government of Somaliland. Strengthening the democratic government of the Republic of Somaliland will promote regional peace in the horn of Africa. It will bring enormous trade, economic and developmental benefits to the country and will discourage other tribes in the south and central Somalia from fratricidal warfare. To follow a peaceful developmental agenda instead of allying with the Al Shabab and al Qaeda may ultimately become the goal for Somalia. In the last meeting of Trade Ministers of IOR-ARC in July, 2014, the Resolution that they passed included the importance of maritime security.[8]

MEKONG GANGA PROJECT

The Mekong Ganga Suvannaphoom Project was launched in 2000 on the sidelines of the ASEAN meeting when six ministers representing India, Myanmar Thailand, Laos, Vietnam and Cambodia decided to go to for greater cooperation. This was a further extension of India's LEP. It was formally launched in Vientiane on November 10, 2000 by India's External Affairs Minister, Jaswant Singh. This project is expected to build better infrastructure between the six countries along with greater cooperation in science and technology, culture and educational exchanges, and promotion of tourism between the countries.

Out of the six countries five have sea openings in either Bay of Bengal or South China Sea but there is, unfortunately, no provision of maritime exchanges or trade promotion through sea routes. The emphasis has been on an Asian Highway to connect these countries. Mekong- Ganga initiative should have greater emphasis on sea based trade and coordination with BIMSTEC where there are parallel projects under planning. Civil Aviation cooperation is also essential to allow connectivity. This regional initiative does not hold so far any major role for Andaman & Nicobar Islands.

CONCLUSION

The rise of regional groups described in this chapter in IOR shows the growing awareness about the region by its neighbouring countries. The realisation that has come is that safety, security and trade between them will lead to harmonious development. Further the countries in the region are seeking comfort from each other by forging regional groupings. Regional cooperation is the only way to grow in a safe and orderly manner.

NOTES

1. Admiral Arun Prakash, "Maritime Security—An Indo-Pacific Perspective", *Defence Watch*, March, 2012.
2. Kanwal Sibal, "The Divided Portion:Towards a Larger Asia-Pacific Security Architecture" *India-US Dialogue,* December 13, 2012 at www.india-usdialogue.com
3. According M.D. Nalapat, India was approached to become a member of ASEAN in its initial constitution in 1967 by Singapore. However, Prime Minister Indira Gandhi was briefed not to join ASEAN as it was considered to be an "anti-communist alliance".
4. MOU signed between the Lt. Governor of Andaman & Nicobar Islands and the Governor of Phuket in Phuket on June 29, 2005.
5. According to Rajiv Sikri, "India's early assessment of the potential of South East Asian Countries was faulty which explains why India did not take up the invitation to join ASEAN". Rajiv Sikri, *Challenge and Strategy, Rethinking India's Foreign Policy*, Sage Publications, 2009, p. 113.
6. Asia-Pacific Defence Forum at www.apdforum.com/en_GV/article/rmiap-articles/online/ featured 20.03.2010.
7. For a full study of BIMSTEC, see Amita Batra, "Asian Economic Integration and Sub-Regionalism: a case study of BIMSTEC", *International Studies*, 47, Sage Publications, 2010, pp. 1-25.
8. *Indian Express*, July 06, 2013.

CHAPTER 7

Indian Naval Diplomacy and Defence Initiatives

Defence initiatives are a very important aspect of a strategic dialogue. As already described in Chapter 4, India has in place agreements on maritime boundaries with all its maritime neighbours in the east of India except for Bangladesh. It is important that this also gets finalised soon. Arbitration proceedings are progressing in this respect. Meanwhile, there are two multilateral and three bilateral naval pacts and exercises which are great in confidence building and bringing about camaraderie amongst the defence forces which also relate to Andaman & Nicobar Islands. Naval diplomacy has a very important role to play, especially in context to India and China. With China developing a so called "string of pearls" policy by developing ports in Bangladesh, Myanmar, Sri Lanka and Pakistan and a base in Seychelles, India's Look East Policy needs a naval dimension in the Indo-Pacific which can, perhaps, counter balance Chinese initiatives in the Indian Ocean. Some of these are described below.

MILAN EXERCISE

Indian Navy can be complimented in starting this very important biennial function in Naval Diplomacy called 'Milan' a Hindi word meaning get together. This brilliant idea is now in its 17th year. Milan basically is a biennial conglomeration of Asia-Pacific maritime navies, hosted by the Indian Navy at Port Blair in Andaman & Nicobar Islands, to foster bonds of 'friendship across the seas', boost interoperability and share views on common maritime issues. From four navies in 1995, it has grown to 14 navies in the last exercise held in Port Blair in January 2012.[1] Although, China is not invited, it is not anti- China in its approach. An important priority in the Asia-Pacific region is the protection of sea lanes around Straits of Malacca since over 60,000 ships sail through it every year, transporting around 30 per cent of the world trade in goods. The 14 countries that took part in January 2012 are Australia, Bangladesh, Myanmar, Brunei, Malaysia, Maldives, Indonesia, Sri Lanka, Thailand, Singapore, Seychelles, Philippines, New Zealand and India. Seven out of 10 ASEAN members took part. Vietnam could not take part but it had done so earlier.

For India, the advantage of holding the Milan Exercise in Port Blair is to show India's central location in the Indian Ocean, astride these major commercial routes and energy lifelines which also makes India a major stakeholder in the region's security and stability.

On the purpose behind the exercise, Chief of Naval staff Admiral D.K. Joshi, elaborated "Terror by non-state actors, gun-running, drug-smuggling, poaching in the EEZ and illegal migrants are common troubles that the nations in the region face. We have to come together and work jointly, learning from each other's experience and expertise".

The Milan naval exercise hosted biennially by the Indian Navy is becoming popular as more and more countries join and could easily convert itself to a joint taskforce for Asia-Pacific region including Australia and New Zealand, with India having a leading role in combating maritime terror, poaching, gun and drug-running.

The four-five day naval exercise also has a seminar where issues of common concerns and threats are discussed with a day-long table-top simulated exercise to arrive at a consensus on "jointmanship and inter-operability". It is also giving prominence to Andaman & Nicobar Islands.

"Milan-2010 is a joint exercise. We are looking at a Joint Task Force (JTF) against piracy in the region in which all these nations can contribute," Australian patrol boat HMAS Glenelg's Commanding Officer Lt. Cdr. Shane Doolin said, when asked about the future roadmap for Milan.

The event witnessed participation of Bangladeshi offshore patrol vessel BNS Kapatakhaya, Malaysian patrol vessel RMN KD Perak, Myanmar's Corvette UMS Anawrahta, Thailand's patrol Anti-Submarine Warship (ASW) Longlom, Indonesian Mall Corvette KRI Imam Bonjol, Sri Lankan offshore patrol vessel SLNS Samudura and Singaporean mine sweepers RSS Katong and Punggol.

New Zealand's Maritime Component Commander Commodore Ross Smith, when asked about 'Milan', said the initiative was good in the sense, India's role as a major naval power in the IOR was acknowledged by all nations. "Indian Ocean is your (India's) ocean. You need to man it. We are always looking for opportunity for joint exercises with Indian Navy, which is big in size," he said.

While it is not an anti-China group, but presence of China in such an exercise would not be welcome by all in view of the belligerent postures being adopted by the Chinese Navy in South China Sea. Further, though the grouping may not transform into a "military bloc" or a grouping against any country including China, it would ensure inter-operability among the Milan nations so as to work side-by-side in times of need and provide India a strong foothold among the naval forces of the region. Two more countries pertinent to this region are South Korea and Japan. They have also not joined Milan as yet.

As a result of the success of the last Milan exercise with 14 countries in February 2012 China has woken up. Consequently, the Chinese Foreign Minister Yang Jiechi called on the Indian Foreign Minister in Delhi with a suggestion for maritime cooperation between the two countries. The Chinese Defence Minister also called on his counterpart in Delhi in September 2012 and finally, during the visit of the Indian Defence Minister, A.K. Antony in July, 2013, the Chinese took up the issue of restarting joint military exercises, which had been suspended since 2009, and was agreed to by the Indian Defence Minister. This time the joint exercises would include navy and air force.[2]

INDIAN OCEAN NAVAL SYMPOSIUM (IONS)

Another excellent move by the Indian Navy to involve the navies of the Indian Ocean, the IONS has also grown since its initial start in 2008 as a voluntary initiative that seeks to increase maritime co-operation among navies of the littoral states of the IOR by providing an open and inclusive forum for discussion of regionally relevant maritime issues. The popularity of this symposium can be gauged by the fact that there are now 35 countries participating in it.

That this regional initiative was able to meet with such wide acceptance across the length and breadth of the Indian Ocean was in itself a unique phenomenon. There are 35 members - navies of the IONS which have been geographically grouped into the following four sub-regions:

35 Countries

South Asian Littorals—Bangladesh, India, Maldives, Pakistan, Seychelles and Sri Lanka.

West Asian Littorals—Bahrain, Iran, Iraq, Kuwait, Oman, Qatar, Saudi Arabia, UAE and Yemen.

East African Littorals—Comoros, Djibouti, Egypt, Nigeria, France, Kenya, Madagascar, Mauritius, Mozambique, Somalia, South Africa, Sudan and Tanzania.

South East Asian and Australian Littorals—Australia, Indonesia, Malaysia, Myanmar, Singapore, Thailand and Timor Leste.

The inaugural IONS was held on February 14, 2008 in New Delhi, India. The Chief of Naval Staff, Indian Navy was designated the Chairman IONS for the period 2008-10. A 'Charter of Business' was mutually agreed to by the Chiefs of the member-navies, which has been forwarded to all the member navies-Indonesia, Thailand and Singapore, for ratification. The theme of the IONS-2008 was "Contemporary Trans-national Challenges – International Maritime Connectivities".

IONS is held every second year in a different member country which hosts the event. The 2nd IONS symposium i.e. IONS-2010 was held in Abu-Dhabi from May 10-11, 2010, wherein the baton of IONS Chairmanship was handed over to the Commander, UAE Navy. The theme of IONS-2010 was "Together for the Reinforcement of Maritime Security in the Indian Ocean". The 3rd IONS was held in South Africa from April 12-13, 2012. The activities of IONS include cooperative activities and mechanisms like workshops, essay competitions, lectures, etc. IONS takes place without any naval vessels.

MALABAR EXERCISE

Malabar Exercise was the start of a bilateral military exercise between the Indian and US Navy on an annual basis. The annual Malabar series began in 1992, and includes diverse activities, ranging from fighter combat operations from aircraft carriers, through Maritime Interdiction Operations (MIO) Exercises. It is held in various locations around the world. In 2007 the operational area of Malabar-2007 stretched from Vizag on the eastern seaboard to the Andaman & Nicobar Islands that guard the approaches to the Strait of Malacca, considered one of the world's busiest waterways. The US Navy had the largest representation during Malabar-2007 with 13 warships, including the nuclear powered aircraft carrier *USS Nimitz*. The other vessels included the conventionally powered carrier *USS Kitty Hawk*, the nuclear submarine *USS Chicago* (SSN-721), two guided missile cruisers, and six guided missile destroyers. Eight warships of India, including the aircraft carrier *INS Viraat*, represented the Indian Navy. *Viraat's* Sea Harrier jets and Sea King helicopters, and the IAF's Jaguar deep-penetration strike aircraft were also seen in action. In 2007, countries like Australia, Singapore and Japan were also invited. Australia was represented by a frigate and a tanker; Japan by two destroyers; and Singapore by a frigate. The 2012 exercise was a 10 day affair in an area of 450 nm of air and space in the Bay of Bengal with only the navies of US and India participating.

China had not officially commented on the drill initially but was known to be unhappy over the event as it was being conducted in the Bay of Bengal for the first time. China has been undertaking naval cooperation with Bangladesh and Myanmar to gain access to the Bay of Bengal and has also been strengthening military cooperation with Sri Lanka. In June 2007 China had issued a 'demarche' to India, US, Japan and Australia seeking details about their four-nation meeting, termed a Quadrilateral Initiative. India and Australia had quickly assured Beijing that security and defence issues did not form part of the meeting's agenda.

SIMBEX WITH SINGAPORE

Soon after becoming independent Singapore leader Lee Kuan Yew approached India in 1965 for help in building up its military. They were also worried over China's subversive role in instigating communist insurgencies. Singapore did want an Indian role as a guardian. The main cooperation, however, started in the

1990s after P.V. Narasimha Rao took over as India's Prime Minister and introduced the Look East Policy. Post-9/11 there has been growing cooperation between India and Singapore. India has been policing waters of the IOR including straits of Malacca and has been welcomed by Singapore as a balancing presence.[3]

India and Singapore have been carrying out joint exercises for the last 19 years. The last one was held in 2012 off the Andaman & Nicobar Islands in the Bay of Bengal. The Indian Navy and the Republic of Singapore Navy (RSN) completed an annual joint naval exercise, codenamed Singapore-Indian Maritime Bilateral Exercise (SIMBEX) 2012, off the Andaman & Nicobar Islands in the Bay of Bengal.

Hosted by India, SIMBEX 2012 was 19th in the series of bilateral exercises that have been held between both nations since 1994. The sea phase of SIMBEX 2012 was held from March 21–April 1, 2012 and involved participation of naval and air assets from both the countries.

The Indian Navy's destroyer, a corvette, a replenishment tanker, two fast attack craft, a frigate and a submarine participated alongside a RSN frigate and a missile corvette. The exercise also involved maritime patrol aircraft and naval helicopters from both RSN and the Indian Navy to conduct air surveillance and simulated aerial attacks. Over the years, SIMBEX exercise has transformed from training-oriented anti-submarine warfare exercises to advanced naval warfare exercises that involve air, surface and sub-surface missions.

During SIMBEX 2010, the Indian Navy's Rajput-class destroyer *INS Ranvir*, the landing ship tank *INS Mahish*, the patrol craft *INS Batti Malv*, the tanker *INS Jyoti* and a submarine participated alongside RSN's Formidable-class multi-role stealth frigate *RSS Intrepid* and the missile corvette *RSS Victory*.

JIMEX WITH JAPAN

Japan and India have been moving closer to each other on the maritime front. The first bilateral maritime exercise between India and Japan, 'JIMEX 12' (Japan India Maritime Exercise) took place in June 2012 in Tokyo. Units of the Japan Maritime Self-Defense Force (JMSDF) participating were two destroyers; one maritime patrol aircraft and a helicopter. Indian Naval units participating were *INS Rana*, *INS Shivalik*, *INS Karmukh* and *INS Shakti*. The four ships entered Tokyo on June 5, 2012 after visiting Singapore, Vietnam, Philippines and the Republic of Korea en route. The three day stay in Tokyo coincided with commemoration of 60 years of diplomatic relations between India and Japan.

The four ships of the Eastern Fleet of the Indian Navy were on a sustained operational deployment to the South China Sea and North West Pacific. The two month long deployments commenced in end May 2012 to enable navy-to-navy cooperation with the numerous navies across the region as well as demonstrated the Indian Navy's operational reach. On completion of the exercise, the ships visited Beijing, China and Port Kelang, Malaysia in June, 2012.

The focus of 'Passive Exercises' is primarily in the sphere of Maritime Security Cooperation. These include Humanitarian Aid & Disaster Relief (HADR) operations and Visit, Board, Search and Seizure (VBSS) drills, which form a part of Anti-Piracy operations. Exercises of these nature enhance inter-operability thereby enabling the two navies to smoothly function together in the sphere of maritime security / HADR operations, should the need arise. However, the JMSDF has 16 submarines, 44 destroyers and eight frigates. It has recently added 2 new types of helicopter borne destroyer ships and another four to six are on order.

In addition, during the port visits, the Fleet Commander along with the Commanding Officers (COs) of the ships, meet high-ranking officials of the navy, state administration, port management, coastal security organisation, police, and other stakeholders of maritime security in the countries in order to share professional experiences and exchange best practices in areas of mutual interest.

The Chinese would perceive this as a direct threat especially if Japan, South Korea and India decide to proceed with a Joint Defence Action Plan and elicit more members to join their forces from the Philippines, Taiwan, Vietnam, and Thailand.

India and Vietnam

This bilateral relationship is most important and interesting for India. Besides the fact that India and Vietnam have strong bonds of friendship going back to 1954, India was also a member of the International Commission for Control & Supervision (ICCS) of Vietnam under the UN. Both India and Vietnam have suffered from Chinese misadventure in 1962 and 1979 respectively. India's support to Vietnam during the Vietnam War and during its invasion of Cambodia and Vietnam's support to India during the Indo-Pak conflict has given a lot of confidence to each other.

Chinese hegemonic designs over South China Sea in which Vietnam comes into direct conflict with China is a major cause of concern for Vietnam. ASEAN countries i.e. Brunei, Malaysia, Philippines and Vietnam have issues with Chinese claims over South China Sea based on unnecessary historic claims. Indo-Vietnamese economic and military relations are crucial requirements for both the countries. Chinese unease at the present Indo-Vietnamese relations could only bring comfort to India in view of the growing closeness between China and Pakistan. The 15 point Mutual Defence Assistance Agreement (MDAA) of 2002 between India and Vietnam and the joint Declaration of Comprehensive Cooperation between India and Vietnam in 2003, led to a formalised strategic partnership between the two countries. India has been providing Vietnam with assistance in enhancing its naval and air capabilities which is possible as both countries have Russian equipment and Russia also encourages it. India and Vietnam have also engaged in joint patrols by their respective coastguards and both have SU-30 aircrafts of Russian origin with which India can help train them.[4]

Joint Patrolling of the Maritime Borders

This is a very important task being undertaken by the Andaman & Nicobar Command. This involves maritime engagement with littoral countries. It involves joint patrols and military exercises. The joint patrolling involves preventing illegal fishing, immigration, drug trafficking, movement of arms and ammunition. It also involves prevention of piracy and conduct of search and rescue operations.

India and Thailand conduct a common patrol along the maritime border every six months with ships of either country moving together on its side of the maritime border. Similarly, India and Indonesia also conduct a joint patrol along their maritime borders. India and Singapore also have joint exercises.

As a result of the military challenge coming from China, countries of East and South China Sea i.e. Japan and some ASEAN countries, are coming closer to India and bringing India onto a common platform. All the countries mentioned above are spending more on defence. Australia, Malaysia, Singapore, South Korea and Vietnam all have submarine acquisition plans.[5]

Other Bilateral Defence Exercises which take place but are not directly connected to the present issues are the following:

- Varuna with French Navy
- Konkan with Royal British Navy
- Indra with Russian Navy
- IBSAMAR 2010 with South African and Brazilian navies

There is tension between India and China on the Tibetan border. While there is no border agreement, there is an unwritten LAC in Eastern Ladakh as well as on the Arunachal Pradesh-Tibet border. However, India and China have been holding joint military exercises as a confidence building measure. The first round was held in Kunming in China and the last round was held in Balegaon in India. However, in 2009 India suspended the defence exchanges after China refused a visa to the Head of the Indian Army's Northern Military Command.

NOTES

1. *Vayu Aerospace & Defence Review*, November 11, 2012, see p. 20 for more details.
2. *Times of India*, July 06, 2013.

3. Bilveer Singh, "Security Issues in South-East Asia: A Singapore Perspective", in *Emerging Asia: Challenges for India & Singapore,* Manohar and India International Centre, New Delhi, 2002.
4. A.V. Chandrasekaran, "Indo-Vietnamese Relations: Exploring Collaboration in China's Backwaters, Defence and Diplomacy in Pursuit of National Security", *Air Power Journal,* 2(1), 2012.
5. Ashok Sawhney, "Indian National Effectiveness". RSIS Working Paper No. 197, May 7, 2010, S. Rajaratnam School of International Studies, Singapore.

CHAPTER 8

A Strategic Shift in India's Defence Policy Post-LEP 1991 and Andaman & Nicobar Islands

> "Andaman & Nicobar Islands provide the key to the eventual success of India's 'Look East Policy' enunciated by the Prime Minister Narasimha Rao in 1990s."
>
> —*Prof. Aparajit Biswas*

For all the talk of India Rising in recent years, it is yet to define clearly what it stands for as a power rapidly rising in the global firmament. For the claims of a great power to be legitimate in the eyes of the world, it is essential that the fundamental moorings of that power be in place. It is time India should articulate its views and not appear to be a fence sitter.

There has however been a strategic shift in the defence policy towards these islands. Up to the seventies the strategy was one of keeping a minimum strategic force to ensure that there is no threat to these islands. The Indian Navy maintained a Naval Officer in Charge (NOIC) at Port Blair and a small contingent at Karmota, in the Nancowry harbour in the Nicobars. The Air Force also maintained a Staging Post at Car Nicobar with no permanent aircrafts based in it since 1956 when the Royal Air Force (RAF) handed over the base to them. The IAF was allotted land for another airstrip at Indira Point (erstwhile Pygmalion Point) at the Great Nicobar Islands as a forward airstrip facing Malacca Straits but they never got around to building it. Reportedly, there were objections from Indonesia. However, this land may not be suitable post-Tsunami, when some parts of this land got submerged under water. In 2012, however, the navy had declared setting up of a naval air base called BAAZ at Campbell Bay in the Great Nicobar Island. However, this airstrip will not be a full airstrip of 12,000 feet due to limitations of land.

US TILT TOWARDS INDIA

In a rare appearance at the Pentagon US President Barack Obama unveiled a document titled 'Sustaining US Global Leadership: Priorities for 21st Century Defense' which identified China as one country which poses a security threat to the US in long term.[1] "The US is investing in a long-term strategic partnership with India to support its ability to serve as a regional economic anchor and provider of security in the broader IOR" said the document.

"Over the long-term, China's emergence as a regional power will have the potential to affect the US economy and our security in a variety of ways," said the eight-page document.

"Our two countries have a strong stake in peace and stability in East Asia and an interest in building a cooperative bilateral relationship. However, the growth of China's military power must be accompanied by greater clarity of its strategic intentions in order to avoid causing friction in the region," the document said. As a result of US thinking of China as a potential security threat, they find that India should be a natural partner, in their efforts in the Indo-Pacific Region. While India is unlikely to become a US ally like Pakistan did by joining CENTO and SEATO in the 1950s and 1960s, India's common perceptions and security concerns do turnout to be more or less identical with the US. Where there are differences like that over Iran and Myanmar, it appears that the US is willing to rely on India. As a result, a reliance of convenience is emerging between the US and India and along with it a number of countries like Singapore, Japan and Australia.

Consequently, the new US strategy also replaces the decade-old policy of maintaining a force capable of fighting two wars at once. It calls for a small and lean American Army. "Even when US forces are committed to a large-scale operation in one region, they will be capable of denying the objectives of—or imposing unacceptable costs on—an opportunistic aggressor in a second region," it said.

India should also appreciate that ever since the 1962 conflict with China over the Himalayan frontier, after their accession of Tibet by armed aggression, the US has been backing India on the issue of McMahon Line. In a statement in 2012, Nancy Powell, the US Ambassador to India reiterated the American position that McMahon Line stands as it was in 1962. However, the US position is silent on the western front of Kashmir and Ladakh including Aksai Chin. With the US position backing India on McMahon Line, there is a strong case for India to be firm on other fronts and not go shy on its relationship with Vietnam.[2]

India and Japan: Convergence of Views

Shinzo Abe, while addressing the Indian Parliament in 2007 as Japanese Prime Minister introduced the concept of "a confluence of the two seas"—a phrase drawn from the work of Mughal prince Dara Shikoh is 1655. The concept of "confluence of two seas" implies that peace, stability and freedom of navigation in the Pacific Ocean are inseparable from peace, security and freedom of navigation in the Indian Ocean. The globalisation of world trade makes operations between the two oceans inseparable. He had further pointed out that Andaman

& Nicobar Islands sitting on the western entrance of Straits of Malacca deserved greater emphasis. He had emphasised regular bilateral military to military dialogue between India and Japan as a great assurance and had further emphasised the need for a trilateral dialogue to include the US.[3]

During the visit of the Japanese Prime Minister Yoshihiko Noda to India in 2012, the two nations renewed a bilateral currency swap agreement in which Japan agreed to make US$ 15 billion available to India to help it in stabilising the Indian Rupee which had witnessed a more than 16 per cent decline in its value over the year. This was a major concession by Japan. Japan has also decided to make huge investments in India in infrastructure projects. The Delhi Mumbai Industrial Corridor (DMIC) a US$ 90 billion project covering 1,483 km is one example of a major Indo-Japanese project. As a return gesture, India signed an inter-governmental agreement in 2012 for supply of rare earths from India, which has one of the world's largest reserves, and which the Chinese have tried to deny to Japan in the recent past. India and Japan also signed a Maritime Security Agreement during 2007.

The political fallout of Senkaku islands issue in South China Sea with China has led to closure of plants of leading Japanese companies. The Japanese Prime Minister had announced that China has more to lose from the Senkaku dispute as Foreign Direct Investment (FDI) will shy away from China if they encourage such belligerent policies. Further, All Nippon Airways have announced cancellation of 40,000 seats on their China-Japan flights. It is, therefore, natural that Japan would be looking towards countries like India for absorption of substantial direct investment by Japan as well as cooperative securities.

Despite the budgetary tightening in Japan post the Fukushima disaster, India remains the largest recipient of Japan overseas development aid.

With deteriorating relations between Japan and China including a boycott of Japanese made goods in China, both imports and local production, there is rethinking on the part of Japan towards improving its military relations with India. Strong economic relations, Indo-Japanese Naval relations are bound to improve, especially when the US is also favourable. In March 2005, an Indo-Japanese agreement was signed to jointly explore the Andaman Sea for natural gas. While not much progress has taken place, this is yet another step.[4]

India and Australia

The Australian tilt towards China seems to have got corrected slightly. The Australian decision to review and change its policies regarding the sale of uranium to India announced during President Obama's visit to Australia cannot but go unnoticed. This happened after Secretary of State Hillary Clinton coined a new term, "Indo-Pacific", to describe the Asia-Pacific region during formal bilateral discussions with Australia.

CHINA IN INDIAN OCEAN REGION

China has announced setting up its first military base abroad in the Seychelles to "seek supplies and recuperate" facilities for its navy. The Seychelles has defended its decision by suggesting that it has invited China to set up a military base to tackle piracy off its coast, and Beijing has played it down by underlining that it is standard global practice for naval fleets to re-supply at the closest port of a nearby state during long-distance missions. But there should be no ambiguity: Chinese footprint in the Indian Ocean has got bigger and will continue to get bigger in the coming years. This is the first articulation of China's 'string of pearls' strategy. The second one is the Gwadar Port in Pakistan as Singapore Ports, who were managing it so far have left and Chinese have taken over.[5]

China's foreign policy thinkers and political establishment have long been trying to convince the world that Beijing's rise will be a peaceful one, that it has no expansionist intentions, that it will be a different kind of great power. Of course, their aggressive takeover of Tibet in the 1950s makes this largely a charade. But there are, however, in India a number of people in the Nehruvian mould who would have us believe China is actually a different kind of great power and that if the West could simply give China a stake in the established order, Beijing's rise would not create any complications. Many in China, however, have been advocating the creation of overseas bases for some time now. Shen Dingli, an influential professor at Fudan University in Shanghai, had asserted sometime back that "it is wrong for us [China] to believe that we have no right to set up bases abroad". He argues it is not terrorism or piracy that's the real threat to China but the ability of other states to block China's trade routes. To prevent this, China, according to Dingli, needs not only a blue-water navy but also "overseas military bases to cut the supply costs". Of course, Dingli also wraps this up in the widely accepted world peace diplomacy, asserting that the establishment of such military bases overseas would promote regional and global stability. It is a familiar diplomatic wrapping that other superpowers should easily recognise. As China emerges as a major global power, it will expand its military footprint across the globe, much like the US which has bases surrounding China. The rapid expansion of China's naval capabilities and broader military profile is a classic manifestation of its great-power status. China's new naval strategy of "far sea defence" is aimed at giving Beijing the ability to project its power in key oceanic areas, including and most significantly the Indian Ocean. Chinese hegemonic and bullying tendencies are well established to need more elaboration.

China's expansionist behaviour has long been evident. It has been keen to acquire naval facilities along the crucial choke-points in the IOR not only to serve its economic interests but also to enhance its strategic presence. China realises its maritime strength will give it the strategic leverage to emerge as the regional hegemon and a potential superpower. Beijing's growing dependence on maritime space and resources is reflected in the Chinese aspiration to expand its influence and to ultimately dominate the strategic environment of the IOR. China's growing reliance on bases across the IOR is a response to its perceived vulnerability, given the logistical constraints it faces due to the distance of the Indian Ocean waters from its own area of operation. Given that almost 80 per cent of China's oil passes through the Straits of Malacca, it is reluctant to rely on US naval power for unhindered access to energy. So it has decided to build up its naval power at choke-points along the sea routes from the Persian Gulf to the South China Sea. Yet, China is also consolidating power over the South China Sea and the Indian Ocean with an eye on India. However, Straits of Malacca remained a Chinese dilemma in spite of it adopting a strategy to bypass it described earlier in Chapter 3. With Singapore at one end of the entrance with a strong US tilt, Indonesia having problems with China over its maritime border as also Malaysia and India at the western entrance of Straits of Malacca, the Chinese can be checkmated in this crucial SLOC if need arises. Herein, lies the importance of building a strategy towards Andaman & Nicobar Islands.

This is a wake-up call for India. This situation is similar to the 1950s when Sardar Patel as Deputy Prime Minister and Home Minister of India wrote a detailed letter dated November 7, 1950 to Prime Minister Nehru who was also Foreign Minister expressing his reasoned misgivings about China, but Nehru chose to ignore it and Patel died soon after. China's growing naval presence in and around the IOR, beginning in areas such as China's Hainan Island in the South China Sea, should be troubling to India. Of particular note is what has been termed as China's "string of pearls" strategy—some elements of which are no doubt hyped—that has significantly expanded its strategic depth in India's backyard. It is possible to explain the construction of these ports and facilities by China on purely economic and commercial grounds; but regional and global powers like the US, Japan and India inevitably view the sum total of China's diplomatic and military efforts in the Indian Ocean as projecting power vis-à-vis competing rivals. Moreover, most of Chinese naval facilities in the Indian Ocean are dual-use in nature and no serious strategy can discount their future military use.

Chinese scholars have expressed strong reservations against India's quest to reach out strategically to democracies in East Asia. They have denounced multilateral (Australia, India, Japan and US) naval exercises aimed at enhancing maritime cooperation in the Asia Pacific and the Indian Ocean as being aimed at the strategic encirclement of China. The Chinese have been aggressively opposing even a non-military Indian presence aimed at prospecting for oil and gas in the South China Sea while themselves seeking naval bases in the Indian Ocean.

Chinese sensitivity towards the Dalai Lama is yet another thorn in India-China relations which could be a trump card for India if India can make a clever diplomatic move. The Chinese abruptly postponed the 15th round of boundary talks between the special representatives in November 2011 as India refused to relent on the Dalai Lama's participation in a private conference on Buddhism. Chinese diplomatic, political and military assertiveness at the tactical level is likely to continue in 2012 and beyond. However, at the strategic level the relationship will remain stable.[6]

Such Chinese rhetoric is not confined to India alone. China's neighbours that contest its irredentist claims of the entire South China Sea being an area of its "core interest" have experienced similar behaviour and rhetoric. Incidents in the East China Sea across disputed maritime boundaries with Japan have led to Japanese vessels being rammed by Chinese ships, followed by a ban on exports of rare earth materials by China to Japan. The Philippines has witnessed the Chinese using force to enforce maritime boundary claims, and Vietnam has periodically been subject to Chinese military force over disputed boundaries. China adopts a similar approach to issues of maritime boundaries in its dealings with South Korea and Taiwan. The Chinese now openly boast about possessing missile power to target aircraft carriers of America's Pacific Fleet.

Along with strong arm tactics with its neighbours in South China Sea it insists that it would handle the differences on its maritime boundaries with countries like Vietnam, the Philippines, Brunei and Malaysia bilaterally. India made the point at the ASEAN Summit in Bali that issues involving maritime boundaries and the freedom of navigation had to be settled in conformity with the provisions of the UNCLOS. Roughly 40 per cent of India's trade with the US traverses through the South China Sea. Moreover, its entire trade with Japan and South Korea traverses through the waters claimed by Beijing to be areas of its "core interest". In these circumstances, undefined and contested maritime boundaries, where one party appears ever ready to use force, are seen as an impediment and inhibiting factor in the freedom of navigation.

To add to China's concerns, reflected in the Chinese media, President Obama announced that Mrs. Hillary Clinton, US Secretary of State would soon visit Myanmar, regarded by the Chinese as their backyard. Since then both Mrs. Hillary Clinton and President Obama have already visited Myanmar. Myanmar's new dispensation is showing signs of wanting to get free of China's embrace. These developments have vindicated India's view that Myanmar unlike Pakistan does not wish to become a Chinese client state. India quite rightly resisted American pressures at the highest level to ostracise Myanmar's military rulers in spite of President Obama mentioning it in his address to the Indian Parliament in 2011.

Chinese Apprehension

China is apprehensive of a possible India-US partnership along with Japan and Australia. It must realise its own strategy to isolate India by encircling it will, of course, have its reaction. Nationalistic but realistic Chinese foreign policy experts including those within the state apparatus understand that India has been proud to follow an independent foreign policy since 1947. That is how the NAM was formed.

There is however little doubt that US has tilted towards India as stated earlier in this chapter. The former US Secretary of Defense, Leon Panetta had stated in 2012, that India will be the lynchpin of America's new defence strategy. Panetta has stated "America is at a turning point. After a decade of war, we are developing a new strategy. In particular we will expand our military partnerships and pursue in the arc extending from western pacific and East Asia into the IOR and South Asia. Defence cooperation with India is a lynch pinch in this strategy."[7]

At the same time India has to look after its national interests which can extend to any part of the world. A survey of the Indian voting pattern at the UN will show New Delhi voted more against the US than otherwise. Yet in a recent voting in UN India trounced its Chinese rival for a senior position. Therefore, China must understand that India has every right to promote relations with China's small neighbours as China has done with India's neighbours. The only difference is that India has no intention to transfer nuclear weapons technology and delivery systems to China's neighbours as China has done with Pakistan including promoting a vicious anti-India policy among India's neighbours. Nor has India made wild claims to its borders based on nebulous history like China did in Tibet and is now doing in South China Sea.

From China's point of view, Indian Prime Minister Manmohan Singh's answer to Chinese Premier Wen Jiabao's query in Bali that India will continue to explore for oil and gas with Vietnam in its territorial waters was perceived as an assault on Chinese sovereignty. They call their claim their core interest which is indisputable.

There is no question that China has for long misconstrued history, interpretations of international laws, and used force to falsely claim territory that does not belong to it. Increasingly, Chinese experts have begun to question these claims especially on the South China Sea, to Beijing's embarrassment.

India's rising profile in South East Asia, especially with Vietnam including a defence agreement is perceived as a challenge by China.

THE ASEAN CONUNDRUM

The last ASEAN Summit at Bali also saw another significant development. Despite Chinese reservations, five ASEAN member-states—Singapore, the Philippines, Brunei, Vietnam and Thailand—along with India, Australia and the US raised the issue of maritime boundaries and the freedom of navigation. Russia, Indonesia and five other members talked in general terms about maritime security. Only Myanmar and Cambodia avoided any reference to the issue. An embarrassed Chinese Premier became conciliatory, but did not give up Chinese insistence on dealing with each neighbour separately and bilaterally. But, with the Americans deciding to participate actively in the Asia Summit and reinforcing their security commitment in the Asia-Pacific, by agreeing to the deployment of forces in Darwin in Australia, the ASEAN states now appear satisfied that Chinese "assertiveness" will not go on unchallenged.

China-India Conflict in South China Sea

As already brought out in chapter 5, the Chinese Government has stated that China enjoys "indisputable sovereignty" over the South China Sea and its islands. It has further stated that it does not want other countries to get involved in the dispute and that it hopes foreign countries will allow it to solve its dispute bilaterally. This is contrary to its own practice of getting involved in that part of Kashmir which is presently under occupation of Pakistan, which they have accepted as a disputed territory in the Article 6 of Border Agreement with Pakistan in 1963 (Appendix 1, page 201) However, India has never taken up this issue with the Chinese Government.

ONGC Videsh, a leading Indian public sector oil company working with Petro Vietnam in oil exploration off the Vietnamese coast has attracted Chinese Government's ire. The Chinese are opposed to any country engaging in oil and gas exploration activities in waters which they consider under their jurisdiction.

The Indian spokesman in reply to the Chinese statement said, "Our cooperation with Vietnam or any other country is always as per international laws, norms and conventions. Cooperation with Vietnam in the area of energy and to secure India's energy security is very important. There are a number of Indian companies already operational and we are looking at further enhancing cooperation in the years ahead."

Some recent incidents with China in the South China Sea are significant. An unidentified caller on an open radio channel hailed an Indian naval ship *INS Airavat* as it was leaving Vietnam after a "goodwill visit", and advised it to stay away from the South China Sea. The Chinese denied Beijing's involvement in the incident. India kept silent over the incident, which the Western media played up.

Post-26/11 Developments and the Andaman & Nicobar Islands

The Mumbai terror attack of November 26, 2008 shook the Indian Government, the defence forces and the naval establishments. Similar to the pre-1962 situation when the Indian Government had evolved a theory of the Impenetrable Himalayan Range, the security establishment in India never envisaged that there could be an attack on India from the sea. Government of Pakistan trained irregulars/terrorists arrived from sea into Mumbai in a small boat and managed to bypass the navy, coastguards and local police. About 2000 people died in five locations in Mumbai. It appears that the same complacency of 1962 and 2008 has engulfed India with regard to these islands. The policy of Masterly Inactivity and Benign Neglect may prove to be a disastrous policy. As George Fernades, former defence minister of India had stated "India's farthest frontier in the most insecure region with 300 uninhabited islands in the region that are highly vulnerable and could be used for dumping arms and equipment."[8] It must be, however, stated that the Ministry of Defence under George Fernandes did take action and set up the first Joint Command of the three services for the first time in India in the Andaman & Nicobar Islands in 2001. This has been working successfully but no other joint command has since come up. Bharat Karnad in his article in *Asian Age*[9] on August 8, 2012, had stated that the shelving of an embryonic idea of mountain strike corps by the Indian Army is unfortunate. He further stated that the air force and the navy have therefore become the new main elements for tackling the Chinese threat. Karnad's hypothesis is largely correct and the Indian Navy will now be the most strategic force to counter any Chinese threat and the emphasis on Andaman & Nicobar Islands as a strategic theatre will increase.

Incidentally, the Japanese who occupied these islands for three and half years during World War II, seem to have a much better appreciation of the strategic value of these islands. This is perhaps because they themselves were an archipelago, at war with the Allied Powers. As already mentioned, the present Prime Minister of Japan Shinzo Abe has already reiterated the need to give greater emphasis to these islands.

The Indian Maritime Doctrine of 2007, updated in 2009 is an attempt to set up a "three-dimensional blue water force" able to ply on water and in air. The purpose is also to counter emerging threats and protect the SLOC. The Straits of Malacca is the obvious one for India. The doctrine highlights the need to control the choke points, important islands and vital trade routes which are significant for India. In the overall military balance between the army on the one side and navy on the other, with the air force common to both, India is vulnerable on the land front. With particular reference to China, India should be able to control the western entrance in Straits of Malacca to ensure that in case of a Chinese attack on the Indian land border, India should be able to choke/blockade the Malacca entrance thereby stopping oil bearing ships and other valuable items.[10]

According to some experts the Indian Army is vulnerable to a Chinese land attack but unfortunately the current stock of advisors in the government are in the mould of the old China Study Group (CSG) of Nehru days which want China and India to live peacefully and therefore, India should not anticipate any threat from China.

As Rajiv Sikri, former Secretary East, Ministry of External Affairs of India writes "On the military side, India must evolve a calculated and calibrated policy to put China under some pressure to safeguard its interests and concerns. India must urgently build up its missile capabilities to bring China's major population centres within reach as well as its naval strength so that China's energy and trade flows can be disrupted in a crisis. India should eschew its current defences, timid and somewhat legalistic approach in dealing with China."[11]

How Ready Are We Today? Possible Blockade of the Straits of Malacca

A question raised by Gaurang Bhatt[12] is that in an event of war with China, there must be sufficient Indian Naval power and assets to blockade the Straits of Malacca which is a transit point for oil to China. The *Business Standard* in its editorial of September 7, 2012 has also come out with a similar proposition. It has stated that with the Chinese Military build up in Tibet and its locational advantage being at a height, it can "indulge in a sharp war to grab a chunk of territory such as Tawang in Arunachal Pradesh". It further states that "China's advantage of land however is offset in the Indian Ocean". It further states that "An Indian Naval Blockade on China's oil and trade flows would take time to bite–especially given China is building a US style Strategic Petroleum Reserve (SPR)–but it is agreed that a longish Indian blockade would have a calamitous effect on Chinese economy."[13]

India's drive over blue water should be to checkmate China in the vulnerable Straits of Malacca. In order to prevent a Chinese incursion from the Himalayas, India must be in a position to blockade the Straits of Malacca. With India's naval build up in the last 10 years and its recent purchase of US made Submarine Hunter-Killer Plane – Boeing P-8s equipped with harpoon missile, two aircraft carriers (one Russian and one Indian), French Scorpene attack submarine and Indian built nuclear submarine (Arihant) with missiles reaching 160 km (100 miles), the Indian Navy does emerge as a formidable force which the Chinese Navy may find difficult to cope with. To add to this force is also the acquisition of the formidable Russian origin Akula II Class submarine called "Chakra" in India. Armed with supersonic cruise missiles and torpedoes, it is capable of diving deep and going faster. According to R. Adm. Raja Menon, if India can have six such attack submarines it will leave no one in doubt about who controls the Indian Ocean as "the country needs power in Indian Ocean as an arbiter of assuring a peaceful environment for India's domestic international growth."[14] A strong naval and air presence in Andaman & Nicobar Islands, and in particular the Great Nicobar Island with a potential for blocking the Straits of Malacca is therefore, becoming an immediate requirement. A mention of the Nancowry-Karmota harbour in the Nicobar Island also needs to be made. Its utilisation for naval purposes finds little mention in naval literature though it is an outstanding deep water harbour protected from all sides with two entries. It could easily be a forward naval base, especially, for submarines. With India having 134 ships, 14 submarines and two aircraft carriers checkmating China on the choke point of Straits of Malacca could be possible. However, only 13 ships are based in Port Blair.[15]

In this connection India needs to examine China's frequent flirtation with its neighbouring countries. The foreign policy adopted by China by setting up a string of ports starting with Gwadar in Pakistan, Hambantota in Sri Lanka, Chittagong in Bangladesh,[16] and Sittwe in Myanmar also needs to be checkmated. On this issue, it may be mentioned that India is helping Iran in financing and building Chabahar Port, about 100 km from Gwadar. This port is already being used for supply to Afghanistan and would also counter the Chinese move to control Gwadar Port in Pakistan.[17] Along with this, we have used confidence building exercises both on the civil side with ASEAN, BIMSTEC, IOR, MEKONG GANGA and on the military side with Milan, IONS and Bilateral Exercises. All this will be useful in case of confrontation. It has also been reported in the Indian Press that unknown submarines were detected in the Indian Ocean. Both Indian and US assessment is that these submarines are Chinese.[18]

With the opening of a forward naval base called 'Baaz' in Campbell Bay in July 2012 in Great Nicobar Island overlooking the six degree channel, India has made a great strategic and significant move. The construction of a naval air base at Campbell Bay and extending the airstrip to 6,000-9,000 feet along with the existing air force base in Car Nicobar does send strong signals both to China and India's friendly neighbours in the Bay of Bengal and ASEAN countries. It has also been announced by the Chief of Indian Navy that *INS Kardip*, located in the most wonderful natural harbour of Nancowry-Karmota Islands will be augmented in its infrastructure. *INS Kardip* is very strategically located in the Nicobar and has a deep natural harbour—one of the finest in the world.[19] This is a natural corollary to the announcement of Baaz.

The Chinese Defence *White Paper* of 2010 has recognised access to raw materials as a major security concern and therefore wants to focus its attention on SLOCs. This will include the Straits of Malacca also. According to Shikha Aggarwal,[20] two factors that have dominated China's security concerns since 1990 is Taiwan's move to declare independence and vulnerability of China's oil supplies coming from Middle East. Since China has not been able to find a total substitute for Straits of Malacca for its oil supplies, Malacca remains the crucial choke point. China further feels that if the US Navy conducts a naval blockade of China in China's SLOCs, it would paralyse the Chinese economy. Its plans to bypass Straits of Malacca are therefore very serious. At the same time China's popularity among ASEAN nations is diminishing.

It is necessary at this stage to look at the possibility of China and Pakistan joining hands to keep India busy with skirmishes along the India-China border.

The threat becomes even more dangerous as both China and Pakistan are nuclear powers. China is supplying military hardware including nuclear hardware to Pakistan. While China may be vulnerable to blockade of Straits of Malacca, India's current dependence on imported energy supplies at about 70 per cent of its requirement which is likely to go up 85 per cent in the next few years, is dangerous from its security point of view. There is a need to quickly build up a strategic reserve of petroleum and also increase exploration on land and offshore including Andaman & Nicobar Islands, especially as oil has already been found offshore in Sumatra.

China's financial ability to expand its defence capacity is much higher than India because of its higher GDP, Foreign Exchange Reserve (FOREX) and expenditure on defence. India also has a dubious distinction of being the biggest defence armament purchaser in the international market because it has not been able to indigenise a large portion of its arms requirement. The Indian Navy has, however, taken a bold step and has decided to develop and build ships and submarines indigenously. Over the next five or six years, the Indian Navy expects to induct five or six ships built indigenously per year. Further, the construction of an aircraft carrier in India is also underway. China's defence budget for 2012 is US$ 92 billion. Generally, the declared budget is half of the actual in China as it camouflages it with other expenditures like internal security. According to Jane's, China's defence budget will be around US$ 238 billion. India's defence budget is insignificant compared to China. Further, it has 40 divisions in the army compared to India's 28; 7,660 MBT compared to India's 3,900; 18,000 artillery pieces compared to India's 10,000. In Navy, China has gone in for modernisation by 2020-25. It could have three aircraft carriers and 60 submarines including 10 nuclear compared to India's two or three aircraft carriers and 16–18 submarines with two nuclear armed only. In Air Power, its J-10 is supposed to be the equivalent of F-16 fighters of US. By 2020 it will have 2300 4th–5th Generation Combat Aircrafts compared to India's 750. In space warfare, it has already tested Anti-Satellite Missiles twice. It is also building Space Mines and even reportedly a Military Space Station.[21] All this said above establishes China's military build-up in its PLA in all its wings of Army, Navy, Air Force and Space.

The Chinese PLA Navy has an impressive arsenal with nine nuclear submarines with five ballistic and four attack types. It also has 48 conventional submarines, 29 destroyers, 51 frigates and 350 patrol vessels and fast attack crafts. Its missile capability with MaRV is also very high. It has already inducted an air craft carrier Varyug or Shi-Lang.[22]

MUMBAI ATTACK: LESSONS

By the early 2000s, it became obvious that India's conceptual settings were already out-of-date and failed to correspond to the contemporary international climate and Indian policy. *The Indian Maritime Doctrine*, published in 2004 and revised in 2009, became a corpus of fundamental principles identifying the use of naval power to achieve national policy goals. The Indian Navy's vision statement and a Roadmap for Transformation in 2006 and in 2007 is a document called 'Freedom to use the Seas.'

Since the November 26, 2008 attack on Mumbai from the sea by terrorists, allegedly supported by the Government of Pakistan, Government of India decided to improve its land and sea border monitoring capacity. It has done so by launching an all Weather Radar Imaging Satellite RISAT-II built by Israeli Aerospace Industry (IAI) in April, 2009 which enables close monitoring of land and sea borders. This was succeeded by RISAT – I, an indigenously built satellite which can determine under water submarines, aircrafts and movement of nuclear weapons.[23] However, with Pakistan acting like a client state of China, it may easily indirectly provoke India in case China does not want to do it directly. With China taking over management of Gwadar Port from the Port of Singapore Authority (PSA) this Gwadar Port will also become a base for Chinese Navy.

The Mumbai attack of November 2008 by Pakistani trained irregulars became the first time Pakistan was using irregulars for attacking India through the seas. The use of irregulars trained and sponsored by Pakistani military has been going on since 1947. It was in October, 1947 that Pakistanis sent irregulars in Kashmir along with their military officers in plain clothes. This led to the biggest airlift of troops in the world at that time and the valley of Kashmir was saved by the Indian Army. The Mumbai attack for India is comparable to the 9/11 attack in the US. This is so because in 9/11 the terrorists attacked the iconic World Trade Center (WTC) and the Pentagon in Washington. In India they attacked the iconic Taj and Oberoi Hotels and the Chhatrapati Shivaji Railway Station earlier known as Victoria Terminus in the heart of India's financial capital, Mumbai. However, it is ironic that no report or white paper has come out with regard to the attacks or India's preparedness. The only comment that came was from the Chief of Naval Staff who said that intelligence received by them prior to this attack was not actionable. It is strange that even many years after the Mumbai attack, no responsibility has been fixed for any lapse. The navy has, however, been made overall in charge of coastal security.

In fact, the Mumbai attacks of 2008 should be an eye opener vis-a-vis India's coastal security including that of Andaman & Nicobar Islands. As a matter of fact it was reported by very senior officers in Andaman & Nicobar Islands that Myanmar's fishermen who come to Andaman & Nicobar Islands to poach sea cucumbers from beaches have permanent fixed places in various locations of the islands where they keep their equipment, fuel, and spares hidden at some locations. A few of these locations have been discovered. This revelation is shocking as these fishermen are acting on behalf of big dealers. Soon the same locations can be misused for more serious incidents including terrorism.

Post the Mumbai terror attack of November 26, 2008, the navy was put in charge of overall national coastal security. Therefore, in its 2009 Maritime Doctrine, the navy subtly stresses on the "principles of war" and expanding it to include synergy and intelligence sharing. While it continues to cover the fundamental framework of the principle practices and procedures that govern the development and employment of military maritime power, the latest document makes a conscious effort to move forward from the commonalities of maritime thought as applicable to most sea faring nations and address India and its navy's specific concepts, concerns and development.

What are the options for India? India's options as seen today are to make strategic partnerships with its maritime neighbours on the east up to Japan and Australia and reinforce the Andaman & Nicobar Islands and in particular the Great Nicobar Island so that any provocation by China directly or indirectly can be retaliated by a naval exercise including blockade of Chinese ships at the western entrance of Straits of Malacca. India's existing good relations with its neighbours on the east including Bangladesh and Myanmar and Sri Lanka, its friendly relations with the US, need to be reinforced. Further to counter the Chinese Naval build up at Gwadar, India should seriously accept the offer of Vietnam for setting up a naval facility.

The AGNI V missile capable of 3,100 miles has been called by Defence Research & Development Organisation (DRDO) of India as an Inter-Continental Ballistic Missile (ICBM). It is capable of hitting Beijing from India and is considered a game changer in the Sino-India defence relationship. However, even after AGNI V, India remains at a disadvantage compared to China in military terms as it does not and nor it is likely to have in the near future the missile inventory backup that China has. In addition, China's anti-satellite tests done twice, shows its capability of destroying an enemy satellite in mid-air.[24]

With the acquisition of Akula to be renamed *INS Chakra* SSN Submarine from Russia on a 10 year lease, the third leg of the nuclear triad widely regarded as a most survivable mode of launching nuclear weapons from the sea is now in place. It is reported that similar submarines will be indigenously built. It is also reported that India is to get two more such submarines. These submarines will be assigned the prime role of anti-submarine warfare in company of Indian Navy's Aircraft Carrier. With a speed of 35 knots and deep diving capacity of 600 metres, it is a great asset, especially when armed with PJ-10 BrahMos, anti-ship cruise missiles.[25] Meanwhile, an indigenously developed nuclear power submarine—*INS Arihant* was launched in July, 2009 at the Indian Navy Dockyard at a cost of US$ 2.9 billion. It will go for sea trials and will be commissioned by 2015. Once successful, more such submarines will be developed in India. This will be India's first Ship Submersible Ballistic Nuclear Submarine (SSBNS). This is also capable of carrying nuclear missiles. This signifies a leap forward for the Indian Navy.[26]

History of Defence Establishment in Andaman & Nicobar Islands

The first military base set up in the Andaman & Nicobar Islands was by the IAF in Car Nicobar in 1956. This air strip was originally built by the Japanese during their occupation during World War II. On their departure, it was taken over by the Royal British Air Force (RAF) as a Staging Post with their air couriers touching Car Nicobar for refuelling on the way to Singapore. The RAF continued in Car Nicobar up to 1956 when they handed the Staging Post over to the IAF. It must be said to the credit of IAF that they maintained excellent relations with the tribals of Car Nicobar. In addition, over the years IAF has given air lifts to the entire football team of Car Nicobar to play in the Subroto Mukerji Tournament. They have turned out as national champions many times.

The Indian Navy opened its account in Andaman & Nicobar Islands in 1954 with commissioning of their base in Port Blair called *INS, Jarawa*. By 1972, the first infantry brigade of the Indian Army was also set up in Port Blair. This was upgraded to a brigade in 1991 when 108 Mountain Brigade was formed. In 1973, the Indian Navy opened up its account at Nancowry-Karmorta Islands of Nicobar Group with a base called *INS Kardip*. Nancowry and Karmorta are two Islands which are like two horse shoes facing each other with a deep water harbour in between. This is an outstandingly good location for India to keep its naval feet under protected waters. In 1978, the coastguards set up its first regional headquarter in Port Blair. Prior to this there was very little surveillance of these waters except for the IAF which used to do limited aerial surveillance. In 1985, the navy took over the airfield at Port Blair from the Airport Authority of India (AAI) and setup a naval air base called Utkrosh.

In 1985 again, the first station called COMDIS 10 was set up in Campbell Bay followed by COMDIS 9 set up in 1987 in Diglipur in north Andamans.

From 1981 to 1987, the Andaman & Nicobar Islands had the concept of a Fortress Commander which was headed by a naval admiral and the other two services came under his overall jurisdiction. In October, 2001 the Fortress Command concept was replaced by a Tri Command called Andaman & Nicobar Command (ANC). This was for the first time India had a joint command of the three Services in which there was a rotation of the Commander-in-Chief, Andaman & Nicobar (CINCAN) Andaman & Nicobar Islands from each of the Services.

Therefore, army, navy and air force get an equal opportunity to become CINCAN. It was also decided that when the CINCAN is not a naval officer the number two will remain the naval officer. The CINCAN also commands the Coastguard in Andaman & Nicobar. The role and functions of the CINCAN are to ensure the defence of Andaman & Nicobar Islands, that the eastern approach to Indian Ocean remains free from threat (both surface and aerial) for safe passage of own and friendly shipping, provides seamless security interface with all commands in the oceanic theatre of Bay of Bengal, Andaman Sea and Eastwards, protection of EEZ, ensure post defence and provide disaster aid. Two major roles that the ANC is performing are civil military interface and regional cooperation.

Abandonment of Policy of Benign Neglect and Masterly Inactivity by Defence—Unified Command Established in 2001

The Formation of a Unified Command on October 8, 2001 was a major step forward in giving shape to India's military preparedness and advance planning. In fact, this is the first Unified Command in the history of Indian Defence Forces and it appears to be a success. In the author's informal discussions with officers this pattern was acceptable to the three Services. Each wing of the Defence Services takes by turn the position of CINCAN, with the understanding that when the army or air force officer is CINCAN the number two would be a naval officer. This system has been accepted by the three Services. The Coast Guard also works under the CINCAN but is not a part of his office. The role and function of the joint command is:

- Defence of Andaman & Nicobar Islands
- Ensure eastern approaches to the Indian Ocean remain free from threat (surface and aerial) for safe passage of own and friendly shipping.
- Provide a seamless security interface with all commands of Indian Ocean Theatre of Bay of Bengal, Andaman Sea, Bay of Bengal and Eastwards.
- EEZ
- Ensure Coastal Defence
- Disaster Aid

A mention needs to be made of the Coast Guards in Andaman & Nicobar Islands. Set up in 1978 it celebrated its 36th anniversary on February 1, 2013. The role of coast guard in the islands is very crucial as it has to police the vast 2 million sq km of high seas under India's EEZ. The coast guard has been growing in India with 110 ships, 12 hovercrafts on order. By 2013, it should have 79 vessels and 57 aircrafts/helicopters. By 2020, the coastguard should have 20,000 men, 150 vessels, 150 aircrafts/helicopters. It however needs much better technology input to cover the vast EEZ of India by using Unmanned Aerial Vehicles (UAVs), balloons and satellites. The poor coordination between the Indian Navy and the Coast Guards has been commented upon by the Auditor &

Comptroller General (CAG) of India (Report No.7 of 2011-12) who has quoted the Parliamentary Standing Committee Report on defence (2008-09) (14th Lok Sabha – 36th Report) and has stated "events in the recent past have highlighted lack of coordination between navy and coast guards resulting in a national catastrophy. This is a serious observation which needs to be taken note of.

The concept of maritime domain awareness introduced in the Coast Guard Organisation involves a static sensor chain project with fitment of high end surveillance gadgets like Frequency Diversity (FD) Radars, Electro-Optic Sensors, WHF sets, MET equipment in Lighthouses at 36 locations including four in Andaman & Nicobar Islands.[27]

Importance of Nicobar Islands

The importance of Nicobar Islands in the present scenario should not be underestimated. While the Andaman Islands remain the area of main action as both the civil and military base are in these islands, the Nicobars need a much greater emphasis as they are near the Straits of Malacca close to international shipping lines. Good relations with Nicobarese tribals are also crucial. They have also proved to be an asset to the navy and other forces who have recruited them. They are keen also to join mainstream India.

Need for Greater Naval and Air Force Presence in Andaman & Nicobar Islands

Surveillance of India's territorial and economic zones is crucial to its security. India has today the threat of poachers, secessionists, terrorists and fishermen all together in various parts of Andaman & Nicobar Islands. There is a need for a much higher level of surveillance to ensure that any of the above do not exploit the situation and misuse India's uninhabited islands and waters. With a large number of islands and creeks it is not possible to send security personnel especially when only about 37 islands in the Andaman group are inhabited and another five islands of the Nicobar group are not inhabited. It is, therefore, essential that India may design a policy of surveillance which may utilise both civil and military sources including tourists and which may be economically more viable. Here, the question comes up as to how much can you guard these islands without economic activity.

Surveillance over the islands-use of technology: The mammoth task of surveillance over these islands is difficult to comprehend and implement. Also such surveillance can be very expensive. The navy, the air force, the coast guard and the marine police are all performing this task. However, to maintain a surveillance over 35,000 sq km of territorial waters and 6,00,000 sq km of economic zone is no easy task. Besides, it is also very expensive. However, technology does provide cheaper and better solutions. One such solution is to use UAVs. In this connection, it may be mentioned that the current US thinking on the subject of surveillance of their waters is the concept of Broad Area Maritime Surveillance (BAMS).[28] At a cost of US$ 1.16 billion the United States is developing a persistent maritime Intelligence, Surveillance and Reconnaissance (ISR) data collection and dissemination capability that fulfils the maritime war fighter's requirement for continuous battle-space awareness. Modern balloons equipped with cameras have also been deployed elsewhere. However, due to monsoon weather in this region, all such equipment will need to take into account adverse weather conditions.

Capt. Bob Dishman, programme manager for the US BAMS programme has stated that this represents the navy's largest investment in unmanned aircraft systems to date. The extraordinary efforts leading to this announcement have helped the BAMS UAS programme begin to develop a persistent surveillance capability never before available to the fleet.

India also needs a better aerial surveillance over Andaman & Nicobar Islands. A network of UAVs and balloons is perhaps an obvious choice.

With Kashmir and Tibet in stalemate and Pakistan becoming a close ally and a client state of China, what is it that India can do? India has basically one option, which is to redefine its maritime policy keeping in mind its advantage of having Andaman & Nicobar Islands—the forgotten islands. While the Indian military is aware of these issues, it is the government that is caught up in a time warp, confused thinking and focusing only on issues of pristine forests and environment. *While the environment of Andaman & Nicobar Islands is worth preserving and it can be done, a strategic opening of these islands is a must to make the world realise the assets belong to India.*

Civil-Military Interface

On the issue of civil-military interface, the earlier strict divisions are less and there is now greater cooperation at the training and operational level. For one, the Andaman & Nicobar Police has some common training programmes with them. During the author's stay in 1991-93 besides the social interface between the military and civil administrations, which was very good, the cooperation at the professional level was minimal because the civil and military work was very different from each other. This was because at that time it was felt that there was no need for it. The threat perception was minimal except for some poaching in which there was cooperation between the civil police, the coast guard and the navy. However, Andaman & Nicobar police and also the department of forests had no skills in swimming and scuba diving. Further neither the civil police nor the department of forests were sufficiently equipped for safeguarding the marine wealth.

Employment of local youth both tribal Nicobarese and non-tribals has been a great success in the defence forces, police and other government departments. Nicobarese have a general reputation of easy going 'Holchoo' a friendly name given to them by others. However, the defence authorities are pleased with them as they turned out to be very hard working after good and strict training.

Another good and interesting aspect that the author discovered during his visit was the interaction between the defence forces and the fishermen community. The navy had also provided the fishermen with some alarm which they could use in an emergency and also signal with it when they came across an unauthorised boat while fishing.

Besides humanitarian and disaster relief, the Civil-Military interface involves intelligence sharing with the local people, training of Andaman Police, recruitment camps, medical camps, distribution by Coast Guard, interaction with fishing community and medical camps in remote areas. These interactions have been extremely good and it keeps the defence forces in contact with the civil population promoting cordial relations. Medical camps have also had a good response.

THE FORWARD POLICY IN THE INDO-PACIFIC

Like in the 1950s when India adopted a "Forward Policy" in the North-East Frontier Agency (NEFA), India needs to have a new Forward Policy in its maritime domain in keeping with India's LEP of 1991. Indian defence forces appear to have already adopted a Forward Policy in the Indo-Pacific Region starting with a concept of Indian Far Eastern Command in the Andaman & Nicobar Islands which came into reality in 2001 as a Tri-Command described earlier in this chapter. With Car Nicobar as a full-fledged air force base and Campbell Bay in Great Nicobar Island as a new Naval Air Command, the strategic shift is getting implemented. Kamorta-Nancowry the deep sea and safe harbour in the Nicobars, is considered one of the best natural harbors in the world and is yet to be leveraged. Its future development will be watched with interest. The strategic location of these islands needs to be developed as a springboard for power projection in the region using both hard and soft power to complement each other. *India needs to convert the Malacca Dilemma of China into the Malacca Advantage of India and, therefore, there is a need for an integrated civil-defence policy in its maritime domain.*

NOTES

1. www.defence.gov/news/defence_strategy_guidance.pdf
2. C. Raja Mohan, *Indian Express*, December 21, 2012.
3. Asia's Democratic Security Diamond, *Mint* Special Issue, January 1, 2013.
4. Brahma Chellaney, *Asian Juggernaut: The Rise of China, India and Japan,* HarperCollins India, New Delhi, 2006, p.145.
5. Chris Debanshire, "China's 'String of Pearls' Strategy, *China Briefing*, March 18, 2009.

6. *Times of India,* January 2012.
7. Rajat Pandit and Sachin Parashar, "US-China woo India for control over Asia-Pacific", TNN, June 7, 2012.
8. *The Tribune,* Chandigarh, January 11, 1999.
9. *Asian Age,* August 30, 2012.
10. Bharat Karnad, *Asian Age,* August 30, 2012.
11. Rajiv Sikri, *Challenge and Strategy, Rethinking India's Foreign Policy,* Sage, New Delhi, 2009, p. 282.
12. Gaurang Bhatt, "A blueprint for a future Indian Navy," July 03, 2005 at www.htpp.// www.boloji.com/rt2/rt178.htm
13. "Indian Ocean: Navy Dominates Crucial Sea lanes", *Editorial, Business Standard,* September 11, 2012.
14. Raja Menon, "Stealth Queen – INS Chakra shows significance of Nuclear Attack Submarines", *Indian Express,* April 6, 2012.
15. Suman Sharma, "Navy Ready to Flex Muscle in South China Sea", *The Guardian,* December 4, 2011.
16. "China offers to build and fund", *The Daily Star,* September 28, 2012 at www.thedailystar.net/ newdesign/news-details.php
17. "Pakistan Ka Khudahafiz" at www.pakistankakhudahafiz.com/2012/05/06/iran-opens-chahbahar. Also see Rahul Bedi, "India begins use of Chahbahar Port in Iran despite international pressure", *The Telegraph,* April 12, 2013.
18. *Mail Today,* August 11, 2013.
19. *Vayu Aerospace & Defence Review,* November, 2012, p.24.
20. Shikha Aggarwal, "China's Naval Strategy: Strategic Evolution and Emerging Concept of Warfare", *Air Power Journal,* 7 (2), 2012.
21. Lt. Gen. Kamal Davar (Retd), *Vayu Aerospace & Defence Review,* January, 2013, pp. 112-117.
22. Rakesh Kaul, "PLA Navy in 21st Century: Development and Implications", *Defence & Diplomacy Journal,* 1 (2), Jan-March 2012. See also Jayadev Ranade, "China expanding maritime ambition and growing naval power", *Issue Brief,* August 29, 2011.
23. Hari Saran, *Defence & Security Alert,* December, 2012.
24. A. Vinod Kumar, "Does India really need ICBMs?" *Vayu Aerospace & Defence Review,* January 2013, pp.120-121
25. "Third leg of the nuclear triad : Arrival of NERPE", *Vayu Aerospace & Defence Review,* November 2012, pp. 52-54.
26. "Indian Defence Consultants", an IDC Report of August, 2012. See www. allmilitaryweapons.com/2011/01/arihant-classsubmarine and also www.indiadefence.com/ arihant.htna.
27. "Indian Coast Guard's Coastal Security Surveillance: Chanakya Aerospace", *Defence & Maritime Review,* February 2013.
28. BAMS at www.as.northropgrunnan.an/productivity/bams

CHAPTER 9

Leveraging Soft Power: A Tourism Policy for Andaman & Nicobar Islands that Compliments the Forward Policy

"The world's biggest power is the youth and beauty of a woman."

—*Chanakya*

In this chapter an attempt has been made to show that while India may build up the Andaman & Nicobar Islands in military terms, if India can attract people to these islands from abroad by creating world class eco-tourism resorts with top class amenities, keeping in mind all environmental constraints, India would dramatically change the perception of both Indians and foreigners with regard to India's reach in the Indian Ocean. India needs to leverage this soft power.

"Soft Power" as a concept was developed by Joseph Nye of Harvard University who described it as ability to extract and cooperate rather than coerce, use force or give money as a means of persuasion. In his book *"Soft Power—The Means to Success in World Politics, 2004"* Nye says that "Seduction is always more attractive then coercion and many values like Democracy, Human Rights and Individual Opportunities are deeply seductive." Therefore, it is better to co-opt people than coerce them. Soft Power is not merely the same as influence. Soft power is also more than just persuasion. It is the ability to attract and attraction often leads to acquiescence.[1]

COMPLEMENTARITY BETWEEN TOURISM AND SECURITY

Tourism can be a means to display India's soft power. Similar to what Bollywood films have done to India's image abroad, by encouraging high end tourism into Andaman & Nicobar Islands from foreign nations with direct flights from South East Asia, India will display its soft power. Such display of soft power in Andaman & Nicobar Islands will complement the prowess which India should project in the Bay of Bengal. Tourism as a weapon of soft power can be used to compliment the military. It will make other countries, non-state actors and poachers realise and appreciate that India has effective civil jurisdiction right up to Straits of Malacca. Mere show of naval strength is not the best manner of befriending other nations. Opening these islands with a welcome will make them realise that Bay of Bengal is truly Indian but all are welcome to visit. This display of soft power will, however, have to be conditional to environmental considerations of a fragile eco-system and the Supreme Court's order.

It is ironic that while the defence apparatus in the 1970s and 1980s did not allow tourism to come up in these islands for fear of 'foreign power', in the 1990's they turned this hypothesis upside down and realised that tourism can be a good source of intelligence. With 572 islands and islets and a large EEZ to guard against poachers, pirates, non-state actors, it is a near impossible and very expensive task as only about three dozen of these islands are inhabited. Therefore, a strategy of tourism development with security and environmental sustainability in mind needs to be evolved. This is possible when tourism resorts are developed with specific locations which command a position for surveillance and are not put together at one or two islands as is being done now. Similarly, tourism requires highly skilled and trained staff coming out of hotel management institutes. Some such locals or others can be picked and trained by security agencies for providing accurate intelligence also while they work. Therefore, tourism and security should be intertwined to achieve the best results.

Complementarity between Environment and Security

Over time India's EEZ and islands have been misused by fishermen coming from countries like Thailand, Myanmar and beyond violating its marine wealth and forest environment. These encroachments upon Indian territories were minor in nature as these fishermen normally came in small boats and would set up a temporary camp in a remote island and go away when their boat could not take any more fish, sea cucumbers, coral etc. They would certainly go back before the sea got rough during the monsoons. Sometimes, however they would come in distress to a habitated island to seek refuge, food or water. Most of the times villagers would help them with food and water and they would go away, especially in the Nicobar Islands as Nicobarese tribals are simple and helpful people. However, once in a while they would come onto an inhabited island in distress and land up in police custody. They would be put in jails while their ships/boats would be confiscated. When a critical mass of such prisoners had collected in Port Blair, their country would be informed through the Foreign Ministry and the country concerned would send an aircraft or boat to have them collected. However, this arrangement was possible in case of innocent fishermen poaching in Indian waters getting into distress due to breakdown of their boat or bad weather. However, over time poaching got more organised with 'mother ships' waiting on the High Seas within India's EEZ to collect the fish and other marine products from their smaller ships. But increasingly there are many cases where these islands started getting used by terrorists and other organisations for purposes of arms, drug transhipments or any such similar activity. Leaving these islands alone with poor surveillance is more dangerous than using them. It is, therefore, necessary to have a policy of proper surveillance which could also be cost effective.

As already stated in chapter 2, this theft of marine products and environmental damage could be worth US$ 100-200 million.[2] Prevention of these activities could, perhaps, be achieved by having a tourism policy which at one end would support and compliment the security issues and on the other end take care of environmental issues.

TRADE-OFF BETWEEN SECURITY AND ENVIRONMENT

At times there is also a need for government to consider the trade-off between security and environment. For example, Narcondum Island in the Andaman Group is a strategically located uninhabited extinct volcano. The defence forces want a radar located in this island due to its specific location. Jutting out in the open sea it provides wide area coverage that no other island can give. However, the Ministry of Environment & Forests (MoEF), without appreciating the strategic location of this island has taken a stand that fixing radars will disturb the small number of Hornbill Birds which are endemic to this Island. The National Security Advisor has also maintained silence. National security concerns cannot be given such secondary treatments. Does India need to wait for an unforeseen incident to take place before the blame is put on MoEF for being rigid and not giving permission?

PRESENT CIVIL POLICY—ENVIRONMENTAL ISSUES DOMINATE

India inherited these islands from the British 60 years back, but kept them isolated and undeveloped. The MHA which was directly responsible for the development of these islands did not encourage any major improvement. Post-independence, the political prisoners were released and penal settlement abolished. The iconic "Cellular Jail" building continued as a local jail till it was declared a national monument. The policy of government towards these islands was to maintain the minimum needed to keep sovereignty over them. Subsidised shipping for the islanders to keep a link with mainland, a bit of inter-island shipping, re-settlement of a few ex-military soldier families in the Great Nicobar Island to keep vigil, an attempt to grow rubber in Katchal Island of Nicobar and re-settlement of east Bengali refugees in the Andaman Islands were some steps taken. The tribal policy to keep the tribals away from exploitation by non-tribals followed by the British in these islands was retained. All other proposals to develop these islands like a free port in Great Nicobar Islands or opening a medical college in Port Blair was discouraged.

SUPREME COURT OF INDIA AND ENVIRONMENT OF ANDAMAN & NICOBAR ISLANDS

Over time unauthorised immigration took place with unimaginative and uncontrolled growth. As a result some environmentalists took up the matter in courts. The Supreme Court of India in a Public Interest Litigation (PIL) delivered a landmark judgment. The PIL was filed in 1995 by Society for Andaman and Nicobar Environment (SANE), Kalpavriksh an NGO and Bombay Natural History Society (BNHS).[3] As SANE leader, Mr. Samir Acharya stated, "this order is like a boon to us; granting all our prayers, the issues we had been working for during the last decade. The order if and when implemented, will drastically alter both the development and conservation scenario in the islands and one hopes will make the islands a much better place for the islanders to live in and will protect this biodiversity hotspot for the nature lovers across the world."

Professor Shekhar Singh of Indian Institute of Public Administration (IIPA) was appointed by the Supreme Court to give a report on this issue. On submitting his report, the Supreme Court accepted most of his recommendations. The major recommendations mentioned in the report and accepted by the Supreme Court are:

(a) Closure of two stretches of the Andaman Trunk Road
(b) Making locally available raw material the main medium of construction
(c) Promoting pulverised stone as a sand substitute
(d) No felling of trees for whatsoever reasons or justification should be carried out to supply to, or to meet the raw material requirement of, plywood, veneer, blackboard, match stick or any other such wood based units except to local small-scale units (including saw mills) solely for meeting the local requirement for sawn timber and other wood based products.
(e) There should be a complete ban on the establishment of any new wood based unit for the next 10 years.
(f) All existing small-scale wood based units (saw mills) should be relocated within industrial estates or, where industrial estates are not feasible, in locations contiguous to forest offices or otherwise convenient for the forest department to monitor. This relocation should be completed within one year, after which the non-complying saw mills should be closed down.
(g) No subsidy of any type, including transport subsidy, should be given to any wood based unit.
(h) Existing medium and large scale wood based industries (including plywood, veneer, and match industries) can be allowed to function provided they import their entire requirement of wood and other forest based raw materials from the mainland or from abroad. No subsidies should be allowed to them.
(i) No timber, either as logs or as sawn timber or plywood/veneer, or in any other form, should be transported out of the islands through any means whatsoever.
(j) In order to prevent any further encroachments and rampant immigration, the administration should, within three months, regulate the entry of

people to the islands by having the islands declared as an inner line area and by imposing relevant restrictions under section 3 and other provisions of the Environment (Protection) Act of 1986. In accordance with this, non-residents entering the islands should have to invariably register themselves so that those who do not return to the mainland within a reasonable time can be traced and, where they have illegally encroached on land, can be evicted from these encroachments at the earliest. In addition, entry to the more vulnerable and forested areas of the islands should be restricted.

(k) Once this regulation is in position, the administration should in a time bound manner issue identity cards to all the residents so that there is no gap in the period of identification and issuance of ID cards. This would ensure that fresh illegal encroachers are easily identified. Subsidised travel to the islands should, once identity cards have been issued, be available only to bonafide residents of the islands.

(l) The extraction of sand should be phased out and no further extension should be granted after the current extension is over on September 30, 2002.

(m) As already mentioned earlier, alternate material for construction, including treated bamboo and soft woods, should be encouraged as this is less damaging to the environment and safer in case of an earth quake. Stone dust should be utilised where use of concrete is essential.

Most of the items of the report have been implemented. However, the contentious portion regarding closure of Andaman Trunk Road has not been implemented so far.

Environmental Concerns and Development

Environmental concern is another major issue which is coming in conflict with development. The environment policy towards the Andaman & Nicobar Islands has not allowed any activity so that the pristine forests and the coral reefs are not disturbed. The Supreme Court's orders of 2001 to control depletion of forests in Andaman & Nicobar Islands is a good intention, but had led to some complications. For example, they are hardly any new wooden buildings due to the ban imposed on cutting of forests. All the new construction is in cement concrete which not only looks ugly but also uses sand which depletes the beaches. As a result there is now a restriction on extracting sand from beaches, which in any case is saline in nature and not good for construction. Sand is now being imported from mainland along with wood with a transport subsidy. With sufficient wood available within the forests of Andaman & Nicobar Islands, it is really not necessary to import wood or sand for local construction.

Another example of environment concern is with regard to the airstrip at

Port Blair. After the British left these islands in 1947 the airstrip at Car Nicobar went to the air force and the other at Port Blair to the navy after initially being with the civil side. With the introduction of Boeing 737s a direct flight to Port Blair from mainland India (Kolkata) started from 1976-77. Although, the Boeing aircraft was inducted into service, only senior commanders were sent as the airstrip was short, unidirectional and with a hill feature at one end. As a result, the aircraft could only land with a load penalty and that too before noon due to strong winds. This inadequacy of the airfield was felt by the civil administration but the navy was indifferent to it as they had small aircrafts for which the existing 6,000 ft of length was adequate.

It was in 1991-92 that discussions were held between the Indian Navy and the Andaman & Nicobar Administration to facilitate the civil administration to extend the airstrip to accommodate bigger jet aircrafts to land without load penalty. The navy agreed so long as the civil administration was prepared to fund it. Consequently, it was found that the airstrip could be extended to 11,000 ft without much difficulty and costs, as levelling of earthwork required could be done in such a way to extend it up to 11,000 ft. This was, perhaps, one major case where the civil authorities and the military were able to complement each other's requirement for the common good.

It was, at this stage, that the MoEF of Government of India became hesitant to give environmental approval. The committee on Environmental Impact consisting of experts examined the report on environmental impact due to extension of the airstrip from 6,000 ft to 11,000 ft and found nothing objectionable but initially refused permission on the grounds that a long airstrip will invite bigger aircrafts, which in turn will bring in more tourists. *To them tourism by itself was anti-environment.* It was argued that if a proper type of eco-sensitive tourism is promoted it will lead to greater environmental protection. The degradation of environment is already taking place by uncontrolled in-migration into these islands from mainland India, by people who find better living conditions and also are prepared to squat in the forests of Andaman's, cut wood illegally and spoil the environment. After much discussion, the proposal was cleared and work started on the airstrip. This anecdotal reference shows that the attitude of the environmentalists then towards tourism was very biased.

As an another anecdotal reference when the author was leaving for his posting to Andaman & Nicobar Islands, he met the Minister of State, Home Affairs and the Commerce Secretary with regard to his assignment. Both wished him well and expressed their apprehension because they felt that the environment lobby in India will not allow any development.

Island Development Authority (IDA)

The IDA was formed in 1986 after the visit of Prime Minister Rajiv Gandhi to these islands, by a government order in which the Prime Minister was the Chairman with about a dozen Cabinet Ministers including ministers of home and defence as members. From its formation in 1986 it has had just over a dozen meetings and produced some reports which were hardly implemented. It is housed within the Planning Commission. It is unfortunate that such a high level authority has achieved so little. It has certainly not looked into the strategic and environmental aspects of these islands even though defence and home ministers were members. The policy of Benign Neglect and Masterly Inactivity continued in spite of IDA.

IDA had set up a sub-committee under the MHA to look into the aspect of security considerations of movement of population into these islands. The sub-group in its report had suggested a two pronged strategy:

1. to neutralise the factors that have led to the influx (viz impression regarding availability of land, job opportunities, and better economic conditions etc).
2. to make ingress of unwanted people into the islands difficult.
   The main issue regarding influx into these islands are twofold and need to be addressed in its proper perspective;
   Since there is inadequate security and surveillance of these islands by the civil administrations and coast guards, there is illegal migration from neighbouring countries especially Myanmar, Bangladesh and also the very poor from the Indian Mainland. The wages in the islands are generally higher than of mainland which is a great attraction. These migrants move into remote islands through ordinary boats and hide in the forests. The forests offer them a better security and life than what they were leading in their country. Further, since these islands are practically inaccessible even to the Andaman & Nicobar Islands administration, they are not detected. Some of them also merged with the settlers in some of the habited islands as there are common racial problems. Keeping the uninhabited islands closed for tourism does not guarantee stoppage of in-migration.

Second, the in-migration from mainland India has to be seen in the light of our shipping policy for mainland-island service. A huge subsidy is being given to passengers, especially deck/bunk passengers. The ticket charge of a mainlander coming into the island as a bunk passenger is only Rs.1,960/-. This carries an average subsidy of nearly Rs.10,000/- per passenger. This is a major incentive for the poor and the marginalised in the mainland to travel as bunk passengers and try their luck in settling down in the Andamans. There has been little thinking on this issue and even less policy making. Not much has been achieved by IDA reports. However, a differential fare with subsidy has been introduced for islanders and for mainlanders.

ENVIRONMENT AND TOURISM: THE SOFT OPTION

The Report of Prof. Shekhar Singh on Environmental Issues of Andaman & Nicobar Islands in so far as tourism is concerned states:

> "Eco-tourism: The landscape of Andaman & Nicobar Islands has good potential for eco-tourism: Interpretation Centres, camping facilities, bird watching, cruise in the creeks and trekking programmes should be provided under eco-tourism development. Rich flora and fauna sites could be added attractions for tourism in the islands. Potential for *low volume, high value eco-tourism* aimed at promoting education and appreciation of nature should be exploited. It is important to check growing commercialisation of eco-tourism through introduction of environment audit system."

It would, therefore be correct to say that the Supreme Court judgment gives a direction to tourism which is eco-tourism and in that it qualifies that it should be "low volume—high value". However, the present tourism policy followed by Andaman & Nicobar Islands has not taken into account the "low volume—high value" tourism concept.

Tourism has an outstanding potential in these islands as there are very few archipelagos left undisturbed in the world. It also has excellent airfields and is close to South East Asia. It was the MoD in the 1980s which did not allow tourism to grow in the islands due to fear of security. They changed their views by early 1990s but by that time MoEF became the protector of these islands. Today, eco-tourism sites with built in environmental safeguards are a major attraction and are found in all parts of the world. The business of eco-tourism is to sell environment in its full beauty and not allow it to be degraded. In the US, the National Park Services (NPS) are well known to provide excellent facilities for eco-tourism which are very popular but at the same time take into account environmental safeguards. Over 6.2 million tourists visited the national parks of US in 2007.[4]

Of late, even leading and respectable Indian magazines like *India Today* have condemned some acts of over enthusiasm by MoEF and described self-proclaimed over-enthusiastic environmentalists as *green terrorists.* There is also a need to review the various amendments carried out in the Andaman & Nicobar Islands under environment to ensure that strategic and developments issues are not sacrificed in the garb of environmental protection.[5] However, the author fully supports that the existing dense forest cover and the coral reefs of the islands must be fully protected.

WHY TOURISM?

(a) Risk of Uninhabited Islands in Present Scenario

Keeping the islands locked up is like keeping a house locked up. It invites burglars. Out of 572 islands and islets/rocks only 37 are inhabited and out of these only

13 are with settled population and the rest with military/police personnel.

It is necessary that India should show greater occupancy of the uninhabited islands to establish its actual presence. This is in spite of the fact that about 90 per cent of the land mass is declared forest and some islands are entirely declared as forests. In view of the fact that land is not available in these islands to settle new population which in any case would be an environmental disaster, the only way out is to allow some eco-tourism facilities. This will also provide additional safeguards to environmental protection. The best way will be to have up market eco-tourist hotels in some of these islands mainly on the coastal fringe run under the supervision of the Forest Department (where revenue land is not available). Many islands which may have very good beaches do not have fresh water. However, this issue can be resolved by various means. Incidentally, Chinese, who claim 9,300 islands in South and East China Seas, have 6500 uninhabited islands. They have conducted island census and passed a legislation called Law of Island Protection on March 1, 2010 for better island protection and management of uninhabited islands.[6]

In an alarmist article by M.H. Ahsan, the potential of a Kargil type foreign invasion of Andaman & Nicobar Islands has been mentioned, as already over 50,000 illegal immigrants are settled in various islands. He has suggested that an inspired takeover of some of the islands should not be ruled out. With Coco Island already under control of the Chinese with Myanmarese sovereignty it is possible that some foreign nationals could take over some more islands in the northern region of Andamans. It is stated in this article that Chinese are encouraging Myanmarese to take up residence in the Andamans.[7]

The Hon'ble Supreme Court in its order, while keeping these islands green cover has allowed "low volume—high value" eco-tourism to come up. The security scenario having undergone a change with terrorists having their own ships, human trafficking by boats taking place in the Bay of Bengal, theft of Sea Cucumber from the beaches and sands of Andaman & Nicobar Islands taking place by organised syndicates, there is a need to take a fresh view of these islands from a security and strategic point of view.

(b) Eco-Tourism as a Protector of Environment

The real eco-tourism of these islands lies in its fabulous coral wealth and the big fish which will attract scuba divers and deep sea anglers from all over the world. Of course, the eco-system of these islands is fragile and needs careful management. This means that limited tourism can flourish in these islands without necessarily opening the hinterland.

The sport of scuba diving is a major specialised tourist attraction. Only in a few places in the world coral reefs are available as they have to be within a specific water temperature zone. Andaman & Nicobar Islands have considerable underwater corals and of good quality. However, the Andaman & Nicobar Administration has really not understood the value of these corals for tourism promotion. Often divers and scuba diving centres report damages caused by theft of corals. Connivance of local authorities in such activities cannot be ruled out. Even the Indian environmentalists have not understood the advantages of scuba diving as a sport as it is a lever for environmental protection. This sport requires preservation of marine environment and corals and therefore, scuba divers always report damages to coral reefs. This is similar to wildlife tour operators who keep an eye on poachers. A Scuba Diving Society with the Professional Association of Diving Instructors (PADI) was started by the administration in 1992-93 to train police and forest officers amongst others but was later closed down due to indifference. Now only a few private diving schools operate for tourists charging much higher rates than neighbouring Phuket with lesser facilities.

United Nations Development Programme (UNDP) Report on Development Strategy for Environmentally Sustainable Tourism in the Andamans (1996)

In order to meet the objections of 'environmentalists' a seminar was held in Port Blair by the Administration on the 'Environmentally Sustainable Tourism Policy for Andaman & Nicobar Islands' in 1992. The outcome of this seminar was that UNDP whose Resident Representative also attended the seminar, offered to prepare a report on the same subject. Initially, the preparation of such a report was resisted by MoEF and surprisingly, also by the Tourism Ministry but was finally approved. A detailed report on the subject was then prepared by World Tourism Organisation (WTO) under UNDP funding. However, this report has never been implemented and is gathering dust in Port Blair. The author managed to salvage it from the archives of the Port Blair Secretariat.

The UNDP along with WTO submitted the Report on the subject in August 1966. The consultant chosen by UNDP was Shankland Cox Entec, a consultancy based in Hong Kong and UK. The report is in six volumes and goes into previous literature, draft perspective master plan for Tourism for Andamans prepared by the administration, its views on it and the various laws/rules in India pertaining to environment issues. It goes into the issues of coastal regulation, national parks, protected forests, reserve forests, development areas, marine parks and crocodile sanctuaries. There are today 91 wildlife sanctuaries in Andaman Islands covering 456 square km of which 83 of them cover entire islands, notably Sir Hugh Ross, Cinque, North and South Brother, Bluff, Spike, Ross and Latouche. The report also describes threatened species like Olive Ridley Turtles at Cinque Island, Olive Ridley at Cuthbert Bay, Green and Olive Ridley at western coast of Rutland Island.

The UNDP report also identifies five threats to the environment which need to be examined. These are degradation of forests through logging and encroachment, quarrying of sand, discharge of pollutants into sea, erosion of beaches, sedimentation and subsequent degradation of corals and poaching activities. Such degradation continues even now as steps taken to stop it are inadequate.

Nils Finn Munch-Petersen who had submitted the preliminary project formulation framework for UNDP in 1992 had stated that "Present Trends in International Tourism Market indicates that travellers comprising of upper sections of the market are becoming more sophisticated and search for destinations that not only offer sun, sand and entertainment.... Diving, sports, fishing and nature oriented tourism (Eco Tourism) comprise significant special interest in the market". He further states "*In Tourism Industry, down market drives out the up market*". He gives the example of Bhutan and Galapagos as up market, Maldives as mid-market and a planned tourism area, while Nepal was an example of unplanned tourism. He emphasised the need and importance for planned tourism development as "well planned tourism may be a vehicle for growth". In this context, he further states that "*Andaman & Nicobar Islands are dangerously close to defining themselves as a down market destination in the future.*"[8] The report has gone into details of tourism sites like grading of beaches with sand quality, water, gradient and character, marine parks, national parks and sanctuaries with area plant and wildlife available. It has also identified potential markets. The UNDP report on Environmentally Sustainable Tourism Policy carried out under supervision of the WTO has been ignored by the Andaman & Nicobar Administration.[9]

However, Andaman Islands as also Nicobar Islands can become international high end tourist destinations if full environment safeguards are introduced and implemented. What is happening at present is that neither a policy towards environmentally sustainable tourism nor any policy to integrate tourism with strategic vision is being followed. The shipping services from mainland to Port Blair are causing more damage to the environment because they are encouraging in-migration into these islands. A subsidised policy of ship fares means an encouragement to mainlanders to come to these islands for settlement. On the contrary, free pricing of air tickets has made these islands too expensive for even upper end tourists from mainland India who prefer to go to Thailand, Malaysia or Singapore rather than come to these islands. There is a serious need to examine the policy towards connecting these islands to mainland and to foreign destinations at a reasonable cost to attract tourists.

Amitabh Kant, a well-known tourism expert and policy maker in India, in his book *Branding India* states that Andaman & Nicobar Islands attract back packers who come by boat to these islands "a single bag packer consumes a total subsidy of Rs.12,000 whereas he spends only Rs.9,000 during his stay in the islands.... The upscale tourist spends US$ 1,500 or more during one week's stay as compared to US$ 200 spent by a bag packer. From both the yield as well as ecological perspective, it is necessary to promote high value tourism to provide an impetus for growth of tourism in the islands". He further states "a network of world class resorts with high quality diving and water resorts, will make the Andamans the most sought after destination in the world". He also states that Shekhar Singh's report which has been upheld by the Supreme Court, has already recommended that tented accommodation which can be dismantled should be encouraged. He further recommends that travel to these islands be made easier. A visa holder should not be asked to take a restricted area permit on arrival and permit for investors and employees should be issued for a period of five years.

The last major study carried out on Andaman & Nicobar Islands was in 2003 by AF Ferguson on Tourism and Environmental issues of Andaman & Nicobar Islands. The salient issues of this study are the following:

> "Andaman & Nicobar, by virtue of their location holds security considerations for the country. Naval security already imposes restrictions on entry and movement of foreigners. The proposal to set up the Strategic Nuclear Command (SNC) and base all air and sea submarines at Andaman & Nicobar Islands would take A&N into the 'critical security zone" and impact the entry of both domestic and foreign tourists".
>
> This factor has been assumed by the study but neither verified nor consulted with the defence authorities.
>
> The Supreme Court ruling on banning tree felling and touching on a variety of related aspects will similarly limit avenues of tourism development. The key points of the ruling include:

SC Ruling	Impact on Tourism
Banning of felling of trees in A&N except in designated and used forest areas and that too for local consumption.	This has unfortunately led to shortage of wood and has been replaced by concrete structures which are neither aesthetically pleasing nor long lasting because of salinity in local sand. Salinity in sand causes rusting and reduces life of buildings. With ban on extraction of local sand things have become worse and now sand is being imported from mainland India.
Regulate entry of people into islands by imposing relevant restrictions under Sec. (3) and other provisions of Environment Protection Act.	While entry of foreign tourists is restricted, no restriction has been imposed on entry of Indians from mainland who then settle down and seek local certificates.
Ban on extraction of sand. No concrete/permanent infrastructure for tourism in the islands	This has led to import of sand from mainland India. Even with subsidised shipping there has been a major increase in cost of construction.

The restriction on permanent construction, even wooden, for tourism area is unnecessary and needs to be revised. Local forest industry has sufficient wood available within their accepted principle of revival and restoration and therefore, this order needs revision. Export of wood from these islands, which has been banned, is acceptable but within the islands use of local wood should be encouraged instead of use of cement concrete used as building material.

A major lacuna of this study as well in the Supreme Court order has been that there has been no interaction with the defence authorities. The islands are not only environmentally fragile but sensitive from a security perspective. The Supreme Court has not consulted defence and security agencies in passing this order.

Further, this study has not considered all the islands, specially the far off remote islands where development of a tourist resort to show presence is important. This can be considered as a security requirement where tourists will compliment security and enhance Indian presence. This will also provide a cheaper option than having a police post. In a couple of remote islands the police has opened posts with a few men. A special ship goes every couple of months to provide rations etc. to the men posted. The expenditure on this is substantial and can be saved. A comparison can be made with the strategy followed by Government of India in the 1970s when they settled 300 ex-servicemen with families in then isolated Great Nicobar Island for securing the far off territory. In a similar manner, India should now open up tourism resorts in remote islands to exhibit its actual presence without permitting any new settlements. This will also provide much needed surveillance without additional cost of security setup.

During the Author's discussions with Lt. Governor of Andaman & Nicobar Islands and the Commander-in-Chief of Andaman and Nicobar Tri Command (CINCAN) there appeared to be openness on the idea of tourism in remote and uninhabited islands. Further, it was felt that there is a need to show presence in some uninhabited islands. This can be best achieved if India allows some eco-friendly resorts of three, four or five star status to come up in selected location with all environmental safeguards including of waste disposal etc. Few of these resorts may even require some incentives or subsidies to open up. Tourism and Forest Departments of Andaman & Nicobar Islands may consider such a scheme in consultation with defence authorities. With amphibious aircrafts, communications to such cut off and remote islands should not be a problem, especially during good weather. Already one such aircraft is taking tourists to a few destinations.

Another aspect which has been mentioned earlier is the stand taken by Government of India to not to allow uninhabited islands for development of tourism. It was a policy driven by the Intelligence Bureau of MHA not to allow opening of uninhabited islands for tourism under a mistaken belief that tourists and foreign tourists, in particular, can be a liability rather than an asset. When Madhavrao Scindia visited the Andaman Islands in 1992-93 as Minister of Tourism he found it very difficult to convince the IB that there is a need to open up uninhabited islands to foreign tourists. Maldives in the Indian Ocean had taken a diametrically opposite view and did not allow foreign tourists in their islands where there was a settled population in order to avoid conflict of cultures. Instead, they allotted full islands to well-known Resort Hotels who have established credentials as eco-friendly hotels on payment of royalty.

There is very little appreciation in India of the fact that its marine wealth is getting poached from its EEZ running into a couple of hundred million dollars. With poaching becoming sophisticated with mother ships and strollers with long nets which can collect huge quantities in a single season, the wealth of India's EEZ is getting eroded.

Professor Aprajit Biswas of Centre of African Studies, University of Mumbai in an article on Small Arms and Drug Trafficking in the IOR has shown how Andaman & Nicobar Islands has been used by drug traffickers, ISI of Pakistan and LTTE of Sri Lanka. The potential complementarity between security, environment and tourism needs to be studied in a holistic manner for Andaman & Nicobar Islands. While security is paramount but environmental protection is equally important. There is a need to fine tune the meeting ground of security and environment and shows how controlled eco-tourism can complement the needs of security and environment of these islands. Once security becomes lax, as it is today, with insufficient surveillance over the 572 islands and islets, the encroachment that starts to take place without the knowledge of the authorities by illegal immigrants leads to degradation of forests and environment. Since many of these islands and islets are not visited by the government authorities for years there is no way of finding out the encroachment. The lower functionaries of government, be it tehsildars of revenue department or forest inspectors do not have any independent means of transport between islands and activities on some uninhabited islands goes unreported. The example of Myanamarese fishermen collecting sea cucumbers illegally in these islands even these days and having permanent hideouts for spares and equipment in uninhabited islands has been mentioned earlier. Such hideouts are serious security threats. While the MHA remains conservative, the military has now realised that opening the islands to tourism is advantageous from a security point of view. There is a need to reconcile these two views.

The degradation done by illegal immigrants and low end tourists is far more damaging than that done by high end tourists. This is so because high value tourists are far more eco-conscious than low value tourists or illegal immigrants and can be better regulated. Further, low end hostels, one or two star hotels do not have the facilities, funds or even the desire to manage sewage and waste which is necessary. Further, locating resorts in inhabited islands can easily lead to conflict of cultures and its consequences. Creating high-end resorts in uninhabited islands will have its virtues and potential intelligence gathering to ensure that nothing anti-national or illegal happens.

It is unfortunate that the existing master plan of 2003 is a very restricted one and has considered only the following islands. The locations covered as part of the study included only:

- Port Blair
- Havelock
- Baratang
- Rangat
- Mayabunder
- Diglipur
- Little Andaman
- Nicobar District

The study covered hitherto uncovered destinations like Little Andaman, Car Nicobar, Katchal and Great Nicobar.

Environment Conundrum becoming a Deterrent to Security and Tourism

Two recent issues show how powers provided under Environment Protection Acts have become a deterrent to security and tourism. First is the case of Narcondum Island (already discussed earlier), where the navy has been refused from setting up a radar due to a population of about 300 Hornbill birds which are, perhaps, endemic to the island. The second is the case of land allotment to a leading Five Star group for a resort in Havelock Island under a duly approved scheme and with proper process. Having got the land for the resort they are unable to do anything with it as the rules regarding coastal regulation changed which makes it difficult for them to construct. When the tender was issued rules provided for no construction up to 250 metres of high tide line. After the award of the tender, the rules changed and disallowed any construction up to 500 metres of high tide line. This will lead to respectable hoteliers with a good and environment friendly record shying away and unscrupulous entrepreneurs taking over. Inconsistency of government policy and frequent changes in it is of course the bane of India's economic model and applies to Andaman &Nicobar Islands also.

Environmental Issues

There are 27 forest and environment related legislations/regulations/notifications/ plans etc. applicable in the Andaman & Nicobar Islands which are as follows:

The rules, regulations, instructions, manuals and records, held by it or under its control or used by its employees for discharging its functions.

Department of Environment and Forests of ANI is primarily concerned with the implementation of policies and programmes relating to conservation of bio-diversity, forests and wildlife for enhancement of human well-being. The objectives of the Department of Environment and Forests, A&N Administration are supported by legislative and regulatory measures aimed at the preservation, conservation and protection of the forest and environment. The important legislations are:

(i) The Indian Forest Act, 1927.
(ii) The Andaman & Nicobar Islands Fisheries Regulation, 1938.
(iii) The Andaman & Nicobar Islands (Protection of Aboriginal Tribes) Regulation, 1956.
(iv) Andaman & Nicobar Islands Forest Produce Transit Rules, 1966.
(v) Public Premises (Eviction of Unauthorised Occupants) Act, 1971.
(vi) Public Premises (Eviction of Unauthorised Occupants) Rules, 1971.
(vii) The Wildlife (Protection) Act, 1972.
(viii) The Wildlife (Protection) (Andaman & Nicobar Islands) Rules, 1973.
(ix) The Andaman & Nicobar Forest Department Code, 1973.
(x) The Andaman & Nicobar Islands (Wildlife Transit) Rules, 1976.
(xi) The Forest (Conservation) Act, 1980.
(xii) The Environment (Protection) Act, 1986.
(xiii) Andaman & Nicobar Islands Protected Forests Rules, 1986.
(xiv) The National Forest Policy, 1988.
(xv) The Coastal Regulation Zone Notification of 1991.
(xvi) Environmental Impact Assessment Notification, 1994.
(xvii) National Eco-tourism Policy, 1998.
(xviii) National Forestry Action Plan (NFAP), 1999.
(xix) National Forestry Research Plan (NFRP), 2000.
(xx) The Coimbatore Charter, 2001.
(xxi) National Wild life Action Plan, 2002.
(xxii) The Biological Diversity Act, 2002.
(xxiii) Forest (Conservation) Rules, 2003.
(xxiv) The Biological Diversity Rules, 2004.
(xxv) Resolution on Joint Forest Management, 2005.
(xxvi) A&N UT Biodiversity Strategy and Action Plan, 2005.

Such a maze of legislation and policy directives can hardly be conducive to a pro-active approach. What is needed is to produce a comprehensive fresh legislation which will take into account all the above legislation, allow a single window service and sort out the conflicts that take place within this maze.

The following four are the main legislations which control the environment issues of these islands and which require that most development activities should take place within its purview:

1. Forest Conservation Act,
2. Environment Protection Act,

3. Coastal Regulation Act, and
4. Protection of Tribals Act.

The Forest and Environment Department of Andaman & Nicobar Islands has to work within these Acts and all tourism related activities must fall within them.

82 per cent of Andaman & Nicobar Islands is under declared forest land while about 90 per cent of land is under green cover based on satellite pictures. Within the declared forests there are three categories as follows:

1. National Parks
2. Sanctuaries
3. Reserve Forests

These three categories take away 7,000 sq km of land surface out of 8,249 sq km. While it may be difficult to go in for tourism activities in national parks and sanctuaries, reserve forests do allow limited use for eco-tourism. However, the Forest Department of Andaman & Nicobar Islands has as yet no plans for development of tourism inside reserve forests which is a practice worldwide. Once this issue is sorted out there is possibility of limited high end eco-friendly tourism in remote locations. Worldwide reserve forests have been developed for eco-tourism under certain rules and guidelines which are strictly followed. Wildlife sanctuaries like Kruger National Park also have enclaves for tourists where they can stay under strict rules of not making noise or throwing garbage etc.

Tourism Development

According to the 2003 report the position of land availability for Tourism Resort building is as follows:

Total no of islands/islets	572
After deducting small islets, rocks	160
Islands with non-forest lands	24
Less exclusive tribal reserves	11
Areas available for development	13

Small islets and rocks have been left out. However, sometimes these can be good for development of resorts. Further, a tribal reserve area like Nicobar can certainly have controlled tourism which will be discussed later. And lastly, there should be no bar on developing eco resorts in reserve forests as is being done worldwide as long as it conforms to some guidelines which are properly enforced. Even the Supreme Court has endorsed this view after accepting the Shekhar Singh report mentioned earlier.

DRAFT TOURISM POLICY

The main features of the existing tourism policy are as follows:

	Policy	Comments by author
I. Vision	To develop the Andaman & Nicobar Islands as a unique eco-friendly tourist destination and simultaneously to generate revenue and employment for local youth.	A good vision but does not restrict itself to high value tourism as orderrd by the Supreme Court.
II. Mission	The Tourism policy of Andaman & Nicobar Islands aims to promote tourism by developing eco-friendly tourist infrastructure of international standards through public and private sector initiative (taking into account the carrying capacity of the islands and limited support infrastructure) for generating local income & revenue and local employment.	There is no mention of high value and low volume tourism. Carrying capacity of the islands has been mentioned but does not indicate whether it will high value only.
III. SWOT analysis	Based on the SWOT analysis in the following paragraphs, it will be the policy of the Department to leverage the strengths and explore the opportunities, while at the same time addressing the weaknesses and being prepared for the threats inherent in this location.	
	a. Strengths	
	• *Large number of good, sandy and safe beaches, beautiful meandering mangrove creeks, lush green forests.*	Andaman & Nicobar Islands do not have long beaches like Goa. There is also an emerging crocodile problem which needs to be checked.
	• *Variety of flora, fauna, including tropical forests and coral reefs.*	Andaman & Nicobar Islands offer one of the best variety of coral reefs. This is a major tourist extraction and is also eco-friendly.
	• *Unique tourist spots not available on the mainland, such as mud volcano and only active volcano i.e. Barren Island etc.*	Forests trails and treks attract a lot of specialised tourists.
	• *Not much variation in climatic conditions, thus facilitating a year-round tourist season.*	Not correct. There is eight months of rainy season and four months dry season. However, monsoon can be sold as a special attraction too.
	• *Communal harmony.*	Correct. No communal tension or crime.
	• *No crime or anti-social activities.*	
	• *Unexplored Destinations.*	A very important issue. Because of a large number of uninhabited islands the tourism potential for opening of new islands overtime and thereby offering new destinations is very high.

Policy	Comments by author
b. **Weaknesses**	
• *Distance from the mainland.*	These islands are closer to South-East Asia like Phuket which is a major tourist destination. Only direct flights from South East Asia are wanting. Incidentally, there is an agreement of Friendship/ Cooperation with the City of Port Blair and Phuket Province of Thailand signed in Phuket on June 29, 2005 which talks of exchange of tourists, education, solid waste management but there has been no implementation of this agreement as yet. Direct international flights from Phuket, Bangkok and Singapore can cut down the cost.
• *Lack of basic tourism infrastructure.*	Very correct. A good airport at Port Blair exists. A new terminal will come up by 2015. Airstrips Diglipur and Campbell Bay need to be lengthened, Car Nicobar is fine. Scuba diving with live-on-board facility has great potential but nothing being done. Uninhabited islands should be opened. No boat of reasonable quality available for this purpose or for deep sea fishing.
• *Lack of adequate accommodation both in terms of numbers as well as categories.*	Serious issue with MoEF as they keep changing their policy. Example: After auctioning of a beach site for a resort, the MoEF has changed its policy of coastal development. Further, only high value accommodation needs to be allowed as per Supreme Court's order.
• *Uncertainty amongst potential investors about future tourism scenario.*	Serious issue with MoEF. Example: After auctioning of beach site for a resort, the MoEF had changed its policy of coastal development.
• *Poor inter-island connectivity, Lack of availability of speed boats, helicopter and other faster modes of transport for tourists.*	Andaman & Nicobar Islands should also consider leasing out inter-island ferries and air routes under their supervision with or without subsidy.

Policy	Comments by author
• *Investors find it difficult to obtain clearance for tourism related projects from different departments in the absence of single window system for clearing tourism projects, high cost of development of infrastructure.*	Poor infrastructure connectivity discourages private investment. No direct international flights despite Port Blair being an international airport.
• *Huge expenses on travelling.*	Unless direct international connectivity is provided from South-East Asia this problem will remain as domestic flights in India are expensive. The subsidy provided to shipping could be reduced and subsidy could be given to air services as was done for Haj Travel in India.
c. **Opportunities**	
• *Scope for promotion of adventure sea sports*	The administration has even shut down the Scuba Diving Society started by it in 1992. This needs to be started by Andaman Administration. No encouragement to private scuba operators. No adventure campaign carried out by Andaman & Nicobar Islands in spite of adequate funds like in Kerala.
• *Marketing unexplored destination*	No campaign has been started. Lessons to be learnt from Kerala experience.
• *Leisure tourism*	Negligible due to scarcity of hotels.
• *Game fishing*	Very high scope however no effort by the administration.
• *Coastal threat and jungle trekking*	Same as above.
• *Creek Cruise Tourism*	No efforts by administration. New problem of crocodiles.
• *Meetings, Incentive Conferences and Events (MICE)*	Infrastructure not sufficient. Not encouraged.
• *Cruise Tourism*	Foreign cruise ships have come to Port Blair earlier. In 1992, they came and were invited to LGs House for tea. Next year somehow, they were not encouraged on security grounds and they have reduced coming.
• *Medical Tourism*	Proposal to setup a super specialty hospital by a well known private sector company, who were also allotted land by local administration, was turned down by MHA.

	Policy	Comments by author
IV. Objectives	*Deriving from the Mission, it is the stated objective of the A&N Administration to promote sustainable tourism in the Andaman & Nicobar Islands in such a way that it would generate local employment and contribute to the economic growth of this Union Territory without bringing imbalance in flora & fauna and also without adversely affecting the carrying capacity of these islands. To this end it would endeavour to:*	There is hardly any visibility on this end. Port Blair Town and other areas are full of open garbage. There is no policy for garbage disposal for wet and dry garbage. Sustainable tourism policy should emphasise on high value tourism only.
	i. Promote Eco-tourism with a view to protect the fragile eco-system.	Fortune Bay Island Hotel run by ITC hotels at Port Blair has done an excellent job in water conservation. They also use sea water for all their flushing and recycle it. They also harvest rain water which is sufficient to meet their requirement during the lean period. This and other good practices need to be duplicated for all other hotels as a model practice.
	ii. Create self-sustainable jobs for the local youth of these islands.	Tourism will bring demand for skilled people. Hoteliers in Port Blair have expressed their unhappiness at the lack of availability of skilled youth and they are being forced to import hotel staff from mainland at a higher cost.
	iii. Generate substantial revenue for A & N Islands and project a friendly tourist image to the world at large and make this union territory one of the best tourist destinations.	Tourism activities will generate such revenues. However, as per Supreme Court Judgment, only high end tourism to be allowed and there is no need to encourage mass tourism.
	iv. To be the number one Indian destination by per capita market share of visitor's expenditure.	Only high end tourism to be encouraged as per Supreme Court's order.
	v. Encourage domestic tourism with a view to provide to the people of the country the unique feature of unity in diversity, secularism—a perfect example of national integration.	No. This will lead to mass tourism which is not permitted as per Supreme Court's order.
	vi. Offer opportunities to the youth not only for employment but also for taking up activities of nation building character.	Introduce items like International Award for Young People Programme (IAYP) for character building in schools and colleges.
	vii. Bring socio-economic benefits to the people of these islands.	Tourist demand for vegetables in Andaman Islands has been met from Islands of Haveloc and Neil and has benefited the local people.

	Policy	Comments by author
		Availability of fish is also met by local catch.
	viii. *Preserving and enriching our cultural heritage in all its manifestations and causing accretion and strength rather than degrading social and cultural values.*	Cellular jail and Ross Island needs further restoration.
	ix. *Develop places of interest as tourist destinations. The uniqueness of features such as mud volcano, the potential of beaches such as at Havelock and Neil Islands for acqua sports, the peace and tranquility of the back waters would be developed in their own light.*	A must
	x. *Provide quality services to all domestic and international tourists.*	Only high end tourism to be allowed.
	xi. *Diversify and expand the marketing of the islands' tourism potential while preserving its fragile ecosystem.*	Yes but in the Nicobar Islands allow only tribals to develop tourism.
	xii. *Encourage people's participation in tourism related activities so that it is community-based, thereby generating synergies between guests and locals. Some such roles for the local community could be to run paying guest accommodation, house-boats etc.*	This would be more appropriate in the Nicobar Islands. However, in Andamans only well established hotel chain with green tourism background should be encouraged.
	xiii. *Focus on promotion of international tourism by including these islands in the South East Asian packages offered by tour operators from the West and Japan, Australia etc.*	Yes. MOU signed between Lt. Governor and Governor of Phuket lying unimplemented.
	xiv. *To develop world class infrastructure i.e. hotels, resorts, connectivity by road, air, ship etc to cater to the demand of foreign tourists.*	Invite tour promoters, leading hotels on familiarisation tours.
	xv. *Encourage the private sector, including international corporates, to invest in tourism related projects, through FDI, either fully owned or in collaboration with Indian partners, either private or governmental, as per the prevailing enactments.*	Last allotment of land to hotels was a disaster as after allotment major change in Coastal Regulation was done.
	xvi. *To encourage traditional artisans and the handicraft sector*	Agreed.
V. Strategy	*The Government will have to withdraw from its present role as a tourism-service provider, but steadily perform as a facilitator and regulator. It would be required to provide support and infrastructure facilities such as tourist information centres & kiosks, facilities for holding Conventions for MICE, drawing up an annual calendar of events, transportation services etc.*	Government to sell privatised hotels.

The draft tourism policy of Andaman & Nicobar Islands contains all the ingredients of a policy which is populist but does not give direction nor does it provide the relationship between forest lands and development of tourism. It also does not seem to be aware of the Supreme Court directive of high value low volume tourism policy. A reality check gives an entirely opposite picture. The present inter-island infrastructure of ferries is old and inefficient. One sea plane has been leased by the administration recently to run a service between these islands with differential tariff rates for islanders and visitors. The same type of sea plane was purchased in 1993 but it met with an accident and was not replaced. Anyhow, this is a good beginning and this would go a long way to improve inter-island connectivity. A Scuba Diving Society was set up by the administration in the early nineties but was allowed to waste away due to bureaucratic indifference. Luckily, private scuba diving centres have since come up but their charges are substantially higher than those in Thailand.

Tourism policy mentioned with other government departments/agencies:

The Environment and Forest Department website mentions eco-tourism in its introduction as follows:

> "Mother Nature has been extra generous to Andaman & Nicobar Islands in endowing it with phenomenally rich biodiversity which is displayed in its varied assemblage of flora and fauna on land and in water surrounding the islands. Their uniqueness lies in high degree of endemism, particularly, in fauna. Forests cover about 84 per cent of the islands' geographical area."

Andaman & Nicobar Islands is also a great attraction for bird watchers as well as for its rich, unique and endemic bio-diversity. As many as 270 species and sub-species are reported by ornithologists. These islands are part of the 218 Endemic Bird Areas (EBA) of the world. Its mangrove vegetation protects these islands from soil erosion. Its wildlife consists of wild pigs, dugongs, elephants, turtles, snakes. Coral reefs, sea cucumbers, and shells of various types form part of marine wild life. It has 96 wildlife sanctuaries, nine national parks and one bio-sphere reserve. This can be a great attraction for nature loving tourists only if facilities for stay are provided and tours under control conditions are made mandatory.

Another place where we find mention of tourism as an objective is in the website on Andaman & Nicobar Integrated Development Corporation (ANIIDCO). This public sector entity is supposed to facilitate industry, fisheries and tourism as a common objective. It states:

> ANIIDCO was set up in 1988 at the instance of IDA with the objective to develop and commercially exploit the nature resources of the territory for the balanced and environmentally sound development of the territory. The ANDIICO which is a fully government owned corporation, undertakes a wide range of departmental activities such as tourism, fisheries, supplies, marketing, industries and finance under one umbrella.

Tourism

The basic objective of the tourism division is to develop, operate and maintain the tourism infrastructure. It has one tourist guest house, the Megapode Nest and a number of catering units and restaurants. Efforts are being made to ensure better maintenance of tourist lodges, recreational facilities and develop shopping centres at the tourist points/places. The tourism section of the Andaman & Nicobar Islands is poised for significant growth and it has to play a catalytic role in creating and maintaining the tourism infrastructure along with the other agencies. However, it should get out of managing resorts which it is unable to do mainly because of governmental rules and regulations. It also does not mention water based activities like scuba or deep sea fishing.

It is unfortunate but ANIIDCO has not been able to provide any quality in its management. Its facilities can best be judged as three stars or less.

Fisheries

The corporation has started this division for commercial exploitation of abundantly available fish in the Andaman & Nicobar Islands, and to provide good marketing network to the local fisherman. A subsidiary company namely M/s. AFL, the first 100 per cent Export Oriented Unit (EOU) in the Andaman & Nicobar Administration has been promoted by Andaman & Nicobar Islands which has recently gone into commercial production. The potential for deep sea fishing is immense. However, on ground there does not appear to be any actual improvement. The coastline of all the islands adds up to 1,962 km in length. It is bordered with luxuriant mangroves and magnificent coral reefs on the fringes.

A clean and pollution-free environment and lush green forests of the islands surrounded by blue sea water should make Andaman & Nicobar Islands one of the most favoured destinations for eco-tourism in the world. However, this is not so. The poor quality of infrastructure and in addition, the increasing population of crocodiles in the beaches and creeks is a cause of concern. Crocodiles breed very fast and the ban on their killing is making it more difficult to encourage tourism. There is need to review the ban on killing of crocodiles as it is leading to attacks by them on human beings and many people have died and lost limbs while swimming. Notices at beaches to beware of crocodiles is driving away tourists from the beaches.

What we see is confusion of the administration in developing tourism which does not provide a philosophy or quality control. Should the island's fragile environment allow mass tourism or restricted tourism? Should the various uninhabited islands be allowed to open up resorts? Should India encourage ship based low value tourists (This does not include high value cruise ships) or restrict it to high value only? These questions need to be answered in a policy and a philosophy statement.

THE FINAL VERSION OF TOURISM POLICY[10]

The final document of the Andaman & Nicobar Tourism Policy has bench marked Andaman & Nicobar Islands with similarly placed tropical island destinations in the world. The following table taken out of the policy gives the position of Andaman & Nicobar Islands in comparison to others island destinations for tourism.

Table 1: Benchmarking of Andaman & Nicobar Islands vis-a-vis Large Tropical Islands Nations (Area greater than 1,000 sq km)

Name of island/island nation	*Land Area (km)*	*Population in lakh 2001-05*	*Density of population (net density of population)*	*Per Capita Income in 2005 in US$*	*Area under Forest (%)*	*Area under Agriculture (%)*	*Tourist Arrivals (in lakhs) 2005*
Andaman & Nicobar Islands	8249	3.56	43 (431)	67	90	2.3	0.56
Solomon Islands	28896	5.81	20 (180)	1900	88.8	0.03	0.09
Trinidad and Tobago	5128	10.56	206 (416)	21700	50.5	26	4.63
Fiji	18274	9.18	50 (91)	4100	44.6	35	5.50
Samoa	2831	2.17	77 (122)	5400	37.2	33	1.01
Vanuatu	12189	2.11	17 (27)	2900	36.7	12	0.62
Jamaica	10830	27.8	257 (367)	4800	30	47	14.78
Cape Verde	4033	4.99	124 (157)	7000	21.1	18	1.97
Barbados	430	3.56	656 (688)	18900	4.7		5.47
Maldives	300	3.86	1287 (1331)	4600	3.3		3.95
Seychelles	451	0.82	182 (546)	16600	66.7		1.29
Singapore	707.1	46.08	6517 (679)	49990	3.3		89.43

Based on Tourism Policy issued by Andaman & Nicobar Islands Administration. Net density of population excludes area under forests.
Lakh – One Hundred Thousand.

From the above chart it may be seen that Andaman & Nicobar Islands has the highest percentage of forests at 90 per cent of land surface and lowest percentage of agriculture. This figure should be seen as an advantage as eco-tourism with dense forests and beaches is a preferred option with eco-tourists. In fact, the high level of forest reserves gives Andaman & Nicobar Islands a special place for nature related activities and reduces the pull of social resort tourism. Forest area has a number of restrictions which have to be honoured and generally allow only up market tourism because of these restrictions. Worldwide forest tourism in reserves is becoming popular. However, Andaman & Nicobar Islands have no forest related tourism especially when the forests of Andaman & Nicobar Islands are extremely dense rain forests rarely found in the world today.

Andaman & Nicobar Islands do not have any major animals in the forest which are likely to be hunted. There are iguanas, other reptiles and birds. The list of protected species has already been listed by the Forest and Environment Department. Unlike forest departments in countries like US, Australia and New Zealand and even some forest departments of Indian States, there has been very little work done by the Forest Department to promote eco-tourism in the forest areas. There is a need to plan out the high quality of the limited number of tourists resorts inside these forests. There is a growing breed of nature lovers who travel to all corners of the world to such locations. It will not only be a revenue earner but also bring awareness of the environmental degradation happening inside, if any.

The Tourism Policy document issued by the Andaman & Nicobar Islands clearly states in its strategy to go in for *Strategic Partnerships*. It states, 'Formulate strategic tourism partnerships with neighbouring international destinations like Phuket for leveraging increased visits to these islands.' So far no such partnership has been signed or even negotiated. The only document is the MOU signed between the Lt. Governor of Andaman & Nicobar Islands and Governor of Phuket signed in 2005 but which remains unimplemented. This is unfortunate as this agreement talked of tourism promotion, solid waste management and cultural exchanges amongst other things. (See Appendix 3)

In order to compare tourism policies of other countries, given below is a comparison with Bhutan, South Pacific Islands based on a UN Report, the Maldives Model and Report of Ecotourism Association of Australia (EAA).

Comparative Tourism Policies of Selected Countries

Tourism Development in Bhutan: High Value-Low Volume Tourism Policy

It goes to the credit of The Royal Government of Bhutan that they were aware that unrestricted flow of tourists can have negative impacts on Bhutan's pristine environment and its rich and unique culture. The government, therefore, adopted a policy of "High value-low volume" tourism, controlling the type and quantity of Tourism right from the start. Until 1991 the Bhutan Tourism Corporation (BTC), a quasi-autonomous and self-financing body, implemented the government's tourism policy. All tourists, up to that time came as guests of BTC, which in turn operated the tour, transport services and nearly all the hotels and accommodation facilities. The government privatised tourism in October 1991 to encourage increased private sector participation in the tourism sector. Today, there are more than 75 licensed tour operators in the country.

What Bhutan insists on is a minimum payment/spend by a tourist per day which is about US$ 200.This might vary from high to low season but it acts as a filter to discourage low value tourists who add to volumes but not revenues and may cause environmental damage. This strategy adopted by Bhutan is working well as it keeps this sensitive area free of ill effects of pollution and degradation which comes with low end tourism.

Tourism Development in South Pacific Islands

Ecotourism is a concept that describes a form of development that respects tradition and culture; protects and preserves the environment; and educates and welcomes visitors. In addition, ecotourism should be sustainable economically over the long-term. In American Samoa, this definition is intended to define ecotourism at the national and local level.

A UN Report on tourism in South Pacific has come out with policy recommendations for ecotourism.

The government adopted a definition of ecotourism that was further developed by the Pacific Business Centre at the University of Hawaii.

The American Samoa National Park was established by the United States Congress in 1988. This makes the park part of the US National Park System (NPS). However, the national park became a reality only after lease agreements were signed by all village councils within the park area. The park stretches over more than 6,000 acres and includes the islands of Tatuila and Manu'a, as well as the beaches of Ta'u and Ofu Islands. Tourists to the national park can join home stay programmes to experience the typical Samoan village life. There is also hiking, diving and traditional fishing as part of village activities. There are also educational and recreational ecotourism tours that include observing marine and wildlife, learning about traditional and medicinal plants and exploring archaeological and historical sites.

Mass tourism is considered the main threat to the sustainability of ecotourism, especially since the environment in the national park is so fragile.

There is a national park staff trained to counteract some aspects of this threat. For example, they monitor tourist activities and educate villagers about using the park site for low impact tourism development. Home stay programmes are encouraged and initiated instead of hotel development. Villagers are able to coordinate tours rather than face the risks presented by group tours. Educational eco-tours are also promoted.

The Maldives Model

The Maldives is an archipelago in the Arabian Sea/Indian Ocean which has evolved into a high end eco-friendly tourism destination. In its environmental regulations and standards for the tourism sector, it has adopted certain principles like maximum built up area to be restricted to 20 per cent of land mass. Reservation of aesthetics, integrity of the resorts, with height restricted to the height of vegetation, with as much use of local material as possible. While construction on reefs and lagoons was discouraged, but as water side bungalows are very popular amongst tourists, their construction is permitted if equal size open space is left on the land for each bungalow being developed on the lagoon.

Australian Model

Formed in 1991, the Ecotourism Australia serves as the apex national body for Australia's ecotourism industry. Currently, EAA has approximately 500 members, publishes an annual Australian Ecotourism Guide, and hosts an annual conference. In addition to strengthening the industry network of ecotourism operators, the EAA actively promotes "best tourism practices" through self-regulation and accreditation. Attracting high value visitors in order to develop a more profitable tourism industry rather than just pursuing growth in visitor numbers should be the goal according to Ecotourism Australia.[11]

To provide tourists and the travel trade with a recognisable and authentic ecotourism product, the Ecotourism Australia initiated the National Ecotourism Accreditation Programme (NEAP) in 1996 in cooperation with the Australia Tourism Operators Network (ATON) and the Tourism Council of Australia, with funding support from the Office of National Tourism. In 2000, the certification programme changed its name to the NEAP. Under NEAP, products awarded ecotourism accreditation are required to meet a comprehensive set of core criteria based on ecological sustainability and minimum environmental impact. At this stage, NEAP mostly relies on a self-assessment procedure and four forms of monitoring measures, including random on-site audits. In addition, NEAP requires periodic monitoring and management review for accredited ecotourism operators to ensure continuous improvement of standards. Australian government supports EAA.

Challenges and Opportunities

The development of ecotourism in Australia is still in its infancy, with approximately 600 ecotourism operators (mostly small in size), providing an equivalent of 4,500 full-time jobs and Aus $250 million turnover. Although a plethora of plans and strategies are being developed in Australia to promote ecotourism, the long-term effectiveness of these newly formed programmes and initiatives has yet been evaluated. To contribute towards sustainable development, these initiatives must be able to move ecotourism beyond simply a niche market within nature-based travel. Ecotourism must serve as a vehicle to transform unsustainable mass tourism practices towards genuine "greening," not just "green washing" of the tourism industry. In a highly competitive marketplace, the ecotourism industry is likely to face immense challenges to live up to the promise of sustainable tourism."

A Policy Prescription for Positive Discouragement of Mass Tourism

It may be seen from above examples that Andaman & Nicobar Islands also need to come out with more detailed policy guidelines and regulations for their tourism policy. Its policies have to be compliant to the Supreme Court's order which is very clear on high value-low volume tourism. While it has identified activities for tourists such as scuba diving, cruise tourism, canopy walkway, mass tourism will be a spoiler. As already pointed out in the case of Bhutan, Maldives, South Pacific Islands and Australian tourism, mass tourism can lead to the destruction of the environment, especially if enforcement is weak. India has already seen degradation of the environment in tourism areas in the Himalayas due to mass tourism and lack of enforcement it. The recent 2012 incident reported in all national newspapers that local tour operators in Port Blair in connivance with police have been taking groups of tourists to Jarawa areas and forcing Jarawas to dance before them. This is a case in point that how a laid out policy was violated not only by travel agents but also local administration and police who connived in this activity. Such activities are proof of poor surveillance and show a need for a tourism and environmental regulator for these islands. It would be in the fitness of things to decide upfront how to control decline in the quality of enforcement.

The town of Port Blair is quite shabby because of poor municipal intervention. Maintaining remote locations will be even more difficult. The Bhutan model is perhaps one option. Having kept a minimum expenditure per tourist at about US$ 200 per tourist per day it provides a good filter. Further, there is a need to put minimum requirements on hotels and guest houses for cleanliness and garbage disposal, both wet and dry. As a matter of fact a minimum ceiling on quality should be kept. The existing accommodations should be asked to upgrade so that in a course of a couple of years this destination becomes a high end destination. Further, in remote locations issues of water availability need to be sorted out. With heavy rainfall concentrated over nine months, water harvesting methods can be employed. The issue of electricity remains a problem as Andaman & Nicobar Islands are dependent upon diesel generation and so far no major breakthrough has been achieved in this area. Diesel generation, with the new type of silent generators is still polluting. A Hydel project called Kalpong

Hydroelectric Power Project has started functioning since November 2001 producing 5.25 MW of Hydel Power by creating a 34 metre high concrete dam on Kalpong River.[12] This is an exception and cannot be repeated due to terrain factors.

Infrastructure and Tourism

In order to attract high end tourists minimum quality infrastructure is required. Good air connection, fast travel to islands, clean environment, availability of clean water, clean beaches, low crime rate all form a part of tourism essentials. Expenditure on these need to come mainly from the government but wherever possible, private sector participation should be used.

One of the problems of Andaman & Nicobar Islands is shortage of water for about three months in the year when it is dry there. While there is adequate rainfall, the months from January to March are dry and there is shortage of drinking water in most areas. These are also the best tourist months. For promotion of tourism and to supply water during the dry months, there is need for extensive rain water harvesting technology to be applied in all islands and all areas where people live and tourism is to be promoted. This is a solvable problem as there is adequate rainfall rest of the year. Water barrages can be built from one island to the other during the season, as the sea is also calm during this period.

Responsible Tourism

Responsible Tourism is the current mantra of tour operators. However, it is not enough to allow the slogan but penalties should be kept in the legislation and fines imposed on hotels/guest houses that do not follow it in letter and spirit. Opening of these islands will give a better appreciation to the whole concept of use of tourism for security purposes.

Will tourism development improve or further degrade environment? This is a complex question. Mass tourism has shown in many places that it can degrade environment if policies are not followed. However, limited high end tourism can improve the environment. How does one achieve limited high end tourism? This can be achieved if appropriate policies are put in place and implemented. This calls for a philosophy for Andaman & Nicobar Islands.

In the recent order of the Supreme Court banning tourism in core areas of tiger reserves, it said that it was not averse to permitting regulated tourism activities, subject to revised guidelines to protect the depleting wild cat. It granted four weeks to the centre to evolve fresh guidelines after consultation with states, all stake holders, hotel associations affected by the ban, guides and tour operators.

They also stated "There is always a watch when tourism is allowed. If there is no tourism there will be no human to watch the tigers. Poachers will immediately be caught by tourists and guides. Poachers actually work under cover. If no tourists are allowed, it will be a field day for poachers."

Eco-tourism is a fastest growing segment of the tourism industry. Why is it so? This is so because tourists have *shifted away from casino based tourism to environmental based tourism.* Such tourists are not looking for music, television or evening entertainment but are looking for a quiet peaceful time. As a result, many countries, especially forested countries and island countries have issued guidelines for this specialised tourism. The above is also true for the uninhabited Islands of Andaman & Nicobar Islands.[13]

Tribal Policy and Tourism: Opening of Nicobar Islands for Tourism

Andaman & Nicobar Islands Protection of Aboriginal Tribes Regulation, 1956 and the Rules framed there under provide the framework of the Tribal Policy.[14] There are four tribes in Andaman Group and two in Nicobar. Tribes of Andaman are Jarawas, Adamanaese, Sentinelese and Onges, each residing in a separate region. The Sentinelese reside in Sentinal Islands which are isolated and they are hostile to other human beings. They are still in hunting and gathering stage and do not want to be disturbed. There is, therefore, no problem with them as long as they are left alone. The Andamanese were the residents of Port Blair region about half a century back but are now re-located in Strait Island, shifted by the British Government. They are about to get extinct with less than 20 members left. The Onges are in Little Andamans living under the Tribal Department's Welfare Scheme and there is no issue with them. The only conflict of the people is with the Jarawas Tribe which is primitive and lives north of Port Blair where a road called Anadaman Trunk Road (ATR) has cut through their territory and is causing a lot of problems for them. This has become a case of litigation in the court by leading environmentalists. The Supreme Court had ordered closure of a certain part of the road going through the Jarawas reserve which has not been done as yet. These four tribes are still primitive and the existing policy to leave them by themselves without allowing tourists to go their areas is fully accepted and appreciated. There is no need for tourists to have any interface with them.

The Nicobars however is another story. The Nicobar Group of Islands has Nicobarese tribals in practically all islands of Nicobar. These are progressive tribals who have joined the mainstream. Nicobarese boys have been winners of All India Subroto Mukerjee Trophy in Football many times.[15] The Nicobarese children are all literate and are attending schools. They are also working in various government departments including defence forces and are doing well. In fact, according to a senior Nicobarese officer, Nicobarese are now facing issues of educated unemployment as the children passing out of schools and colleges are not getting absorbed in Nicobars and have to seek a living outside their homes.

Another very small group of tribals called Shompens is found in Great Nicobar Islands. They are still hunters and gatherers and can be called primitive. These tribals are shy and live in the forest areas. Yet they are friendly and come into settled areas to exchange their products like honey. They should be allowed to live their own life. They have some contact with the tribal department in the Great Nicobar Islands but they feel shy to mix with other settlers. There is no problem with them.

Although, the Tribal Policy of Andaman & Nicobar Islands has insulated the primitive tribes (except from some breaches in implementation), the author's position is to respect all the restrictions imposed by the Supreme Court and the tribal legislations by the administration except for Nicobars. The Nicobarese have now reached the stage of development and integration that they need to be more actively involved with the rest of the country. Further, their main activity in the Nicobar Islands is around coconut trade which has suffered due to the tsunami and reached a saturation point. They need a new economic venue to absorb the youth, especially the educated youth and a policy of controlled tourism after taking into confidence their Tribal Council. Leading Nicobarese have stated that their coconut trade has reached a saturation point and they need to start a new economic activity. The obvious choice would be to allow growth of tourism in Nicobars.

As part of India's enlightenment policy adopted towards the Nicobarese there is a need to dialogue with them regarding regulated tourism in these islands. It is necessary that all decisions are taken after due consultation with their Tribal Council, which they respect. As the younger generation looks for jobs and is getting educated, there is a need to allow tourism in these islands but managed by them and not outside companies. They are well organised and capable of managing business themselves.

While the Nicobar Islands are still very remote and isolated, their interaction with foreign fishermen and traders has always been there prior to 1947. The government policy since after World War II of prohibiting foreign boats from entering these islands has made them more insular and isolated. However, reopening these islands to foreign tourists/cruise ships will not be such a major change. The island of Car Nicobar is the most progressive of them and is ready to welcome a limited number of tourists. For the rest of the islands cruise ships stopping for a few hours like in the Greek Islands would be a win-win for both the tribals and display of soft power.

In conclusion, the scope of leveraging India's soft power by tourism promotion and allied activities is immense keeping in mind full environmental protection. Not only that, while hard power is a costly drain on the exchequer, soft power through tourism and its allied activities, is revenue generating for the local economy, the region as well as for the country. Tourism is now the biggest industry in the world and the share of Andaman & Nicobar Islands is insignificant. However, the need for promoting tourism in these islands should not be for generating revenues but for supplementing the LEP and complimenting military power with soft power to increase the strategic vision in the national context.

NOTES

1. Joseph S. Nye Jr., *Soft Power: The Means to Succeed in World Politics,* Harvard University, 2004.
2. Rohini Mohan, "The Great Indian Tuna Robbery", *Tehelka,* March 03, 2012.
3. Judgment dated May 07, 2002 passed by the Hon'ble Supreme Court of India in W.P. No.202/1995.
4. Darren Smith, "National Park Status", see www.usparks.about.com
5. "Green Terror", *India Today,* October, 15, 2012, p. 19.
6. Jayadev Ranade, "China expanding maritime ambition and growing naval power", *Issue Brief,* August 29, 2011.
7. M.H. Ahsan, "Andaman faces Kargil type invasion:, at www.Boloji.com, July 12, 2011.
8. Nils Finn Munch- Petersen was a short-term consultant to Andaman & Nicobar Administration and UNDP. Currently he is working in Bhutan.
9. UNDP-WTO project IND/93/032 Shankland & Cox Entec, August, 1996.
10. Issued by Directorate of Tourism, Port Blair (undated).
11. www.etravelblackboard.com/article136276/focus-on-high-end-tour
12. pib.nic.in/feature/feyr2001/fnov2001/f231120011.html
13. *Indian Express,* August 30, 2012.
14. Even during the British period there was a trader protection policy in the Nicobars. The British introduced licenses to trade in the Nicobars, and cancelled all debts of the traders. Please see Chapter 3.
15. The Air Force Station at Car Nicobar often provides them airlifts to the mainland to participate in such sporting events as a matter of goodwill.

CHAPTER 10

Andaman & Nicobar Islands—Strategic Challenges: A Proposed Policy Prescription

India's LEP of 1991 was a major departure in its foreign policy followed up to that time. However, the LEP remained incomplete without a critical look at the role the Andaman & Nicobar Administration could play in the developing security scenario of the country. The MoD took nearly 10 years to leverage the strategic advantage offered by these islands by creating a Joint Command in 2001. They took another 10 years in announcing a forward naval base called Baaz at Great Nicobar Islands in 2012. However, the civil side represented by MHA remained indifferent to LEP and continued with the policy of benign neglect and masterly inactivity. Therefore, there is *now need for drastic change in the civil policy towards these islands in view of the new challenges.* India is in a similar state today in the geopolitical context as India was in late 1950s and 1960s when China took over Tibet by military aggression while India watched them in quiet acquiescence and its borders became common with China. The peaceful borders with Tibet became full of tension and remain so even now. Western borders with Pakistan have the problem of terrorism. The all-weather friendship between Pakistan and China is yet another known unknown.

The forward policy adopted in 1950s over NEFA gave us effective jurisdiction up to McMahon line and also brought 50 odd tribes of the region into harmonious development with affinity towards India. The twin purpose of the policy was achieved. However, in the western sector of Ladakh, since there was no effective jurisdiction mainly due to the terrain, the Chinese came into Aksai Chin and have stayed on since with 35,000 sq km of area under their control. This shows that effective administration can be used to one's benefit in international relations. In a similar manner, the Chinese aggressive claims and physical occupation in East and South China Sea is a reminder of what they did over 60 years back over the Himalayas and what they are doing now is to increase their influence and effective jurisdiction to consolidate the claim in South and East China Sea.

INTEGRATING ANDAMAN & NICOBAR ISLANDS WITH LEP

In implementing the LEP enunciated by Prime Minister Narasimha Rao in 1991 these islands were completely overlooked for their strategic relevance. While India made moves to integrate with its eastern neighbours in ASEAN and other countries, the civil administration completely bypassed leveraging the advantages of having the islands. In the natural order of things, the integration of these islands with the LEP should have been done at the earliest. The defence authorities, however, did take the initiative and created the joint command in Andaman & Nicobar Islands in 2001 after a gap of 10 years.

In such a scenario, India needs to leverage these forgotten assets to its advantage. With the recent developments in South China Sea over maritime boundaries claimed by China on basis of "historic data", India should seek lessons from it and extend its presence in these islands. This can be done in two ways: (1) India should use its military to fortify these islands and send a message to the world that these islands not only belong to India but are in full occupation, (2) India should open up these islands as a matter of soft strategy to announce to the world that Indian territory extends right up to Straits of Malacca.

SOFT POWER OPTION

To complement India's military strategy India should use the soft power available due to these islands. India should open up these islands, which have been kept locked up due to restrictive policies, by allowing Indian and foreign tourists to visit in a much greater way. This is similar to what China is doing to the islands which it has occupied in South China Sea. It is an effective method of conveying to the world what is yours. This can be done in two ways, either by settling Indians from mainland or by encouraging tourism. The fact that these islands have over 90 per cent forests and are environmentally fragile and many islands are short of drinking water, the idea of any new settlement cannot be considered. The second alternative of encouraging tourism to uninhabited places also has its problems. *If mass tourism is allowed then there will be impact on the fragile eco system and therefore the only possible method is to allow high value-low volume tourism in various islands which also has the approval of the Supreme Court of India.* Price as a filter for tourism will determine this aspect. There is also a need to review the Foreigners Restricted Areas Orders of 1963. While these orders allow a foreign national to stay in these islands for a period of 30 days extendable locally for another 15 days, anything beyond requires the permission of the MHA. Further, Nicobars are completely prohibited to foreigners and require prior permission of the MHA.

The Andaman & Nicobar Islands have a unique location for India for they extend India's land surface and maritime border right up to the mouth of Strait of Malacca. Leveraging these islands can enhance India's relationship with

Thailand, Malaysia and Indonesia and also with ASEAN in general. India's presence in the Andaman & Nicobar Islands determines its standing with these and other South East Asian countries. This realisation has not been felt in the corridors of power in Delhi. In addition, nearly 30 per cent of India's EEZ is derived from the existence of these islands post 1992 when UNCLOS III came into force. This can easily prove to be a great source of underwater wealth besides the huge untapped pool of fish not available anywhere else in the world. With technology for deep sea oil drilling now available, there is great potential in this region.

The Incredible India campaign launched in 2002 by the Ministry of Tourism has been a great success. It brought India into the mainstream of world tourism by a massive brand building campaign which was excellent in quality and impact. However, Andaman & Nicobar Islands were completely left out. These islands were not ready for it as they did not have either the infrastructure or the policy in place. What is required now is to build up brand Andaman & Nicobar Islands on the line of Incredible India. Islands like Cayman Islands or Malta have an online campaign which is on the internet and is very effective.

Amitabh Kant in his book *Branding India: An Incredible Story* writes "the biggest thing that happened to tourism in Kerala was opening of three new destinations—Kumarakom, Munnar, Wayanad. In no time these locations became hot favorites with celebrities ranging from ex-Beatle Paul McCartney to the then Prime Minister of India A.B. Vajpayee holidaying there."[1]

Environmentally conscious hotels like the Fortune Bay Island Hotel at Port Blair have voluntarily adopted eco-conservation policies on their own since 1990s. They use sea water for all flushing and recycling it. They harvest all the rainwater possible and use very limited municipal supply. This is an existing role model, therefore, available in Andaman & Nicobar Islands. The administration however is yet to issue rules for hotels on the above subject. Licensing of new hotels should not only provide them minimum environmental standards but also their credentials as environmentally friendly hotels should be checked up.

The Eco-Tourism and Environmental Handbook: A Ready Reckoner for the Tourism Industry has been issued by Ministry of Tourism, Government of India in 2002 and is based on the National Eco-Tourism Policy of 1998, developed after interaction between governments, NGOs and the industry. It also takes into account the PATA Green Leaf Pledge signed in 1999. It mentions that there is a need to issue guidelines for creating an Environmental Management System (EMS) which has not been done so far. This will include issues like saving water and energy, making the tourism industry more environmentally friendly and ensuring no water pollution by ships, a new architecture policy, waste disposal and to develop the concept of Eco-Lodges in forests which are sustainable with environment. Introduction of an internationally accepted Eco-Lodge programme along with introduction of Global Green–21 as a global benchmarking developed by 182 Heads of States at the UN Rio de Janeiro Earth Summit will go a long way in making tourism sustainable.[2] There is a need to incorporate this in the tourism policy of Andaman & Nicobar Islands. Other best practices like tourist charter planes taking back their own garbage to some other locations can also be considered.

National Security and Uninhabited Islands

As already mentioned in chapter 1, Chinese have surreptitiously set up an outpost in uninhabited islands of South China Sea, filled it up with population, put their military and have established physical presence besides their dubious historic claims. Can this happen in Andaman & Nicobar Islands, especially in some uninhabited island? While there is no clear answer, the best way to ensure that it does not happen is to by establishing India's presence in more islands. The cheaper way to achieve it is by promoting tourism and not settling anymore population from mainland India. For example, Landfall Island is the northern most island opposite Coco Island of Myanmar. So far because of its logistics it is not popular with tourists. However, if defence forces want, a resort could be opened even if transport to it has to be subsidised. In contrast, Hainan Island of China in South China Sea has a submarine base on one side but China has opened it for tourism in a big way.

It has been decided at the highest levels of government in India to encourage mountaineering/adventure expeditions along international borders in the Himalayas. It was felt that this is a good way to convey that India has effective jurisdiction and control over its high mountain borders where there is no settled population due to terrain. Similarly opening of Tawang in Arunachal Pradesh to foreign tourists conveys a similar sentiment. In a similar way it would be wise to encourage and allow visits by boat or seaplanes to the various uninhabited islands, including night halts. Such visits can be used to gather information. Rules should be framed and tour guides/operators should be made to accompany visitors so that a watch can be kept as well as rules on waste and garbage disposal can be followed. Such tour operators should be licensed and made to report to the police any untoward incident and fined for lapses. Forest tours in the reserve forests should also be allowed and encouraged by the Forest Department. The license of tour operators should be revoked when found indulging in any activities against the rules (the recent case of tour operators taking tourists to Jarawas reserves in connivance with local police is one such case in point).

On the environmental front, Andaman & Nicobar Islands have nearly 90 per cent of its land coverage under forest. This is unique and also gives an added charm to the islands. As the UNDP Report states, even with the expansion of tourism the most significant continuing threats of environmental degradation will result from non-tourist activities. The tourism development strategy requires some 60 hectares out of a total forest cover of 5,629 sq km (about 0.01 per cent) for accommodation of new tourist facilities. The impact from the physical takeover of land for tourism is clearly negligible when compared to other threats to the environment. Similarly, environmental disturbances from the construction phase of tourism development will be minimal and transient.

Developing a tourism site/area within a forest reserve is a matter of great importance. In most wildlife and forest rich countries, forest reserves as well as wildlife game reserves provide within their protected area tourism enclaves. The world famous Kruger National Park in South Africa offers a number of enclaves within the forest reserve where there are hotels, guest houses, lodges. Spread over 20,720 sq km it has a number of residential enclaves where guests can stay in comfortable cottages subject to some restrictions like not playing music etc. There is a need to think on similar lines for creating attractive tourism enclaves within national parks of these islands.

Scuba Diving a Source of Surveillance and Environmental Protection

For sea based activities like scuba diving, snorkelling, sailing, deep sea fishing, live-on-board diving a new set of guidelines need to be developed to ensure that while India encourages these activities, the environment remains protected and is improved. Scuba diving as a sporting activity is extremely popular. Coral reefs are found only in warm waters and Andaman & Nicobar Islands are extremely fortunate in having a very large collection all over along with crystal clear water. With warm water good enough to swim without a wet or a dry suit, Andaman & Nicobar Islands offer great scuba dive sites. The only thing is that they are not developed up to the standards found in other countries like Thailand, Caribbean or Pacific islands. Sites all around Andaman & Nicobar Islands like Thailand, Sumatra, Maldives are getting famous and divers are keen on new sites. However, current prices charged by dive centres in Havelock Island are much higher than in neighbouring Thailand due to many factors. This needs to be further evaluated.

It is well recognised that scuba divers and dive resorts/camp owners are also great marine environmentalists. The reason is that their trade is such that only if the natural beauty they offer remains intact or improves that they remain in business. There are many instances of scuba diving clubs becoming defenders of the environment. In Andaman & Nicobar Islands scuba divers have reported to the authorities, an instance of a gunny bag full of plucked corals lying under the sea. It was obvious that some poacher had hidden it underwater in the hope of finding a convenient time to take it away. In another instance, a group reported dead seeing sharks as some unscrupulous fishermen had cut off fins of the sharks and left them to die in the sea.

The Tourism Policy also states that one of the unique selling points of the island is as one of the ideal dive destinations in Asia. To tap this unexplored potential, a well-defined scuba diving policy incorporating adequate safety regulations will need to be put in place. Scuba diving centres with certified instructors need to be promoted in the islands. The emphasis should be on self-regulation but a formal regulator should also be welcomed. However, the government is yet to provide even a single decompression chamber in spite of there being nine dive centres working. They have in fact closed the only state sponsored scuba diving centre. Scuba diving being a dangerous sport requires that a regulator should keep a check on the quality of equipment so that no untoward incident happens.

Private scuba diving centres need to be encouraged all along these islands. Such licensed centres can be run by qualified staff from the Professional Association of Diving Instructors (PADI) which is internationally accepted. Further, these centres can be used to keep a tab on both security issues like poaching etc. and environment issues like degradation of marine life and corals which are otherwise difficult to supervise at no cost to the government.

According to Tourism Statistics of Andaman & Nicobar Islands handbook there are nine dive centres/shops in Andaman of which six are found only in Havelock Island and three in and around Port Blair. There is a need to open up dive centres in remote islands also, wherever the corals are available. This can be done by having a proactive policy on scuba diving by allotting small pieces of land in remote islands or perhaps, the Department of Tourism/Forest Corporation constructing attractive dive centres with accommodation and leasing then out over the long term even at a subsidy, to attract dive centre companies from India and abroad to take then on lease with sufficient safeguards.

Deep sea fishing is yet another sport which offers great potential in Andaman & Nicobar Islands. This is so because availability of fish is plenty. While fish stock is getting depleted in most parts of the world, fishing is highly sustainable in these islands.

Good quality sports boats of all sizes will be required to develop water based activities. Cheap Rigid Inflatable Boats (RIB) can be high performance and high capacity and seaworthy if constructed with solid shaped hulls and inflatable collars. Similarly, Pontoon Boats with triple hulls have proved to be both seaworthy and comfortable. Innovation in boat making is very much required.

Remote location eco-resorts: There is a need to evolve a policy of location of eco-resorts of the high end type which will not only provide exclusivity but a location with an opportunity of surveillance to the security agencies. Such locations will most probably be in uninhabited islands on the coast. Initially a fund will have to be created to subsidise transport to and fro as is already being done by the administration for various inhabited islands. Over time if the resorts become viable, the subsidy could be withdrawn. The land allotment and cutting of trees will have to be minimal and only well-established resorts with background of eco-tourism after being shortlisted should be allowed to apply and compete. There would, of course, be strong environmental safeguards, which are now available under "responsible tourism" described in Chapter 9 or under "eco-tourism and environmental handbook" or under "PATA Green Leaf Pledge" described earlier in this chapter. Allotment of land will have to be minimal and there will be commitment of exclusivity to that resort.

POLICY TOWARDS NICOBAR ISLANDS

India's policy towards Nicobar Islands also needs a review. Nicobarese tribals have come a long way from their isolated days. They have grown as a tribal group, taking advantage of educational facilities offered by the government. The development of their society into cooperatives for sale of coconuts brought economic growth to these islands, especially in Car Nicobar where it was a great success and today the island of Car Nicobar through its cooperative societies owns four ocean going ships. The next stage of the tribals' growth could be led by tourism development and it is felt that they are ready for it provided it is done through their own cooperative societies and only their boys and girls are allowed to work in then after proper training. Car Nicobar is the most progressive of the Nicobar Islands. It also has an airfield belonging to the Air Force and, therefore limited high end tourism should be considered for flying in directly. However, proper consultation with the tribals must precede any such decision. The tribals have expressed their desire through their tribal council that they would welcome tourism. Their youth is already facing problems of educated unemployment. Tourism and deep sea fishing is the next big potential.

The defence authorities have said that they have recruited many Nicobarese and find them very good. Nicobarese are now seeking employment outside their islands. They are at a stage where they need to open new venues and what can be better than limited tourism in the Nicobars run by them. The Tribal Council and EHL have already drawn out plans for limited tourism in Car Nicobar. Now it is the Andaman & Nicobar Administration with MHA that need to change their policies to accommodate the aspirations of the growing Nicobarese. Car Nicobar has the advantage of the Air Force airstrip which is long enough to take any civil aircraft. Direct flights from South East Asia besides Port Blair would be a great opening for the Nicobarese. Limited direct international flights into Car Nicobar should be arranged on pilot basis.

It must be pointed out once again, as brought out in Chapter 2, Nicobarese tribals should be considered a major asset in India's security scenario as their dedication and loyalty to India can be taken for granted. However, the government must be sensitive to their aspirations and the demands of their youth. A mention must be made of the Nicobar youth's jest for sports, especially water based activities. They are great fishermen and go out to sea in their small dugouts whenever weather permits. They make their own snorkel, underwater eye glass and go arrow fishing in shallow waters. They have been winners of All India Subroto

Mukerjee Football Tournament many times and have also excelled in kayaking and rowing.

As brought out in Chapter 9, the main objective of encouraging international tourism and especially from the ASEAN countries is to tell the world and ASEAN countries in particular that India exists physically right up to the Straits of Malacca. The psychological impact of this could be tremendous. Once it is found by the well-heeled people who go to Cayman Islands or the Bahamas for holidays that this place is equally attractive as an eco-friendly destination, it will bring about a change in the attitude and thinking of the world that the geographic limit of India is not just mainland India. However, all this can be achieved by removing the cobwebs of various hues be it defence, environment or tourism. Hard defence strategies must be accompanied by a soft strategy to make the impact. Opening of Nicobars in this respect is important to achieve the objective of soft strategic challenge.

MASS TOURISM VERSUS HIGH VALUE TOURISM

The issue of complementarity between defence and civil policies with respect to these islands and the ongoing tussle between tourism and environment needs to be resolved. How can environmental protection be guaranteed when mass tourism is allowed? The so called 'LTC'[3] tourism had started taking its toll on Andaman & Nicobar Islands as large low income groups started descending onto Andamans. Without proper arrangements individuals opened up boarding houses and allowed large amounts of solid and liquid waste to go into the sea untreated. Such activities need to be stopped. It is necessary that minimum quality of accommodation is ensured so that basic minimum environmental conditions on waste, garbage disposal, liquid waste, water harvesting etc. are introduced. High end but low numbers has to be the guiding principle instead of unnecessary jargon which exists in India's tourism policy with the purpose of boosting figures of tourist arrivals.

India needs to emulate those islands and other destinations which have maintained their environment by strict controls and close supervision. There is also an urgent need to stop the growth of low quality hotels say below three stars, as then only better monitoring will be possible. There is also a need to ensure that existing low quality hotels are upgraded and brought to a minimum standard. Price as a filter can also be used as a mechanism as is being done Bhutan. As Amitabh Kant writes 'research in the US travel industry has revealed that 83 per cent of travelers are inclined to support Green Travel Companies which focus on low environmental impact and energy use and respect culture and well-being of the local population'. Tourists are not always looking for the lowest price provided the quality of the offer is good. These islands are turning out to be a destination for low end travellers both domestic and international. This is so because the administration has allowed mushrooming of one or two star hotels and dormitories. The author met a foreigner on his flight into Port Blair who had plans to go to Havelock Island, a popular destination, and said that he plans to pay Rs.200 or US$ 4 per night for a 30 day stay. Such accommodation could hardly contribute to the economy. The Bhutan example of keeping a minimum daily spend of US$ 200 to keep the low end travelers out appears to be a sensible alternative.

LOCATING TOURISM SITES WITH STRATEGIC VALUE

Location of tourism sites should be based on strategic planning also. While islands like Havelock have come up because of natural market forces, the administration in consultation with defence and police authorities should also set up resorts and forest lodges based on perceived strategic importance of a location. The importance of opening these areas from a strategic point of view will also justify if any subsidy is to be given to the resort or in transportation of guests. Opening remote uninhabited islands needs to be in tandem with security requirements. There is enough evidence as brought out in Chapter 8 that remote locations are being used by fishermen from neighboring countries. Operating in groups to collect sea cucumber they have their hide outs in remote locations in Andaman & Nicobar Islands where diesel, spare parts etc. have been stored. How can one assume that terrorists and people inimical to India will not be able to exploit such glaring lacunae in existing surveillance and use it not for poaching sea cucumbers but for anti-national crimes. While it may not be possible to have a complete surveillance over the creeks and remote locations, opening of small tourist resorts even with subsidies, to keep vigilance may be worthwhile. For example, a resort at Landfall Island in the north Andamans facing Coco Islands could keep vigil over any undesirable activity coming from Coco Islands. Opening of resorts on the west coast of the island where poachers go and hide their equipment is another possibility.

ISSUES OF CONNECTIVITY TO ANDAMAN & NICOBAR ISLANDS

Aviation and tourism, especially high end type, have a very close relationship. If tourism is to be encouraged, direct flights from South East Asia and other places need to be encouraged. Granting of liberal bilateral rights or even declaring open skies for Andamans may be a solution as Port Blair has already been declared an international airport but there are no scheduled flights from any foreign country interested in coming in, due to poor tourism infrastructure.

Use of aviation as a catalyst and an enabler should be employed. This involves permitting and encouraging direct flights from South East Asian countries like Singapore, Thailand, Malaysia or Indonesia. All these countries have developed excellent tourist spots and we need to leverage them to attract tourists directly from there without coming into Indian mainland. Further, there are four airstrips in Andaman & Nicobar Islands namely, Port Blair and Diglipur in the Andamans & Car Nicobar and Campbell Bay in the Nicobars. All this should be put to use for tourism also. Besides this, use of small amphibious aircrafts to take tourists to remote locations in various islands should be encouraged. This will restrict only high end travellers due to higher ticket prices.

Port Blair in the Andaman Islands is about 1,200 km from the Indian mainland. In the 1950s it was connected to the mainland by a ship called *MV Maharaja* which used to make a monthly trip from Calcutta to Port Blair. Inter-island travel was worse. Traders used to bring their own boats to collect coconuts and would take passengers. By 1955 the first aerial service started with the Indian Airlines connecting Calcutta (now Kolkata) to Port Blair with a technical stopover in Rangoon (now Yangon) for refuelling. There are three other airfields in Andaman & Nicobar Islands, they being in Campbell Bay in Great Nicobar Islands, Car Nicobar, and Diglipur in the North Andaman Islands. The Airfield at Car Nicobar, which was also built by the Japanese during their occupation during World War II, is with the IAF and is a full length airfield which meets all requirements.[4] The other airport at Campbell Bay is only 3,000 ft long but with the announcement of the establishment of the forward base called Baaz for the Naval Air Force, it will be extended to 9000 ft. Night landing facilities will also be provided in due course. The Diglipur airfield is about 3000 ft and there are plans to extend it. Presently, an odd private plane from abroad lands in Port Blair with an average of one per month. Domestic schedules have improved and so have the number of flights. It is now possible to come into Port Blair the same day from Delhi or Mumbai and return the same day unlike earlier when one had to compulsorily spend a night in Kolkata or Chennai on the way to Port Blair.[5] There has never been a regular direct commercial service to any another airfield in the islands. Earlier Indian Airlines did start a service to Car Nicobar by extending a flight from Calcutta-Port Blair-Car Nicobar-Madras. But this did not last long due to poor traffic. However, with more prosperity and more government staff, there is a need to have air connectivity from mainland to Car Nicobar by extending a mainland flight to Port Blair even with a subsidy.

Domestic Air Connectivity: Government of India Policy on Connecting Remote Locations

The use of a highly subsidised mainland-island passenger ship service needs to be examined from the angle of in-migration, low end tourism and eventual ecological damage. While one could appreciate subsidised tickets for islanders, high ticket subsidy for tourists and mainlanders needs reconsideration in order to protect these islands from environmental pollution, in-migration and low end tourists.

The Group Dispersal guidelines for Commercial Scheduled Air Services was announced by the DGCA 1994 after the domestic monopoly of Indian Airlines was abolished by repeal of the Air Corporation Act of 1954 in 1994.These guidelines mandated that all scheduled carriers plying on Category I A routes had to compulsorily ply 10 per cent of their flights on category II routes, generally loss making routes consisting of North East India, Ladakh and Jammu and Kashmir (J&K) and Andaman & Nicobar Islands. Category III consisted of remaining routes. It was obligatory on part of the scheduled airlines to deploy on Category II, IIA and III routes, a specific percentage as per following:

- On Category II routes—at least 10 per cent of the capacity deployed on routes in Category I.
- On Category IIA routes—at least 10 per cent of the category deployed in Category II.
- On Category III routes—at least, 50 per cent of the capacity deployed on routes in category I.

Although, some airlines started to ply to Port Blair, it was felt that they either avoided this route or formed a possible cartel to hike up the price. The ticket price from the mainland to Port Blair during season from Calcutta or Chennai could go up as high as Rs.20,000/- to Rs.25,000/- one way. As Port Blair became a preferred holiday destination with Indians, especially due to LTC being given out by the government and public sector, Port Blair being the longest destination from most points of the country became the preferred destination. The airlines made huge profits by increasing the fares.[6] A request was made by the Andaman Government to fix a sub-quota of two-three per cent within the 10 per cent quota under group disbursal guidelines to DGCA but so far there has been no relief. The need to bring air services within reach of the ordinary traveller to Port Blair by way of a reasonable fare is a just demand. There is also a need to connect Car Nicobar.

The huge shipping subsidy being borne by the Andaman Administration makes little economic sense.

Direct International Connectivity

Why is direct international connectivity a necessary requirement for Indian policy of leveraging the strategic potential? It is very significant for various reasons. These islands are closer to Straits of Malacca than mainland India. This aspect needs to be brought out in the international tourist circles and through them conveyed that India' s soft power jurisdiction extends right up to Straits of Malacca. The route to Andamans can be circuitous for foreign tourists who are coming from east of India. They have to travel to mainland India and then take a domestic flight to Port Blair. Further, Indian domestic flights are very costly[7] and a trip from mainland India during the season can be very expensive as prices of domestic tickets tend to fluctuate. The Port Blair tickets during season are often prohibitive. Direct international flights will correct this imbalance.

While domestic connectivity has improved with about 10 commercial landings a day, there is still no international connectivity. In order to expose these islands to high end foreign tourists India needs to have direct connectivity from South East Asia. Otherwise, for a foreign tourist it takes very long to connect to a flight from mainland India. Direct connectivity with Phuket, Bangkok or Singapore may be the answer. This is so because the distance from Port Blair to Phuket is shorter than distances between Port Blair and the mainland. However, efforts by Andaman Trade Association which signed an MoU with their counterpart in Thailand (Appendix 2) failed to get a direct flight to Port Blair because of the reluctance of Civil and Defence authorities to giving clearance.

Port Blair International Airport

Although the airport has been lengthened to 11,000 feet and declared international, the airport terminal at Port Blair has proved to be inadequate. With a peak time capacity of 200 persons it is already experiencing 700 to 800 passengers at peak time. A new terminal complex on 25 acres of land has been designed and approved which will cater to a much higher number of passengers at peak time. It will have two aero bridges and a separation between domestic and international flights. The Planning Commission has approved Rs.540 crores for it and the AAI will start construction soon on a plot next to the existing terminal and hopes to complete it in three years. With this Port Blair will be fully ready and operational to receive direct international flights from abroad in a proper manner unlike the present terminal which is really meant for domestic flights. Separation of domestic and international flights is most essential and the new Port Blair airport terminal will provide this and other modern facilities like aero bridges etc. Customs and immigration facilities will now be provided as international traffic increases.

Shipping Subsidy Versus Air Tickets

Andaman Administration runs a fleet of government owned ships at huge subsidy between the mainland and Port Blair and also between the habited islands. Besides annual dry docking for two months due to inefficient management when they are not available, this subsidised shipping service that gives up to 90 per cent for the 'islanders' and a little less for others is proving to be an inefficient drain on the exchequer. Attempts by the administration to substitute it for charter plane services between the mainland and Port Blair giving islanders about 80 per cent subsidy but providing them 40 per cent seats with the rest on commercial rates is being envisaged. Since the aircraft will be on wet charter there is no capital cost of purchase unlike in shipping in which ships are owned. This innovation, if it takes place, will eliminate the shipping of passengers from the mainland to Andaman & Nicobar Islands and ships will be used for cargo only. Purchase and maintenance of ships for passengers and cargo is a huge expense for the civil administration. If all passengers are made to go by air with local islanders getting subsidy it will be a huge saving for the administration as efficiency of ships is very poor. These savings could be used to improve inter-island connectivity both by ship and air and will be a great benefit to both islands and tourists. The economics of wet charter of aircraft and ships for inter-island traffic can be of great benefit to the administration as well as the public.

The example of a similar commitment by the Government of India towards Indians going for Haj pilgrimage to Mecca can be cited. During British times and even up to early 2000, the Government of India had owned a full time passenger ship for this purpose. By 2000 it was found that the cost of maintaining a ship and running it between Mumbai and Jeddah was very high. Instead if aircrafts were chartered on wet lease they could travel more efficiently and there would be no maintenance cost. This also provided direct embarkation with a large number of cities in India as embarkation points for direct flights, instead of pilgrims travelling to Mumbai to take the ships. This switch over to air travel has worked well and both passengers and the government have benefited from the same. We need to follow a similar strategy for these islands.

MoU WITH PHUKET: SISTER CITIES

The business community of Andaman Islands as well as the tribals on Nicobar Islands are keen on greater economic prosperity for the islands. The Andaman Chamber of Commerce and Industry has been making efforts to increase tourism and other trade. On November 30, 2003 an MoU was signed between Phuket Chamber of Commerce and Andaman Chamber of Commerce with the Governor of Phuket and First Secretary of the Embassy of India as witnesses. This MOU's objective as stated in its preamble is to further the development of bilateral economic relationship by a forum of businessmen to discuss and explore business opportunities in trade, investment, transfer of technology, services and other industrial sectors. This MOU has not had any further advancement or implementation.

Again on June 29, 2005 an agreement was signed at Phuket between the Lt. Governor of Andaman & Nicobar Islands and Governor of Phuket Province to promote and undertake regular exchanges and interaction in the following areas:

Tourism: Exchange of tourist missions for fairs, expositions, tourists' fairs, promotion of tourist destinations for each sister city, and finally promotion of international tourism between one and another.

Education and Culture: Cultural Exchanges-Phuket days in the city of Port Blair and City of Port Blairs days in Phuket Province. Cultural exchanges between students, artists and professionals.

Urban Development: Exchange of expertise in innovative water harvesting techniques; upgradation of water treatment plants; study of old water supply network and rationalisation of water distribution network; desilting-relining of old sewer lines.

Solid Waste Management: Study of modern and sustainable methods of solid waste management particularly in the areas of Andaman & Nicobar Islands, of roads and public places, safe disposal through transportation, development of proper Andaman & Nicobar Islands landfill sites, segregation of bio-degradable solid wastes and recycling.

Commerce: Exchange of Commerce Missions and participation in expositions, fairs and other promotions with increased flow of goods and services between parties.

Investment: Exchange of business missions, information sharing of investment possibilities and business opportunities.

None of the activities mentioned in the MOU have been carried out and both the MoUs are lying defunct.

A major factor which comes in the way of implementing the two MOUs is the indifference shown by the governments and lack of direct connectivity between the two. While Port Blair has been declared a major port and the airfield international, it has made little difference to the present position. No direct scheduled or even charter flights come into Port Blair nor do any international ships.

In this connection a high powered delegation from Phuket consisting of Governor of Phuket and Governor of Krabi along with 30 officers and businessmen came to Port Blair in a RTAF aircraft. They also brought with them some ethnic Indian businessmen and also one diplomat from the Indian consulate in Bangkok. The Andaman Chamber of Commerce made some arrangements for business discussions. The Lt. Governor of Andaman Islands was present. However, the government was not ready for any positive investment proposal. The delegation went back disappointed. In 2006 there was also a press article in the Phuket Gazette of May 12, 2006 that the Governor of Phuket was planning to cancel the "sister-cities Agreement." The Andaman Chamber of Commerce also tried to bring in a direct flight from Thailand but all efforts failed at the government level.

While Thailand is interested in having close relations and commercial arrangements with Andaman & Nicobar Islands, it is India which is dragging its feet. This is yet another confirmation of the hypothesis of masterly inactivity and benign neglect of these islands by India.

TELECOM CONNECTIVITY

Another issue which is related to the development of the islands is good telecom and internet connectivity which are crucial to both growth and tourism. While cell phone connectivity is available in some inhabited islands, the quality and reach is not good enough to reach all the inhabited islands. It is for the Andaman & Nicobar Islands Administration to ensure that there is good connectivity in all the inhabited islands. Even under the Millennium Development Goals (MDGs) bridging the digital divide applies to these islands also. India has under the Telecom Ministry, a Universal Service Obligation Fund (USOF) which can be used to provide cell and internet service to all the inhabited islands. During the author's visit in June 2012 the internet connectivity was very poor in Port Blair, limited in Havelock and non-existent in Neil Islands. It is necessary to lay out a good telecom infrastructure with good quality internet. This is also a requirement of the defence forces and it needs to be taken up in a more serious and urgent basis.

According to Shirangi Narayan[8] during her visit in January 2013, even cell phones were barely available out of Port Blair. Out of the 36 hours she spent in North Andaman she was unable to get cell phone reception for eight hours and internet for 12 hours. However, a project to lay optical fiber cable for Rs.750 crores has been approved and will be completed by 2015. Internet connectivity with broadband is a must for promoting these islands. The USOF for this purpose should be used to connect all inhabited islands up to the Great Nicobar Islands.

THE INDO-PACIFIC AND THE NICOBAR ISLANDS—STRATEGIC ANGLE

The report of the Trade Development Authority on the Great Nicobar Island, the largest of the Nicobar group, produced in the early 1970s needs to be reviewed and revised. This report had proposed that after the British leave Hong Kong and Hong Kong merges with mainland China, a number of rich Indian business groups would look for a location to relocate themselves. It was envisaged that Great Nicobar island as a free port had great potential in attracting such people. As usual, no decision was taken by the Government of India and Hong Kong is now a Special Administered Region (SAR) of China and this option is closed. But Great Nicobar still retains its potential due to its strategic location on the mouth of Straits of Malacca. This island has 400 sq km of land mass with sufficient fresh water. However, about 2/3rd of the Great Nicobar Islands have since been declared as a Biosphere Reserve, consisting of 885 sq km. Within it is the Campbell Bay National Park of 426 sq kms. Therefore, only 1/3rd of the landmass is available. Of this a lot of land at the tip of Straits of Malacca has gone under water including the lighthouse due to the tsunami of 2004. In effect, about 130 sq km will be available for development including defence requirements and land for local settlers. As such, Great Nicobar Islands cannot anymore provide a base for major population as envisaged in the Trade Development Authority Report of the 1970s. But it can provide shipping facilities like bunkering, transhipment etc.

The strategic location of the Great Nicobar Island on the mouth of Straits of Malacca gives it great potential for bunkering of ships with huge tonnage passing by. With the opening of Naval Air Station (NAS) Baaz at Campbell Bay at Great Nicobar Islands, opportunities to fully exploit the geographic location of Great Nicobar Islands in commercial terms in coordination with defence requirements should be carried out without any delay. This will complement the soft power that India needs to display at the western entrance of Straits of Malacca. About one third of the world's sea borne trade passes by Great Nicobar Island. This activity will not disturb the forest and biosphere reserves but will enhance India's status in the Malacca region.

The Nancowry-Kamorta harbour in the Nicobars is yet another fantastic feature of the Nicobar. This harbour is excellent for keeping ships and submarines and is quite close to Great Nicobar Island.

On the economic front also China has become a major factor to deal with. In 2010-11 it exported US$ 40 billion worth of goods to India while India exported only US$ 20 billion worth. Most items of exports from China were value added manufactured goods while India's exports there were mainly raw material with iron ore making up 46 per cent of the basket.[9] Further, India and China have agreed to a trade target of US$ 100 billion. India, would have a serious problem if there is a sudden disruption of supplies coming from China. Such heavy economic dependence does not make sense when political relations between the two countries are far from good. In such a scenario it is very necessary for India to safeguard its maritime domain where so far China has not made a dent. It cannot ignore this anymore.

The Chinese expansionist tendency with use of force, wherever necessary, is also well established. With under water wealth becoming a viable source of oil, gas and minerals, the Chinese have set their eyes on South China Sea and East China Sea by making historical claims and making their presence felt by using both civil and military vessels. In this context, India's role in Vietnam takes new shape as it is also interested in exploring, exploiting and sharing the oil deposits belonging to Vietnam and also providing a counter to Chinese position in South China Sea.

India's legitimate interest in South China Sea with joint exploration in Vietnam is a factor to be taken into account when analysing strategic depth. With this also comes the need to strengthen its position in Andaman & Nicobar Islands.

Eco-Tourism with Security Scenario in Mind

Before the islands are opened to tourism a well thought out tourism policy should be put in place. Within eco-tourism scuba diving and fishing should be encouraged. Strict rules with an implementation mechanism should be evolved. Pollution of the crystal clear water of these islands has to be avoided. With a few precautions like these a good tourism policy can be evolved for the next stage of growth of these islands. The Environment and Forest Department should be more involved in the management of this policy.

During a presentation made to the author by the Tri Command it was brought out in passing that with only 17 out of 572 islands and islets being inhabited, it is very difficult to maintain good surveillance over these islands. Although, joint patrol is conducted with the army, navy, coast guard, marine police and forest department in remote islands and sometimes a camp is set up for a day or so, surveillance in these islands with countless creeks is a gigantic job. It is, therefore, felt that tourism in these islands should be dealt with as a strategic tool and should compliment the defence services.

A New Administrative Set up for Andaman & Nicobar Islands

Can the present set up at Andaman & Nicobar Islands deliver a policy change as proposed in this book?

It is unlikely that the present set up, which is geared towards preservation of the status quo, will be able to do so. The MHA, which is the administrative ministry for the islands has too many problems in hand to look into development, security and environmental issues which if mixed together in the right proportions can bring about a lasting change in India's security scenario without sacrificing the environmental aspect.

Therefore there is, perhaps, a need for a new administrative set up for these islands. The role of MHA over the years has been to keep these islands secure and without trouble. However, if India adopts a forward policy there is a need to seriously review the administrative structure and take it out of the MHA. Like NEFA which was created out of Assam and made into an agency under the Foreign Ministry for a decade, a similar policy should be followed by putting it under a new structure similar to what has been done for North–East India. A new Ministry called Development of North East Region (DONER) has been created for North East India. Therefore, only such a step can bring about the necessary changes in policy and implementation in our forward policy under the LEP for India's security scenario.

Towards a Philosophy and Strategy for Andaman & Nicobar Islands: Leveraging the Potential—Complementing the Soft Power with Hard Power

There are three perspectives on the Andaman & Nicobar Islands. The first is to do nothing in particular and let the things happen at their own pace. This is the philosophy of *Masterly Inactivity*. The second way of looking at these islands is to bring greater connectivity with the mainland to ensure that the islands maintain the minimum link with the mainland. This can be called the philosophy of *Benign Neglect*. The third way is the way the author is proposing. Leverage the location and use the islands as strategic assets for benefit of the islands and the country. This may be called the strategy of *Leveraging the Potential.*

A Philosophy for NEFA

India developed a philosophy and a strategy for NEFA in the 1950s and 1960s. Post-independence, as a forward strategy, NEFA was carved out of the northern hill districts of Assam in 1954 and the Governor of Assam was put directly in charge of the Agency as an Agent of President of India. A new civil service was created out of Ex-military officers called the Indian Frontier Administrative Service. NEFA, as the Agency was called was put under direct charge of the Foreign Ministry with the purpose of extending the administration up to the Indo-Tibetan Border based on the McMahon Line of 1914 and integrating the various tribes of NEFA without destroying their tribal traditions and culture. Dr. Verrier Elwin, a famous anthologist was made the advisor to the Governor of Assam for this purpose. Tribal Welfare and Protection was the cornerstone of this philosophy.

The philosophy for NEFA was to integrate 50 plus tribes in the region with the mainstream but also not to allow their economic or regional exploitation by non-tribals and others. This philosophy has stood the test of time. NEFA was transferred back to MHA in 1965 but much was achieved during the eleven years under the MEA. Subsequently, it was converted into the state of Arunachal Pradesh. The philosophy for NEFA of the 1950s has served the dual purpose of extending India's actual administration up to McMahon line, providing modern amenities like roads, electricity, health facilities and schools to the tribals of these hills in a manner which is not exploitative, preserving their culture and integrating them with the rest of the country.

During its early years NEFA was given very special treatment and massive air support by the air force and some private companies were provided to open up the region which was otherwise inaccessible. Today, after so many years, Arunachal Pradesh is more accessible as a very large number of roads have been constructed and dependence on air support is negligible. This special action is proof of India's actual administration over this territory and has stood well internationally in spite of Chinese claims over the entire erstwhile NEFA and now Arunachal Pradesh.

A Philosophy and Strategy for Andaman & Nicobar Islands

India now needs to develop a fresh philosophy and strategy for Andaman & Nicobar Islands on similar lines to NEFA due to their strategic location and isolation from the mainland. The fact is that these islands are close to countries of ASEAN where tourism is already booming. Direct air and sea connection with these countries is essential to leverage the advantage of their goodwill built up all over the world and also to bring ASEAN closer to India. This will give a fresh impetus to India's Look East Policy. In order to do so India needs to develop a Special Tourism Plan for Andaman & Nicohar Islands with this philosophy in mind rather than the present tourism policy which is aimed more at integrating India's mainland domestic tourism with Andaman & Nicobar Islands with no regard to the quality of tourism or strategic implications. A strategic master plan needs to be redrawn for this purpose after taking into account the various environmental and strategic concerns integrating the civil and military requirements and merging it with India's LEP of 1991.

NOTES

1. Amitabh Kant, *Branding India: An Incredible Story,* HarperCollins, India, 2009.
2. Mandip Singh Soin (Ed.), *Eco-Tourism and Environment Handbook,* Environment and Eco-Tourism Heritage Committee, Pacific–Asia Travel Association, India Chapter, introduced by Incredible India, Ministry of Tourism, Government of India. See www.incredibleindia.org
3. LTC stands for Leave Travel Concession. All government servants and also employees of the Public Sector are entitled to visit with their family any part of India, once in four years. As Andaman & Nicobar Islands is the furthest it has become a very popular destination for such free travellers who form a base of mass tourism.
4. The Japanese had built two air fields in Car Nicobar during their occupation. However, the second airfield was closed down after they left because it was located at the centre of the islands and the tribals did not want it. The present one is at one corner of the island and is with the Indian Air Force.
5. Indian Airlines used to run a weekly service to Car Nicobar prior to 1994 when its domestic monopoly was taken away. This weekly service from Kolkata-Port Blair-Car Nicobar-Chennai and return was of great advantage. This was discontinued after its domestic monopoly was taken away and there has been no replacement by any airline.
6. This also became a scam by travel agents who could manipulate the ticket price and provide cash or other incentives to the users.
7. Domestic Indian flight tickets are very costly due to high taxes on fuel, service tax on tickets, custom duty and many other charges. International flights have lesser taxes and duty free fuel.
8. "Internet in Andamans", *Governance Now,* January 1-15, 2013.
9. *Indian Express, September* 01, 2010.

Appendix 1

The Boundary Agreement Between China and Pakistan, March 1963

The Government of the People's Republic of China and the Government of Pakistan;

Having agreed, with a view to ensuring prevailing peace and tranquility on the border, to formally delimit and demarcate the boundary between China's Sinkiang and the contiguous areas the defence of which is under the actual control of Pakistan, in a spirit of fairness, reasonableness, mutual understanding and mutual accommodation, and on the basis of the 10 principles as enunciated in the Bandung conference;

Being convinced that this would not only give full expression to the desire of the peoples of China and Pakistan for the development of good neighbourly and friendly relations, but also help safeguard Asian and world peace.

Have resolved for this purpose to conclude the present agreement and have appointed as their respective plenipotentiaries the following:

For the Government of the PRC; Chen Yi, Minister of Foreign Affairs;

For the Government of Pakistan; Mr. Zulfikar Ali Bhutto, MEA; who, having mutually examined their full powers and found them to be in good and due form, have agreed upon the following:

Article 1

In view of the fact that the boundary between China's Sinkiang and contiguous areas the defence of which is under the actual control of Pakistan has never been formally delimited, two parties agree to delimit it on the basis of the traditional customary boundary line including natural features and in a spirit of equality, mutual benefit and friendly co-operation.

Article 2

(One) In accordance with the principle expounded in Article 1 of the present agreement, the two parties have fixed, as follows the alignment of the entire boundary line between China's Sinkiang and the contiguous areas the defence of which is under the actual control of Pakistan:

(1) Commencing from its north-western extremity at height 5,630 metres (a peak, the reference co-ordinates of which are approximately longitude 74 degrees 34 minutes east and latitude 37 degrees 03 minutes north), the boundary line runs generally eastward and then southeastward strictly along the main watershed between the tributaries of the Tashkurgan river of the Tarim river system on the one hand and tributaries of the Hunza river of the Indus river system on the other hand, passing through the Kalik Daban (Dawan), the Mintake Daban (pass), the Kharchanai Daban (named on the Chinese map only), the Mutsjilga Daban (named on the Chinese map only), and the Parpik Pass (named on the Pakistan map only), and reaches the Khunjerab (Yutr) Daban (Pass).

(2) After passing through the Khunjerab (Yutr) Daban (pass), the boundary line runs generally southward along the above mentioned main watershed up to a mountain-top south of this Daban (pass), where it leaves the main watershed to follow the crest of a spur lying generally in a southeasterly direction, which is the watershed between the Akijilga river (a nameless corresponding river on the Pakistan map) on the one hand, and the Taghumbash (Oprang) river and the Koliman Su (Oprang Jilga) on the other hand.

According to the map of the Chinese side, the boundary line, after leaving the southeastern extremity of this spur, runs along a small section of the middle line of the bed of the Keliman Su to reach its confluence with the Kelechin River. According to the map of the Pakistan side, the boundary line, after leaving the southeastern extremity of the spur, reaches the sharp bend of the Shaksgam or Muztagh River.

(3) From the aforesaid point, the boundary line runs up the Kelechin river (Shaksgam or Mistagh river) along the middle line of its bed to its confluence (reference co-ordinates approximately longitude 76 degrees 02 minutes east and latitude 36 degrees 26 minutes north) with the Snorbulak Daria (shimshal river or Braldu river).

(4) From the confluence of the aforesaid two rivers, the boundary line, according to the map of the Chinese side, ascends the crest of a spur and runs along it to join the Karokoram range main watershed at a mountain-top (reference co-ordinates approximately longitude 75 degrees 54 minutes east and latitude 36 degrees 15 minutes north) which on this map is shown as belonging to the Shorgulak mountain. According to the map of the Pakistan side, the boundary line from the confluence of the above-mentioned two rivers ascends the crest of a corresponding spur and runs along it, passing through height 6,520 metres (21,390 feet) till it joins the Karakoram range main watershed at a peak (reference co-ordinates approximately longitude 75 degrees 57 minutes east and latitude 36 degrees 03 minutes north).

(5) Thence, the boundary line, running generally southward and then eastward, strictly follows the Karakoram range main watershed which separates the Tarim river drainage system from the Indus river drainage system, passing through the east Mustagh pass (Mustagh pass), the top of the Chogri peak (K-2), the top of the broad peak, the top of the Gasherbrum mountain 8068, the Indirakoli pass (names on the Chinese maps only) and the top of the Teram Kankri peak, and reaches its southeastern extremity at the Karakoram pass.

(Two) The alignment of the entire boundary line as described in section one of this article, has been drawn on the one million scale map of the Chinese side in Chinese and the one million scale map of the Pakistan side in English which are signed and attached to the present agreement. (Not attached in this book)

(Three) In view of the fact that the maps of the two sides are not fully identical in their representation of the topographical features the two parties have agreed that the actual features on the ground shall prevail, so far as the location and alignment of the boundary described in Section one is concerned, and that they will be determined as far as possible by joint survey on the ground.

Article 3

The two parties have agreed that:

> Wherever the boundary follows a river, the middle line of the river, the middle line of the river bed shall be the boundary line; and that wherever the boundary passes through Daban (pass), the water-parting line thereof shall be the boundary line.

Article 4

I. The two parties have agreed to set up, as soon as possible, a joint boundary demarcation commission. Each side will appoint a chairman, one or more members and a certain number of advisers and technical staff. The joint boundary demarcation commission is charged with the responsibility, in accordance with the provisions of the present agreement, to hold concrete discussions on and carry out the following tasks jointly:

(1) To conduct necessary surveys of the boundary area on the ground, as stated in Article 2 of the present agreement, so as to set up boundary markers at places considered to be appropriate by the two parties and to delineate the boundary line of the jointly prepared accurate maps.

(2) To draft a protocol setting forth in detail the alignment of the entire boundary line and the location of all the boundary markers and prepare and get printed detailed maps, to be attached to the protocol, with the boundary line and the location of the boundary markers shown on them.

II. The aforesaid protocol, upon being signed by the representatives of the government of the two countries, shall become an annex to the present agreement, and the detailed maps shall replace the maps attached to the present agreement.

III. Upon the conclusion of the above-mentioned protocol, the tasks of the joint boundary demarcation commission shall be terminated.

Article 5

The two parties have agreed that any dispute concerning the boundary, which may arise after the delimitation of the boundary line actually existing between the two countries shall be settled peacefully by the two parties through friendly consultations.

Article 6

The two Parties have agreed that after the settlement of the Kashmir dispute between Pakistan and India, the sovereign authority concerned will reopen negotiations with the Government of the PRC, on the boundary as described in Article 2 of the present agreement, so as to sign a formal Boundary Treaty to replace the present agreement:

Provided that in the event of that sovereign authority being Pakistan, the provisions of this agreement and the aforesaid Protocol shall be maintained in the formal Boundary Treaty to be signed between the PRC and Pakistan.

Article 7

The present agreement shall come into force on the date of its signature.

Done in duplicate in Peking on the second day of March, 1963, in the Chinese and English language, both texts being equally authentic.

Marshal Chen Yi, PRC and Zulfikar Ali Bhutto, Plenipotentiary of the Government of Pakistan.

Appendix 2

Memorandum of Understanding Between Phuket Chamber of Commerce and Andaman Chamber of Commerce and Industry, November 2003

Objective

The fundamental objective of the MOU is to further the development of bilateral economic relations by providing a forum for businessmen of both the countries to meet, discuss and explore business opportunities in trade, investments, transfer of technology, services and other industrial sectors.

Cooperation

The Phuket Chamber of Commerce and The Andaman Chamber of Commerce and Industry formally undertake to initiate and develop bilateral actions of co-operation within the principle of mutual assistance and support, in line with the following priorities:

- To develop strong institutional relations in order to establish a sustainable mechanism of dialogue and forums of discussions;
- To provide their members with information on the general economic situation, taxation, investments opportunities, trade policies and legislative changes therein;
- To promote the establishment of legal and administrative conditions favourable to the creation of a business climate enhancing the development of trade and economic relations between The Andaman & Nicobar Islands and Phuket.
- To encourage businessmen of both countries to participate in exhibitions and fairs held in The Andaman & Nicobar Islands and Phuket.
- To develop tools for co-operation between The Phuket Chamber of Commerce and The Andaman Chamber of Commerce and Industry which would allow an attractive role of both parties in the implementation of The Andaman & Nicobar lslands/Phuket trade and co-operation agreements.

1. The Phuket Chamber of Commerce and The Andaman Chamber of Commerce and Industry undertake to promote within their respective

regions and institutions all aspects related to economic development and trade relations between Andaman & Nicobar Islands and Phuket.

2. The present agreement shall enter into force upon its signature.
3. Modifications and amendments to this agreement must be approved by the competent bodies of each organisation.
4. This agreement may be terminated by either party by written notice to the other party within a sixty days notice.
5. All agreements on commerce will be ratified by each Chamber of Commerce.

The present agreement has been established in two copies, equally authentic, each party recognising having received its copy.

Signed:

Pamuke Achariyachai.
Chairman, Phuket Chamber of
Commerce.

Mohammed H. Jadwet.
President: Andaman Chamber of
Commerce and Industry.

Witness:

Udomsak Usawarangkura.
Phuket Governor.

J.R. Sharma
First Secretary Commercial
Embassy of India - Bangkok

Date: 30 November 2003

Appendix 3

Agreement of Friendship/Cooperation Between City of Port Blair and Phuket Province, June 2005

The City of Port Blair, Capital of Andaman & Nicobar Islands, Republic of India, and Phuket Province of the Kingdom of Thailand (hereinafter referred to as "Parties");

Desiring to establish and develop relations of friendship between the parties for the good of their citizens; wishing to contribute to the strengthening of relations between the Republic of India and the Kingdom of Thailand as a whole;

Have agreed as follows:

Article 1

The Parties agree to promote international understanding and strengthen the relationship through tourism, education, culture, urban development, commerce and investments.

Article 2

The Parties shall undertake regular exchanges and interactions in the areas which include, *inter alia*:

- Tourism: Exchange of tourist missions for fairs, expositions, tourist festivals, promotion of tourist destinations for each sister city, and finally, promotion of international tourism between one another.
- Education and Culture: Cultural exchanges—Phuket days in City of Port Blair and City of Port Blair days in Phuket Province. Cultural exchanges of students, artists and professionals.
- Urban development: Exchange of expertise in innovative water harvesting techniques; up gradation of water treatment plants; study of old water supply network and rationalisation of water distribution network; desilting—relining of old sewerage lines.
- Solid Waste Management: Study of modern and sustainable methods of solid waste management particularly in the areas of Andaman & Nicobar Islands of roads and public places, safe disposal through transportation, development of proper Andaman & Nicobar Islands land-

fill sites, segregation of bio-degradable and non-biodegradable solid wastes and recycling.

- Commerce: Exchange of commerce missions and participation in expositions, fairs, business forums and other promotions with the increased flow of goods and services between the parties.
- Investments: Exchange of business missions, information sharing of investment possibilities and business opportunities.

Article 3

The parties shall make every effort to contribute to the fostering of relationship and cooperation particularly in the areas of tourism, education and culture, urban development, solid waste management, commerce and investments.

Article 4

The Parties shall utilise any or all of the following methods to carry out this cooperation:

- Organisation Andaman & Nicobar Islandisation of seminars, conferences, meetings, symposiums, workshops etc.
- Exchanges of experts and students in the areas of activity.
- Exchanges of information.
- Exchanges of visits by cultural troupes.
- Technical consulting.

The parties can agree on other means of cooperation other than these referred to in this Article.

Article 5

The Department of Local Self Government (LSG), Government of Andaman & Nicobar Islands, and the Department of Local Self Government of the Kingdom of Thailand, are responsible for implementing the objectives and programmes envisaged under this agreement.

Article 6

The exchange of civil servants and technicians shall be made according to international practice, under which the Party that sends, councilors, civil servants and/or technicians takes charge of the international transportation costs and the host Party takes charge of the local transportation, meals, and accommodation costs of the councilors, civil servants and/or technicians.

Article 7

The agreement may be modified by mutual consent of the parties. The said modifications shall come into effect from the date of their approval and notification by the parties.

Article 8

This agreement shall enter into force on the date of its signature and shall remain in force for a period of five years, renewable automatically for equivalent period, unless one party notifies the other in writing, at least six months before the end of its period, of its desire to terminate the agreement.

Article 9

The termination of this agreement shall not affect the validity of those on-going cooperative programmes and projects made under it.

Done in duplicate at Phuket, Thailand, on June 29, 2005 in the English language.

(Ram Kapse)	(Udomsak Uswarangkura)
Lt. Governor of Andaman & Nicobar Island	Governor of Phuket Province
REPUBLIC OF INDIA	KINGDOM OF THAILAND

(Udomsak Uswarangkura)
Governor of Phuket Province Kingdom of Thailand

Bibliography

Amitabh Kant, *Branding India: An Incredible Story*, HarperCollins India, 2009.

AR Radcliffe – Brown, *The Andaman Islanders*, The Free Press – Glencole – Illinois, 1948.

Ashok Dilwali and Ranjana Kaul, *Andaman and Nicobar Islands in the Sun*, Spantech Publishers Pvt Ltd, New Delhi, 1989.

B.R. Tamta, *Andaman and Nicobar Islands*, National Book Trust, New Delhi, 1992.

Bishop John Richardson, *The Father of Modern Nicobar Society*, unpublished.

Bertil Lintner, *Great Game East: India, China and Struggle for Asia's Most Volatile Frontier*, HarperCollins, 2012.

C. Raja Mohan, *Samudra Manthan: Sino-Indian Rivalry in the Indo-Pacific*, CEIP, Washington D.C., 2012.

Cassim. M. Jadwet, *The Jadwet Saga*, unpublished private circulation.

Census of India: 1901, 1911, 1921, 1931, 1941, 1951, 1971, 1991.

De Roepstorff Fr: *Vocabulary of the Dialects Spoken in the Nicobar Isles*, Calcutta, Office of the Superintendent of Government Printing, 1875.

Dr. Simron Jit Singh, *The Nicobar Islands: The Japanese in the Nicobars.*

Dr. Simron Jit Singh, *Danes in Nicobars*, www.andaman.org/NICOBAR/book/hist-Denmark.html

Eco-Tourism & Environment Handbook—A Ready Reckoner for the Tourism Industry published by Mandeep Singh Soin, Produced by Incredible India, Ministry of Tourism, Govt. of India.

George Whitehead, *In the Nicobar Islands*, Seeley, Service & Co, London, 1924.

Jaswant Singh, *A Call to Honor*, Rupa, 2006.

John Richarson, *My Recollections*, unpublished.

Kiran Dhingra (Ed.), *The Andaman and Nicobar Islands in the 20th Century: A Gazeteer*, Oxford University Press, 2005.

Late Bishop Rt. Rev. John Richardson-manuscript unknown author.

M.G.G. Varghese, *Nicobar: A Cooperative Commonweath*, Deputy Registrar, Car Nicobar-unpublished.

N. Iqbal Singh, *The Andaman Story*, Vikas Publishing House, New Delhi, 1978.

Nandita Haksar, *Rogue Agent: How India's Military Intelligence Betrayed the Burmese Resistance*, Penguin Books, New Delhi, 2009.

R.V.R. Murthy, *Andaman and Nicobar Islands*, Northern Book Centre, New Delhi.

Radha Singh, *Sino-American Relations—Mutual Paranoia*, Palgrave Macmillan 2003.

Rajiv Sikri, *Challenge and Strategy: Rethinking of India's Foreign Policies*, Sage, New Delhi, 2009.

Rev. Canon John Richardson, *Car Nicobar under Japanese Occupation: 1943 to 1945*, June 1947 unpublished.

Robert D. Kaplan, *Monsoon: The Indian Ocean and the Future of American Power*, Random House, New York, 2010.

Index